# miracles for daddy

*A Family's Inspirational Fight Against
a Modern Medical Goliath*

## Erica Kosal, Ph.D.

Burro Publishing
Raleigh, NC

Miracles for Daddy
By Erica Kosal

Published by Burro Publishing
www.bouncetoresilience.com

Copyright © 2013 Burro Publishing

For information, contact the author at erica.kosal@gmail.com

Chapter title definitions
*Webster's Third New International Dictionary of the English Language, Unabridged.*
(1993). Also available at http://www.merriam-webster.com/

Scripture quotations marked (NIV) are from the Holy Bible, New International Version®,
NIV®. Copyright © 1973, 1978, 1984 by International Bible Society. Used by permission
of Zondervan. All rights reserved. (www.zondervan.com)

Library of Congress Cataloging-in-Publication Data Pending

ISBN: 978-0-9856809-0-9
E-book ISBN: 0-9856809-1-6

Editor: Gail M. Kearns, www.topressandbeyond.com

Book and cover design: Peri Poloni-Gabriel, Knockout Design,
www.knockoutbooks.com

Printed in the United States of America

*To Jim Young, my sweet, persevering husband*
*who has taught our children and me much about*
*how to live life and, above all else, to believe.*

✳ ✳ ✳

# Table of Contents

# Preface

SURREAL . . . THIS ONE WORD comes to me often. How could one of the worst times of my life also be one of the best times? I have a terrific son, now age six, and a beautiful daughter, age four. I have a career I enjoy, teaching at a small liberal-arts college, and a solid marriage. My husband is kind, supportive, and we feel connected. Still, during these past few years, we have experienced great sorrow starting with my husband's health decline, followed with a fatal diagnosis and then the quest to uncover the truth and the battle to regain Jim's health. To add insult to injury, we have also had to fight the insurance company and the refusals to pay for treatment as well as struggle with other physicians' opinions on Jim's condition. Jim has also had to fend off mental demons that plague him. Will he live long enough to see his children graduate school? Will he be able to keep his job? Will he be able to make a living? And various other questions that fire at him on a regular basis.

Our story is certainly not unique. Many other families struggle and fight their own wars and some are worse than ours to be sure. Talking with other people that have similar tales to tell, the theme is often the same: the unsupportive medical community, the mental and physical tolls, not only on the person directly suffering, but also on the entire family.

Even though there are horrible events that have happened and continue to happen, there are also wonderful things that occur as well. Even though we cannot control the event—Jim *is* ill—we can control other things and this can make all the difference in the world. From the start, Jim and I have known that there must be a reason why all this is happening to him. There must be some good that will come of this. We can say that for now, one "plus" is that our relationship is solid and we have had to bond and connect with one another in ways unknown to us prior to these health hell days. We have also been touched and helped by so many people. We have neighbors walking our dog, neighbors and friends bringing us meals, people praying for us and sending sweet notes often, and others who have helped with childcare and projects around the house. Good friends have helped tremendously in various roles since Jim's family and my family both live in different states. These friends have helped at the last minute, dropped what they were doing if the occasion popped up, and continue to be a true support system in general. There are other people who have touched us greatly that we don't really know. For example, after an unusual snowstorm in Raleigh North Carolina, a neighbor showed up at our house with his son, shovel in hand. The two of them shoveled the driveway and sidewalk for us and wished us well. I was so shocked and felt so fortunate to have that kind of a neighbor. Additionally, we have experienced many "mini-miracles" and at least one major miracle. As you learn about all these wonderful events, I hope that our story will help others fight through a battle, bounce to the path that is needed for mental and physical health, and learn something about resilience.

When times were really tough in my life and we didn't frankly know if Jim were going to live or die, friends would comment on how strong I was. This never really sat well with me - I knew this really wasn't the case. I was simply doing to survive. I was responding because I had to, not because I was strong. But I also realized, that I was resilient. Truly resilient. Again, I had to be. It is certainly not a gift I have—all people have the ability to be resilient, but I do also acknowledge that not everyone can "bounce back" to their original "state" as efficiently as I have been able to do.

My story is one of resilience, but also my family's story is one of resilience. Jim and I have learned to shake off the negative quickly enough and focus on the positive. This can be very difficult at times, especially when people and signs are saying otherwise, but it is the one thing that has "saved" us over and over. My kids, even though they are young, seem to have this ability to focus on the positives and to believe that things will return to normal in due time. They do not see their father as anything other than their daddy. They seem genuinely thrilled when they have his attention and try best to interact with him when Jim is having a good day. Although our family is now "different" in how it looks and the roles we play, we are still the family we were before. We still love each other, hang out with each other, bother each other at times, and appreciate each other.

I hope as you read the book you realize how inspiring and impressive my husband is. My hope is that you also value your friends and family and know they can make or break you when it comes right down to it. Personally, I know we wouldn't have made it as a family if we didn't have all the help and love and support that we have. As a result of reading the book, I hope you learn something about this crazy health industry in our country that we will all deal with at some point in our lives. I hope you will learn to believe in yourself and to plunge ahead if your gut tells you should (and perhaps when others are trying to convince you to give up). My sincerest hope is that you begin to see the miracles that surround us, every day. Some miracles are small and others bigger, but miracles nonetheless. Once you start looking for them, you will find them, appreciate them, and begin to see life in a new way.

This is my family's story of resilience.

## CHAPTER 1

DECEMBER 2007

# Deflation

*"The act of reducing in size, importance, or effectiveness"*

WE DIDN'T KNOW WHAT TO expect. According to our referring physician, the specialist had "interesting shoes"
and was supposed to be the best in the region. My husband Jim
checked in, and we waited. As wheelchair after wheelchair went
past, I felt my anxiety increasing. Various physicians, nurses,
and staff walked back and forth across our viewing area. As
each one passed, I looked at the shoes. *Those shoes seem standard. No. Those shoes aren't a match.* So it went for several
very long minutes. *Who would this specialist be?* I thought to
myself. My husband's fate rested in his hands.

About ten minutes into this process, I saw some shoes that
I thought might belong to the specialist. I looked at the whole
package and thought this had to be the man. He wore a dark
eggplant-color suit, and he was slender and quite angular in
his movements. Although he didn't look physically like Willy
Wonka of the movie *Charlie and the Chocolate Factory*, he
reminded me of that character. He was eccentric enough to fit
the part. The personality, I learned, that went with this man,
was similarly arrogant to the character of the movie; both men

were overly confident and discounted others around them. The redeeming qualities of Willy Wonka, however, were not found in our specialist. Our physician, Dr. Wonka, did not have a kind heart hidden under all the talk and tests as the movie character does. Dr. Wonka thought he had all the answers and the puzzle already solved. We just remained in the background as props and extras to his movie of design.

We knew before coming to the clinic that Dr. Wonka was not only a practicing physician, but also a researcher. "I'm so excited for this combination, Jim," I said confidently. "He is engaged in the research and will be interested in solving puzzles. He should also have a good handle on the practicality of such situations as he sees patients." I was very optimistic that we would find the combination of scientist and healer in one. Jim, still numb and trying to take in all his crazy symptoms, was unusually quiet during these talks. "Jim," I tried to reassure him. "This is going to be good. The doctor will be able to figure out what is happening with your body, and we can get you healthy again."

Jim shook his head, looking sad, and often stared off. Sometimes, he watched our young son, Braxton, who was a toddler, just learning how to walk. It was Christmastime and our son yearned for his daddy's attention, but Jim didn't have it in him to give. Most of the time, Jim was completely exhausted and mentally fatigued. He was sleeping much of the time when he wasn't at work and had so much going on mentally that he could not engage with his child. "I'm scared, Erica." *What is going to happen?* he wondered.

"I don't know what's around the corner," I tried to reassure him. "But you are strong and have always been able to do things that other people can't. You can do this. We'll figure it out."

I truly believed this. My husband always seemed to have

a handle on his body. He was diligent about what he ate, he exercised on a regular basis, and up until this point, he was healthy. I was convinced that the Christmas season was the time that things would be figured out from a medical standpoint and that we would be able to tackle Jim's condition and start moving down the path of healing. One night over dinner, I said, "Jim, this is our time. My semester just ended. I turned in my students' grades, I am going to start Christmas shopping, and we will spend some more time together as a family. It is the season of light—Jesus' birth—and that brings up a new time. A new perspective. A time for you and healing." I knew in my heart this was true, but as the days rolled on and Jim seemed to get more and more depressed and detached from Braxton and me, my worries increased. I eagerly awaited the specialist's visit and some answers.

My optimism was crushed that afternoon in Dr. Wonka's office. After the interestingly clad physician quickly introduced himself, he directed his attention only to Jim. "Were you ever in the military?" he asked.

"No," replied Jim, as confused as I was at the question.

"Have you ever been around toxins of any kind for an extended period of time?" he continued.

"Not really," answered Jim.

I tried to interject, "Well, Jim grew up in a town in Alabama that is considered by some to be the most toxic town in America." I was pleased to be able to shed some light on Jim's condition and thought this might provide some insight into Jim's situation.

The specialist shrugged me off, leaving me confused. I thought to myself, *why did he ask the question if he really wasn't interested?* But we continued on. It seemed that the specialist was just interested in yes or no answers, without elaboration from the patient. In particular, he didn't want conversation from the spouse. "Okay," Dr. Wonka said to me and then turned to Jim. "Mr. Young," he continued. "Have you travelled overseas to spend considerable time in another country?"

Jim gave me a look of frustration, but answered the specialist. "I travel often enough for my job. I have been to Brazil, Germany, and Mexico recently, but not for any extended period of time."

Dr. Wonka continued, "So I have a report from the neurologist who referred you here and I'll start my own testing right now as well."

"Do you want to know about Jim's symptoms?" I asked quietly. "He has so many more that you haven't touched on yet."

Sharply, Dr. Wonka replied to me, "I have the report here. I have already reviewed it."

Slinking back on my chair, I initially felt timid, but then I grew irritated that this physician didn't seem interested in really helping my husband. Was he taking into consideration not only the fasciculations, these random neuron firings over his whole body, and muscle weakness in his hands, as well as major cramping in various body parts that would immobilize Jim for several minutes? There was also ringing in one of his ears, a major pain in his neck, massive headaches that would stick with him for many, many hours, and overall "just not feeling well."

Dr. Wonka paused his examination of Jim to say to me, "The other symptoms are irrelevant and not of use diagnostically."

He spun his chair around toward Jim again and continued with his physical exam, testing Jim's strength. "Push against my hands as hard as you can, Mr. Young," commanded Dr. Wonka. "Okay now, squeeze my hand as tightly as you can."

After this, the next test was for Jim to walk down the hallway as Dr. Wonka studied his gait.

After this very brief exam, Dr. Wonka explained that there were five things to consider with Jim's case. He sent Jim off to have an MRI scan (looking for renal cell cancer), blood work (testing for Lyme disease, HIV, and Copper Deficiency), and various neurological tests (looking for evidence of ALS/Lou Gehrig's disease). We were to return for a follow-up appointment in a few weeks.

When that second appointment arrived, I found myself convinced that this Christmas season was a sign that Jim was going to get some answers and start moving down a healing path. I was so convinced that after this appointment, I knew we would go celebrate and have a new vision of our future. I was looking forward to having my husband back, thinking that having an answer would bring out his fighting spirit and "can-do" attitude once again.

"I really don't want to go to this appointment, Erica," Jim said on our way to the office.

"I know, sweetie," I replied. "But it's going to be good. I know it. We'll have some answers and we'll move forward."

We sat in the car silent for the rest of the trip, Jim with his thoughts of what was going to happen to his body over the long haul. As we drove down the highway, he was distracted by thoughts alternating between life in a wheelchair and his death. He wondered if this was his time to die and what he would miss out on, especially as it related to his son.

We got to Dr. Wonka's office and waited for many minutes. During this interim, several interns came to see Jim, asking him to perform the various strength exercises Jim was asked to do, many weeks prior. Not one intern explained his or her role, and both Jim and I grew more anxious by the minute. *Why isn't anyone telling us what's going on?* I wondered.

Jim thought to himself, *why is yet another person, and not Dr. Wonka, coming into this office?* Finally, Jim voiced this question out loud. It was as if the other physicians put "mute" on the Jim Young television show. Every single person ignored Jim's question. No one wanted to tell us where Dr. Wonka was, and this made me very anxious.

Still, I tried to convince myself that I was just paranoid. Jim tried to reassure me, "It doesn't mean anything, Erica. They are just busy trying to help with many patients." I looked at Jim, my sweet husband of eight years. At the age of forty-nine, he looked much younger with a full head of dark hair, youthful dancing blue eyes, and up to this point, much energy. I just couldn't believe that he could really be that sick. Jim tried to give me a smile, but from the overall look on his face, I knew he was terrified.

I was frightened, too. What we knew at this point in time was the following: Jim had had a strange nerve conduction test at another neurologist's office. The results weren't abnormal, but they weren't normal, either. Jim had previously been tested for Lyme disease, and this test came back negative. We were also confident that Jim didn't have HIV. So we ruled these out as possibilities. That left us with three other possibilities: ALS, renal cancer, or a rare copper deficiency. A recent hair analysis, initiated on our own accord, showed that Jim did have low copper. "Please let it be that simple, God," I prayed.

Finally, Dr. Wonka came through the door. We exchanged pleasantries as he settled into the chair in front of his computer screen. After a few minutes, he looked up, swiveled around in his chair, and said, "I guess you guys are expecting a few tests results—let me go track those down." Then he left.

Jim and I looked at each other. "Did that really just happen, Jim?" I asked my husband.

"Wow," he replied. "That was weird. Do you think he even knew what exam room he was in, Erica? He acted like he was confused as to where he should be."

I half smiled, welcoming the brief relief this strange encounter brought, but just as quickly as Dr. Wonka had rushed out of the room, he rushed back in again.

With folder in hand, Dr. Wonka studied the report for a few seconds and announced, "I've got great news!" Major relief came to my body.

*I knew it,* I thought to myself. *Jim is going to be all right.*

But then Dr. Wonka's follow-up statement made me nauseous. He proclaimed with a smile on his face, "All of your tests results are negative."

The full impact of those two sentences only took a millisecond to settle in—this was hardly great news. It was the worst blow we could have been hit with, and it was delivered with such insensitivity. I protested, "What about the copper levels? We recently had Jim's hair analyzed and there . . ."

I was cut off before I could even finish the sentence. "Nonsense!" said the specialist. "Hair analysis is not accurate. Tell me, what did the company suggest you take?"

Jim and I nervously commented about various supplements. Upon hearing "adrenal complex" supplements, Dr. Wonka scoffed and commented, "What is *that* supposed to do? If I wrote something like that as an answer in medical school, I would have never graduated. How ridiculous!"

Still, we persisted. Jim and I had been reading enough scientific literature over the course of many months to know better. After digesting copper supplementation studies and positive results shown with patients with neurological problems, Jim started taking high doses of copper several weeks prior to our Dr. Wonka visits. During this self-medication phase, I asked Jim one night, "Are you sure the levels of copper you are taking are safe?"

"I am taking the high dose of what the author cited he used on his patients," he replied.

"Could you get the doctor's opinion, Jim? You could send him an email. Look at the paper again. There should be contact information there."

Jim thought this was a good idea and emailed several researchers. He explained his neurological symptoms and asked if they thought his read of the dose was accurate. He also inquired on the duration of such supplementation.

Jim emailed five authors. He heard back from one researcher. The email was short and direct. "Mr. Young," it started. "While I found copper supplementation to be highly effective in my patients, it is unclear if such supplementation will help in your particular case. The dose you stated was what I gave my patients, but you need to consider other avenues. Have you had blood tests confirming low copper? Hair analysis is not accurate. You need to consult a local physician, but if you do not have the blood results to back up the low copper, you should not be taking extra copper."

As we tried to explain this copper idea, Dr. Wonka grew more agitated. It was evident he was not impressed with our armchair self-diagnosis. I moved on from this argument and returned to Dr. Wonka. "Okay," I said. "So what do we know now if everything is negative?"

"We now know what Jim has. The guessing game is over.

Jim has ALS." I was astonished that this fatal diagnosis was delivered to us in this fashion.

I blurted out, "And that's great news?"

"Well, at least we know what it's not," replied the ever-arrogant Dr. Wonka.

Jim sat stunned in the chair, thinking that once a diagnosis of ALS/Lou Gehrig's disease is made, the average life span for a patient is three to five years. Jim pictured his son, Braxton, learning how to play golf, learning how to read, and going to school all without a father. I could see tears welling up in Jim's eyes. I stared straight ahead, hoping that the specialist would follow up his blow with something encouraging.

I glanced at Jim and then quickly looked away. *If I look at you for too long, sweetie,* I thought to myself, *I will break down and I don't know if I'll be able to pull myself together.*

I was shaken back to the moment at hand and the tasks that needed to be completed by Dr. Wonka, who was asking Jim some more questions. He started, "There is one form of ALS that is genetically based. Would you provide us with a sample of your blood so we can see if you have this form?"

"Ah," sputtered Jim. "Sure."

Dr. Wonka replied, "Great, we'll also test your blood for other indications of stress and how your body is doing at this point. We'll follow up over the weeks and keep track of your progress."

Next, Dr. Wonka asked Jim to breathe into an apparatus called a spirometer, a plastic horizontal tube with a ball in it connected to another vertical tube. "As you breathe into this, Mr. Young, we will be able to see how far you can lift the ball. This will help us understand how well your lungs are doing and we can more easily track your progress as you grow weaker over time."

Moments later, as I was still trying to process what was happening to our lives, a social worker came into the room to ask us all kinds of questions. She had a kind look about her, blond hair, and a pretty smile. She was a nice contrast to Dr. Wonka. She sat in a chair across from me and maintained eye contact the entire time. "How many stairs do you have in your house, Erica?" I stared at her, trying to understand why she cared about my stairs. Another few seconds passed without me saying a word.

"Erica, this is important," she said. "As Jim progresses, it will be harder and harder for him to walk." She continued, "Where do your closest living relatives live? It will be important to get as much support around you as you can."

*Huh?* I thought. *This is all too fast. Why are all these questions coming to me? I can't understand how Jim is so sick?* My head was swirling around and around.

The social worker touched me on my leg, "There are many support groups, too. Just let me know if you want some information on them."

Tears started flowing freely down my face. I could not speak. I could only shake my head and answer very simply with a "yes" or a "no." Then she ended with a blow, "Does Jim have a living will? I'll need to have a copy of that, so if you could bring it in on your next appointment, that would be great." The woman ended the conversation with a smile as she handed us a thick book on living with ALS. It made me queasy just to consider opening the first page.

Before heading to the clinic for the blood withdrawal, Dr. Wonka finished our appointment with a discussion on clinical trials. "But in order to participate," he urged Jim "you can't be taking any of these supplements. There is a pill that you can take that may slow down some of your symptoms, but that is really all you should take."

Jim questioned the specialist, "I am still confused about something. The nerve conduction test I had prior to you was not completely abnormal. In fact, the neurologist wasn't even convinced he should label it as abnormal. Is ALS really the diagnosis? The copper supplements really do seem to be helping."

To this Dr. Wonka ruffled his shoulders, as if to brush off Jim's silly comments, and informed us, "I read every journal article on the subject. I am the one who told you about copper deficiency, if you remember. Every night I come home and read articles. I am an expert. Please don't start thinking you have something else."

Jim protested a little, "What about the book *Eric is Winning* by Eric Edney? Do you know of this person?"

To this, Dr. Wonka said, "Oh yeah, I've read it. There are things in there that don't make any sense. Eric's ALS is probably just progressing slowly. I don't think anything he is doing is really working against ALS. Eric is probably just lucky in that his ALS is not moving as quickly as many patients. Some people do live longer than the average three- to five-year life span, post diagnosis. He is probably just one of those outliers."

Feeling completely blindsided, but a bit more confident, Jim didn't stop, "Well, what is your opinion about what Eric argues for the use of . . ."

Dr. Wonka cut him off and replied, "As I have stated before, I read literature every night over dinner. I am very well versed in the subject." I was so angry, but too stunned to say anything.

Jim managed to continue the conversation. "Well, what

about Lyme disease? Why can't it be that? Maybe we need to revisit that?" Jim followed up his earnest plea with a summary of five people in our small suburban Raleigh, North Carolina, neighborhood who had Lyme disease.

Dr. Wonka smirked, quietly laughed, and said, "**Who** made the diagnosis?"

During this period in North Carolina, people argued that Lyme disease was non-existent in the state. Since this time, it has been moved to the rare-in-occurrence category, even though there is so much evidence pointing to the contrary. Lyme disease is in North Carolina and has been for quite some time.

It was evident that our expert was convinced Jim had ALS and that any other potential disease or issue was not to be considered. Dr. Wonka delivered us our Christmas gift, consisting of an awful package with the label of ALS. We returned home unable to speak to one another. I looked at our Christmas tree and thought, *How can this be happening? I put all my trust in You, God, and how can this be happening? How can You take away my son's father? My son needs Jim. Please save him.*

That Christmas season was bittersweet. "Will this be the last Christmas I have with Braxton?" Jim asked me one evening.

"Of course not," I said. "You will be here for many years. Don't think anything else." But inside, I wondered if I was sure of this myself. It was a time of taking note of what was truly important. It was a season to pay attention to things, to remember, and to appreciate what we had and make the most of the time we had together. I went through the Christmas season routines and soaked myself in inspirational books. Jim gave me a beautiful necklace with a silver cross with diamonds. I bought Jim a picture of a sailboat with the verse from Jeremiah 29:11

written underneath it: "For I know the plans I have for you," declares the Lord, "plans to prosper you and not to harm you, plans to give you hope and a future." (NIV)

✳ ✳ ✳

JIM IS A HANDSOME MAN with a perfectionist streak. He grew up in a loving family with his older sister of three years, a father who encouraged hard work and excellence, and a mother who supported and nurtured kindness. He and his sister Priscilla were close. They shared some of the same friends as they got older, and both Priscilla and Jim looked out for one another. Jim's mom Patricia encouraged this closeness, by her kind acts toward family, friends, and strangers. She taught her children how to be considerate of others through her acts and fostered a connection to God and the church. Jim's dad Harold was a hard worker, who instilled a solid work ethic in his son. Harold worked in the early hours of the day and was home when his kids returned from school. He was often the one making dinners during the week, which allowed for some good family bonding time. Jim grew up in this family learning to be kind, to trust God, and to work hard, expecting the best out of life.

When Jim got to college, he worked full time in order to pay his way through the five years. Before the age of weekend courses, online degrees, and ease of college loans, Jim worked to pay for his education 100 percent. He didn't borrow money from his parents, the bank, or anywhere else. This was a difficult task at times as Jim decided to major in computer science (just as the field was starting to form), a demanding major, as well as join a fraternity. Jim was always popular in school, making friends easily, playing on various sports teams, and having an infectious pleasantness about him. He was the one in school whom everyone wanted to be friends with—he was smart, funny, liked to have a good time, and was an all-around "good guy."

During college, this combination of working strange hours, going to school full time, belonging to a fraternity, and being a perfectionist didn't always work well. For example, during one period, Jim was working with his dad at the local foundry from 4:00 a.m. until 2:30 p.m. After a physically demanding full day of work, he would rush to college for late afternoon and evening classes. One particular night as he attended class, Jim fought the urge to fall asleep and eventually did so. The professor decided to teach Jim a lesson and told everyone to leave the classroom. Some kind soul came back and woke up Jim shortly after class was released. Instead of hiding from this professor, as many students would have done in his small-class setting, Jim didn't let this incident get him down. Instead, the incident actually propelled him to work harder and prove to this professor that he was a good student.

In spite of the drain physically on Jim with running to classes, work, and parties, Jim did well academically in college, graduating in five years. He then started working for a large private software company, moving up quickly in the company and traveling across the country. He lived in Alabama, but spent a lot of time in San Francisco, New York, and various other large cities across the country. He enjoyed these years of meeting people, having fun, and dating many women. He was exposed to many new things and showed appreciation for most. Jim is never quick to say "yuck" to a new food, or "no way" to something that is different from what he knows. Jim wants to learn, grow, incorporate, blend, and make sense of all the interconnections in life.

Our connection came when Jim relocated to North Carolina. I was in graduate school, and we met one November night at a seafood restaurant and bar. Jim had just finished dinner with his cousin, and I was hanging out on the bar side of the restaurant with my roommate. When I saw Jim, our eyes locked. It was hard to resist his sparking eyes, which seemed to be saying, I am dynamic and interesting—come talk to me. The blue shirt he was wearing made his blue eyes stand out even more. He smiled, and I nervously looked away, thinking, *he can't possibly be looking at me.*

After a few minutes, he made his way over to our area. "Hi," he said. "My name is Chip." Or at least that's what I heard over the din in the noisy bar. Instead of the usual "what do you do for a living" questions, we talked about the band, his cousin being in town for the weekend to play golf, and seafood. It was laid-back, refreshing, and seemed easy.

*This conversation is way too "normal,"* I thought to myself. *Chip must be interested in my roommate. That's why it is so easy for me to talk to him.* This revelation put me at ease, and we continued talking about my research in graduate school. I was impressed that this total stranger could talk science. I quickly learned that this man was articulate, fun-natured, and smart. "Why don't you talk to my roommate?" I finally asked him.

"Why would I want to do that?" he said.

I blushed. *Really? He's interested in me?* I smiled a big wide grin.

"May I have your phone number, Erica? Oh, and by the way, my name is Jim, not Chip."

I blushed again, but this time out of embarrassment. When I thought about giving this stranger my phone number, I recalled my mother's advice not to give people too much information, and I felt it would be odd if I were to scribble my phone number down on a napkin. "I'll tell you my last name and you can look me up in the phone book," I said. Somehow this made me feel better, but of course, I wanted him to call me. As an afterthought, I rattled off my phone number in haste, just in case. I figured if he really did like me, he could remember either my last name or my phone number. It never occurred to me that he could have simply walked over to the bar after I left and asked for a napkin and then quickly jotted down my phone number himself.

Fortunately, Jim did phone a few days later, and we had a great conversation. Similar to the connection we felt instantly in the bar, talking on the phone was so easy. It seemed to "fit," like we had known each other for years. My only issue was that Jim was a "pauser." He would be saying something to me, then pause mid-sentence to find a word. As I soon learned, Jim's pauses are a reflection of his perfectionist side. He is searching for the precise, exact word to use. He is careful with his selection and the meaning of his word choice. I'm not sure if he got better at choosing his words more quickly as we dated longer or if I just got used to the pauses, but his fastidious nature is still intact today.

During this initial dating period, Jim was in his late thirties and had never been married. After we got more serious in our relationship, friends and family members would show concern. "How could someone so handsome, nice, and 'normal' never be married?" they asked. The voices grew louder, and at one point, I started thinking to myself, *oh no, he does have a wife and kids and I'm the mistress and don't even know it!* I started probing him with more questions about where and how he lived, looking for clues.

Finally, one night I asked Jim, "Why don't you ever take me to your house? We've been dating a while and I've never seen your house. Are you trying to hide something from me?"

The look on Jim's face was total surprise. "It never occurred to me, Erica," he replied. "We are always going out on your side of town, and I didn't think you'd be interested in seeing my house." The next day, we visited his house. My mind was at ease.

Jim waited many years to find the right person, as I did. I had been through a series of long-term relationships that ultimately never seemed to be the right fit. I reconnected with a college love and had a long-distance relationship, only to be disappointed that he still wouldn't act on his dreams and goals and go after what he thought was important. Another long-term relationship was with a manipulative man, who constantly caused me pain. Another live-in relationship involved a man who was still trying to figure out himself and was not interested in a future with me.

It was after this relationship that I met Jim. Jim was responsible, fun, kind, and driven. He was the nicest person I had ever known and always had time for everyone. Additionally, he let me be myself. Prior to this, all of the men I had been involved with wanted to either control me and have me be someone I wasn't, or be around me all the time, to the point that it was exhausting. With Jim I found a confident man who treated me well. We liked one another and we enjoyed spending time together.

We both knew quickly after initially meeting one another that we wanted a long-term relationship. Jim says he knew he wanted to marry me on our second date. But in practice, we waited two years before getting married. Even though we were older when we married, we wanted to wait to have children. I was just starting in my career and we wanted to enjoy being married first before starting our family. During this time, we traveled and took many vacations with friends, and went out, often locally, to plays and dinners.

One particular trip involved meeting several friends at a beach in North Carolina. It was a grand time of playing beach volleyball, tossing around in the waves, reading, having great seafood meals with friends, and just relaxing and laughing. One afternoon on the beach, while everyone was tanning in the sun, a friend jumped up and said, "I lost my ring. My father's ring—it's gone!" Everyone could see how panicked he was, and we heard the panic in Jimmy's voice. Then I remembered that Jimmy's father had recently passed away, so the ring had extra meaning to him. Everyone began looking in the sand and walking the path up to the beach house.

After many, many minutes, everyone was giving up. "I'm so sorry," they would say. "Are you sure you had it on at the beach? Maybe you left it in your room?" Others commented, "I don't know how we are ever going to find this ring. It could be anywhere. For all we know, it could be in the ocean."

Jim decided that this ring had to be found. His friend needed it, and as the saying goes, "If there is a will, there is a way." At that point, Jim phoned his dad, asking him to overnight to the beach house the metal detector that he owned. Once the detector arrived, Jim stayed on the beach scanning the area, up and down the beach, back and forth, hour after hour.

"Jim," I urged at one point. "You need to stop. I know everyone appreciates you doing this, but I think the ring is gone."

"No, Erica," he replied. "I just need some more time. Just trust me, I can find it."

I shrugged my shoulders and hoped he was right. I turned back toward the house and walked the stairs to the back deck, thinking to myself, *how long will he work on this?* Up on the deck, we all had beers in hand, watching Jim with the metal detector. Our friend started feeling guilty that Jim was still looking for the ring. "I think I'm going to tell him to stop, guys. I'll be right back."

Just as Jimmy was pushing himself off the rocking chair, we all heard some excitement from Jim. He was looking back at us with his hand raised in the air. "I think I found it!" Jim said. We all went running down to the beach and sure enough, the ring had been discovered.

Jim tackles most things in life just like with the ring. His attitude is that problems can be solved if you work hard enough at them. There are solutions to puzzles if you don't get discouraged and if you stick with it.

This attitude was called into play again when we decided we did want to start having children. Unfortunately, I had no luck getting pregnant. Jim and I both read all kinds of books, articles, and tracked cycles, trying to solve the puzzle. But nothing worked. Finally, my gynecologist agreed for more aggressive intervention, so I began seeing a fertility specialist. Fortunately, after several months, we did have luck and I became pregnant, and Braxton was the wonderful result.

Moments after Braxton was born, a nurse came into the delivery room. Jim said to her, "I just want you to know, this is one of the good ones." The nurse looked perplexed, so Jim continued. "Everyone says their child is going to go places and do good things. Well, I know this is true of my son. I'll make sure of it." The nurse smiled and walked away quietly. I knew exactly what Jim meant. He would be sure that Braxton minded his manners, spoke well of others, became a gentleman, and was motivated to follow his dreams. I had no doubt that Braxton would grow into all these things with Jim as a role model and teacher.

Jim's overall attitude that he wanted to teach his son was to take action and make things happen. Jim believes positive mindset can go a long ways to helping people achieve their goals. This type of optimism seems to have served him well over the years. Jim found that if he worked hard enough at something, he could achieve his goals. He had earned awards at work, excelled in sales, was in good physical shape, and his golf game was strong.

Jim loves golf. This may be an understatement. Jim finds so much joy in the game and connects golf with so many life events and character traits. For example, Jim can discuss with such passion how you have to clear your mind in golf to make the shot. You have to block distractions, and you have to concentrate and visualize where the golf ball is going to travel before you even hit the ball. Golf helps keep things in perspective for him. "I love the game so much," he said one afternoon in Alabama, as we were swinging on his father's front porch, watching Braxton play with trucks. "You can't think just about the one shot—you have to think about the whole strategy. The way you approach the game is important. The way you walk on the course and the thoughts you are thinking influence your ability to hit the ball and influence how you direct the ball."

Many of life's moments are like this for Jim. You have to really think through something, focus all efforts on it, and prepare. One of Jim's favorite quotes hung on his office door. The quote is from Abraham Lincoln: "If I had eight hours to cut down a tree, I would spend six hours sharpening my axe."

Jim is a thinker. He prepares and he works on the front end to be sure when he does something, he does it right. As a new father, Jim craved the time when he could teach his son the game of golf and by default this positive way of thinking. Jim was devastated when one of his first symptoms hit him: His hands wouldn't work the way he wanted them to. Over the course of this journey, his hands went from being weak to his muscles physically wasting away. Jim's grip on the golf club was difficult, and controlling where the ball went upon striking it became more and more complicated over time. It was disturbing that after golfing with one of his best friends, Mike Braxton (and one of our son's namesakes) for twenty-three years in an annual golf tournament, Jim could no longer play.

In July of 2009, we ventured to visit Jim's family for the annual golf tournament in Alabama. Jim was sure that the trip wouldn't be too taxing on him and that he could play golf even though he was struggling physically. He knew, of course, that he wouldn't play the kind of golf that he wanted to, or was capable of playing in the past, but that wasn't important. The act of participating, bonding with his friend, being outdoors, and working his hands was important. When we arrived after the long car journey, though, I knew Jim was in trouble. He didn't get out of the car at all during our ten-hour trip, except to use the restroom. He didn't eat much, either. He was exhausted when we got there and he never really recovered.

Still, Jim tried. After the first day out for practice, Jim looked to our son's other namesake, Del Miles, to take his place. The three men have known each other since elementary school and are the best of friends. All three men are equally jolly when in each other's presence, laughing continuously, and always looking out for one another. Mike, with his perpetual smile and optimistic view on life. Del, with his insight, deep faith, and strong love for his family always evident in anything he says. And Jim, the one who connects equally well with all people—the person many turn to for advice and comfort.

I recall the first real interaction with these three men in my presence. Del was telling a story, taking on the voice of a southern comedian of whom I had no idea, leaving me totally confused. As Del acted his scene, up on his feet with theater voice projecting, Mike and Jim were slapping their legs, howling in laughter. After the story, Jim filled me in on what happened and before I could reflect on the skit, Mike and Del were at my side. "Erica," Mike started. "You know this man means the world to Del and me." Mike slapped Jim on the back and Jim nodded in approval.

Del took over, "If you ever need anything from us. If there is ever any trouble, and I mean any problem, you call us." He smiled and touched me on my back.

Mike returned, "Really, anytime at all, Erica. Doesn't matter if it's in the middle of the night. You call us. We'll be here in a heartbeat. We love Jim."

So the love that these three men shared for one another was evident over the years. That love was again shown years later when we were in Alabama at the golf tournament. Del was happy to help, taking Jim's place on the course. Jim rode the cart with his two best friends and tried to remain positive and enjoy the time. After the first day on the course with his two buddies, I asked Jim how he felt. "I want to live, Erica. I don't care about the tournament really. I want to live."

I hugged him closely, wishing I could wave a magic wand and make all the pain go away. I gave him a smile and tried my best to say something of significance. "I know this stinks so much," I said. "As we have both said before, if your symptoms just stop and don't get worse, you can still live a long fine life. A good life. I love you, Jim." We both smiled as best we could and gave each other a squeeze.

## CHAPTER 2

JUNE 2007

# Struggle

*"To proceed with difficulty or with great effort"*

HEADING TO ALABAMA ON AN earlier occasion for a surprise party marked Braxton's introduction to many of Jim's friends. Jim, Braxton, and I drove from North Carolina to Alabama in our first long car journey. We drove casually, taking many breaks along the way. We enjoyed each other, being together, and looked forward to the celebration. Del was turning forty-nine years old, and his wife was having a party to mark the event.

When we arrived at the festivities, everyone was thrilled to see Jim and meet his new son. "I can't believe you have a toddler, Jim. My child is starting college this year!" one of his friends said, lightheartedly. Other friends laughed at this situation as well. They were all roughly the same age, but most had started their families long before. Braxton was one and a half years old and was learning to walk well. He was still crawling some of the time and seemed to enjoy all the attention that was being given to him. Under the table he would go, popping out on the other side to the giggles of women looking his way. "He looks just like you, Jim Young," stated one guest.

"I know," I said. "It's pretty amazing how much he can act like his daddy, too, at such a young age." Sometimes when I watched Braxton, he grinned just like Jim, moved his arms and legs in a manner similar to his dad, and as he grew, took on even more of his personality.

Jim was happy in this party setting. I would glance Jim's way and see a grin of satisfaction, as he moved his body to the music beating in the background. As guest after guest sang Del's praises, recalling stories, Jim shook his head up and down in approval. "Yep," he commented. "That is so Del."

An intense barbeque aroma began to seep through the house, indicating dinnertime was here. People started to move outside, refreshing their drinks and making themselves plates of food. There was chicken, pork, biscuits, corn on the cob, and lots of sweet treats.

Jim had gone to the corner of the deck and was chatting with Mike. He reached over to get a beer out of the cooler and tried to twist off the top. He struggled. The top was not turning well. "Maybe there is some water on the cap from the ice," Jim said and wiped it off on his shirt. He tried to twist off the top again, and again he failed.

Mike laughed and said, "How are you going to handle a kid when you can't even handle a beer?"

Jim smiled, but was growing more and more weary. *What is going on?* Jim thought to himself.

Finally days later, when we were back home in North Carolina, Jim let me in on it. He recounted the story of the bottle to me. "Jim," I replied. "I'm sure it's nothing. I think you are making too much of it."

"No, Erica," he stated firmly. "I'm not." My look gave away

my confusion. "Okay, let me explain," Jim continued. "I have been trying to figure out what is going on with my body."

"What do you mean, Jim? Do you have other things going on?"

"Unfortunately, yes. I have these random nerve firings called fasiculations. If you look at my arm close enough, you'll see what I mean." So I sat there, staring at his arm, waiting for something. Just when I thought nothing was going to happen, pop! A wave moved very quickly over his arm.

"What is going on?" was all I could manage to say. Jim's whole body tensed, his face became contorted, and I could sense he was fighting back tears.

"Every time I google, I get the same results. I try different variations of symptoms and concentrate on some more than others and then reverse my strategy to see what results the computer will show."

"And . . .?" I nervously replied.

Jim continued, "And every time it is the same result. Every time." He looked away for a brief moment. I could hear the baby monitor beep and hiss. Braxton must have been moving about in his crib. I waited. Again, the beeps. Over another hiss, Jim stated, "It's always ALS or Lou Gehrig's disease." Beep, hiss. Then there was another noise in the background. Our dog barked. Another moment of silence.

I was trying to read Jim's face. I couldn't. All I could do was hear the beeps and hisses. Finally I said, "Okay, Jim. Let's figure out what is going on. We need help. You don't really know if it is ALS or not."

Jim started seeing various physicians, and ultimately was re-ferred to a neurologist. The goal was to hook Jim up to electrodes

in order to study how his neurons were working in a nerve conduction test. "Do you want me to go to the appointment with
you?" I asked on the morning of his appointment.

"No," Jim said. "It's all right. You have to work, and I'm
not sure there will be answers for me anyway. It seems like the
norm these days."

It was late in the afternoon when Jim phoned me after this
first appointment. I was driving in my car, coming home from
work and picking up Braxton at daycare, taking in the scenery.
I was traveling on a road that is flanked by a forest on one side
and a horse farm on the other. It was still hot, but not burning
as it can often be in North Carolina during the late summer
months. The windows of the car were down and the warm
wind was coming in gently. I looked in my rearview mirror at
my son in the back seat. I looked outside again, reflecting on
life—trees, horses, and people. I could smell the fresh air, horses
in the background, and the pines. I braced myself for what Jim
might say. He recounted the appointment and the physician's
response after reading the nerve conduction results. "Well,
Jim," the physician said. "Your results from this test are not
normal, but they are not really abnormal, either. I would guess
that if you returned in six months, I might find a totally normal
reading." The physician then explained there is a condition
called benign fasiculation syndrome (BFS). This condition is
bothersome to the person who has it, but it is not life threaten-
ing and can sometimes even go away after a period of time. Still,
just to be sure and for a second consultation, the neurologist
recommended Jim visit our Dr. Wonka, the specialist who gave
us the ALS diagnosis.

"Erica," Jim said, "Wouldn't this be fantastic if I had BFS?"

I was so relieved. "Fantastic is an understatement, Jim. I
knew it though. I can't believe that you could have ALS. I just

think you take such good care of yourself and know your body so well, that you would have been alerted earlier if there was a major problem with your nerves."

"I love you," Jim replied.

"I love you too, sweetie. I'll see you soon."

As I clicked off my cell phone, I thought to myself, *finally. Jim's problem is diagnosed, labeled, and manageable. Life is good again. Things are going to be okay. Thank you, God. Things are going to be okay.*

This elation, obviously, didn't last a long time. We had our second opinion consultation with Dr. Wonka shortly after that, which led to the second and grave diagnosis of ALS. Our life was so uncertain from that point on, moving from ups and downs, with alternating moods of sadness and determination. We didn't know what was happening to Jim nor did we know what to expect of our future. One night, Jim stated firmly over dinner, "I just don't understand why pharmaceutical companies can't collaborate with other scientists. Think how much further ahead we would be as a nation. I really don't think they are looking for cures to diseases. There is no money in it for them. It makes more sense from a business model to manage the problem, rather than cure it."

"Jim Young," I replied. "You are so cynical. You know scientists are good people in general. Things take a long time because research takes a long time, not necessarily because of a lack of collaboration."

"Do you know the story about ulcers?" he replied.

"I think so," I said with a slight irritation in my voice.

"Well, there was a doctor who thought ulcers were caused by bacteria and had the data to support this, but no one else in the scientific world would listen to him," Jim said enthusiastically. "At conferences he was laughed at and no one wanted to believe you could cure ulcers. The goal was to manage them. Well, it turns out that this physician was correct."

"I know," I replied. "But there are many other cases where physicians and researchers are working together to move things forward together and are not working against each other."

"I don't know about that," Jim said firmly.

"Jim, in general, the system works," I argued back. "There are checks and balances in medical research. People do share data and collaborate."

"Well, we can just agree to disagree, Erica," Jim said thoughtfully. With that, we ate the rest of our meal on our back deck. This was one of our favorite spots. We lived in a suburban neighborhood of Raleigh, the capital of North Carolina. We had a small backyard, with a small strip of trees—just enough pines and hardwoods to give you a sense of nature, but still plenty of grass for Braxton to play on. During these late summer nights, the mosquitoes were not as commonplace as earlier in the summer and the temperature was perfect. There were always lots of birds to study—cardinals, sparrows, and chickadees. Every once in a while, we would get a nice surprise of a hawk or woodpecker viewing. A mile or so away was a state park. For this reason we had more birds and wildlife than you would expect for our suburban neighborhood. For several years, we also had deer in our backyard. Today, we still have foxes, rabbits, and many birds show up on a regular basis.

✳ ✳ ✳

## CHAPTER 3

DECEMBER 2007

# Message

*"A communication in writing, in speech, or by signals"*

"PATRICIA, THE DOCTORS SAY JIM has ALS." There was silence. Jim's mom, Patricia, was trying to process my words, just as I had done in Dr. Wonka's office minutes before.

"What do you mean?" she replied.

"The doctor says that Jim has ALS and is going to get worse quickly. I don't understand," I blurted out quickly as the tears started flowing.

"It's all right, Erica," she replied. "We'll figure this out. How is Jim?"

"He's inside right now having vial after vial of blood drawn to check for various things."

"I'm not sure what to make of all this," Patricia said, "but Jim can do this. God will help."

After this call, I phoned my own mom Wilma. "Mom," I started crying immediately.

"What's wrong?" she asked.

"Mom . . ." I could hardly get the words out, I was crying so much. I managed, "It's Jim. He really is very sick." I gave her a version of our meeting with Dr. Wonka and tried to be as calm as I could.

My mom is a strong woman who is used to working hard and seeing the good in things when others cannot. In her most comforting voice, she replied to me with conviction, "It will be all right. Jim is strong. You are strong. Hold this together, Erica. It's all you have right now, but remember, miracles happen every day."

I took her advice to heart, trying to work on autopilot and remaining the strong one in the family. It was imperative for both Braxton and Jim. That night, after I put Braxton to bed, Jim and I lay together on the couch. Silence was the norm, with each one of us in our own dark place. My brain would take me all over—there was the fighter mode, the pity mode, the "what about my son" mode, and the "there has got to be another answer" mode. I was everywhere.

Jim broke the silence first, "Erica, we need to think about the future." My body tensed. I did not want to go here. "Erica, really, what are we going to do?"

I wasn't sure how to answer Jim and tried to say what I was feeling at the moment, "Do we need to start shopping for houses, maybe a ranch so we don't have to worry about stairs? I could also look for a job in Michigan to be closer to my family."

Jim turned his body to face mine more directly and said very seriously, "I do not want you to sell this house. We live in a good neighborhood, and it is important to me that you stay in this house." He paused and then added, "Do you understand what I am saying?"

I could only shake my head for if I spoke, I knew I would lose it and my tears would start to flow. Finally, minutes later, I managed to say, "Jim, I don't understand how you are so sick. This makes no sense to me. You have always been so healthy. You look healthy. This is just so unfair." We both knew it was undeserved and that there were no easy answers.

The void that I felt that night was intense. I'm not sure I have ever felt sadder in my life. After several more minutes of silence, a light bulb went off and I had an overwhelming feeling that Jim didn't have ALS. *It doesn't make sense because the diagnosis is wrong,* I thought. The doctor didn't take into account all the symptoms, and he was too quick to judge. My logical brain continued, *sometimes symptoms can fool you. Just because you have some symptoms associated with a disease doesn't mean you have that disease.*

Over the next several days, as I worked to process what was happening, I realized quickly that many people would think Jim was on a downward spiral and that we might be clinging onto delusional hope. There is a fine, fine line between hope and delusion. I understand that. Still, I firmly believe that if you believe and are willing to work hard, truly work hard, you can accomplish what you want. The body is an amazing machine, too. It works hard to the point that cells need to be replaced on a regular basis from either getting damaged or getting worn out. The cells replace themselves on a regular basis. The cells heal themselves. Once I was reminded of this, I became convinced that Jim's body could heal itself as long as we figured out the pieces to allow his body to do so.

To this end, Jim began his plan to slow down the disease as much as possible and to beat the odds of only living three to five more years post diagnosis. *What toxins are in my body that are preventing my body from doing well?* Jim considered. He wanted to rid his system of mercury (including any found in his teeth's fillings) and any other toxin he could uncover. Jim's problem-solver mindset has served him well over the years, and was now kicking into high gear.

His love to discover and help was stirred in part by inspirational movies. One such movie is "Lorenzo's Oil," based on a true story of Augusto and Michaela Odone, the parents of a boy, Lorenzo, who had a rare disease called ALD (adrenoleukodystrophy). The parents searched for a cure themselves upon reaching roadblock after roadblock in the scientific and health communities, and eventually the father found an oil to add to his son's diet. It proved successful in slowing down and halting the progression of the disease. Although Jim has never mentioned this movie when considering his situation, I think about it often. I know, whether consciously or not, this movie propels Jim forward, reminding him "impossible things are not necessarily so." Jim would take on the role of Augusto Odone and get his hands on anything and everything he could to gain more information.

Interspersed with these "can-do" moments were the dark moments, when the devil would get after Jim and tell him he was dying and fooling himself. If Jim let himself think too long about the future, he froze in anxiety. At times, he would stay in the bed, a mixture of exhaustion from the disease and depression, and slept the day away. My fear for him grew. At times, I caught myself going down the same dark road.

Fortunately, in all cases, sometimes quickly over the course of hours and sometimes more slowly over the course of days, both Jim and I would hear something, read something, be reminded of something, and we would mentally kick ourselves out of these awful, destructive thoughts. Just at the right time, just as either Jim or I or both of us would start going toward that downward spiral, something of consequence and significance would happen. We would sometimes be hit over the head with it and other times, subtle signs were in front of us trying to be seen. These clues and events always came.

For example, Jim eventually crashed about two and a half years after the original diagnosis, winding up in the hospital in January of 2010. Because his diaphragm wasn't working well and because he had lost so much weight in several months, he needed a tracheostomy and a feeding tube inserted into his stomach. The day of his surgeries, my sister emailed me a newspaper article that a friend from California had sent her. The email read: "You won't believe this. Please read this immediately. It is Jim's story." The article was about the surgeries, the confusion of diagnosis, the building back of strength, and most importantly, the man overcoming and winning his battle against something misdiagnosed originally as ALS. This man's symptoms started off the same as Jim's—he was tired all the time and his swimming, something that was a joy to him, suddenly became difficult. His body was getting weaker and his nervous system wasn't cooperating anymore. After searching for answers, another diagnosis was made and the man was growing stronger slowly, but getting stronger. He had to have a tracheostomy and was working to wean himself off the ventilator.

I phoned my sister Monique. "When did your friend email you this?" I asked her.

"She just did today and then I forwarded it on to you."

"Does she know what's going on with Jim today? The fact that he is having the tracheostomy?"

"No," Monique replied, "she doesn't. But that story is Jim Young, isn't it?"

"Yes, it is. I can't believe it."

"Believe it. There's a reason you are reading that article today," Monique replied confidently.

We hung up and I reflected on my sister. As the middle sister of three, Monique found herself in "responsible person" mode early in life. She held the family together when my mom and dad were separated and always seemed to know the right thing to do. She has this amazing ability to say the right thing at the exact time you need it said. Always a beautiful person inside and out, Monique is popular and a perfectionist, being pulled in many ways. She is loving, but puts a lot of expectations on herself, and often runs ragged, trying to get everything done. Because we often have phone conversations on the fly, Monique will cut right to the chase and tell you what she thinks. She always has your best interest at heart, but you might not realize this immediately.

For example, on one such quick phone call occasion, Monique stated a fact: "Your life sucks right now. I am so glad I don't have your life."

At first, it was a sharp slap that struck me. *Did she really just say that?* I wondered. Then, a weight came off my shoulders. *Someone gets it. My life really does stink right now, I thought. I don't have to always pretend things are all right. It is good to acknowledge the bad and immobilize it before it can take over. From that point, you can move on and take more control of a situation.*

We tried to take control after the ALS diagnosis in December and arranged to visit Jim's family in Alabama. "A family visit will be a good distraction. You can rest, Jim, and not worry about work," I commented.

"No one realizes I'm sick at work, Erica," Jim said. "So I don't really have to worry about it."

"You know what I mean, Jim. I want you to rest and enjoy your family. And by the way, you really don't think people notice anything at work?"

Jim recalled a conversation with one of his colleagues at work. "Well, I did tell one person at work the other day."

"Really?" I replied, surprised by Jim's actions, since it was important to him that no one know at the office.

"I decided to tell Michele," Jim told me. "She could tell that I haven't been myself lately and because she knows a lot about me from her coaching role, I decided to tell her a bit." I waited to hear more. "I told her I was exhausted and really concerned about my muscles and my nervous system."

"How did she respond?" I asked.

"Well, I'm not sure. She gave that same look I see a lot these days from people who can't understand that I could be so sick. It's kinda a "I feel sorry for you" look and a "You are probably being too dramatic" look combined." After a short pause, Jim continued, "Michele reminded me that I am a positive person and that I need to wait to find out what is happening before jumping to conclusions."

"So you didn't tell her of the diagnosis then?" I asked.

"No," Jim stated, "I didn't think it was important. But it did feel good to let someone in at work. She gave me a good pep talk in general."

"I'm so glad things went well with Michele. Maybe it's time you let more people know," I responded.

"Oh no," Jim earnestly replied. "We can't do that. I don't want to tell anyone until I know what we are doing—what I can expect."

Over the weeks, we let additional close friends and family know. Because Jim is so positive in general, and because he didn't want to talk about his illness and symptoms, it was hard for people to understand that Jim was truly ill. On the outside,

Jim looked as healthy as ever, so most people were understandably confused. "Jim looks great, how could he be sick?" and
"Oh, come on, there's no way Jim could be that sick. He is
probably just making too much out of something minor. He
needs to stop working so much. You know he is a workaholic.
Maybe his body is trying to tell him to slow down."

Not intentionally, people would make light of Jim's symptoms, suggesting that they could relate. He heard comments like:
"I know how you feel, Jim. I was so exhausted after the babies."
And, "I can relate, Jim, I have been so unhappy with how my
body responds to exercise. I can't seem to lose the weight." And
there were the general statements, too: "We all get sick sometimes. You just have to shake it off, Jim."

But Jim was quite ill, unable to shake his symptoms, even
though he was trying to be positive, trying to say positive
things, and praying that the illness would disappear. Somehow
Jim made it day to day at work. Usually he crashed into sleep
once he returned at the end of the day. This same pattern was
seen when we arrived at his dad's, Harold, house. Once we got
to Alabama, Jim collapsed onto the couch, exhausted from the
journey. With Harold's help, I unloaded the car and tried to
answer the questions about Jim's health. Jim's sister, Prissy, who
had also come for a visit, tried to explain to her dad that ALS
was very serious. "Dad," she said, "people die from ALS. It
is really bad. I think I remember Jim saying about 60 percent
of patients with ALS show their initial symptoms with weak
hands. Jim is concerned because this is where his symptoms
started, too."

Harold couldn't make this register. His son was young, in
the prime of his life. "How do you contract ALS?" he asked.

Prissy explained again, "No one really knows. It is a horrible disease that attacks your nervous system and your muscles.

The weakness usually either starts in your hands or in your feet and works its way slowly across your body until you are paralyzed." I was happy to not have to talk and that Prissy took over at this point.

A few hours later, as Jim was taking a nap on the couch, he woke up and asked God, "What is this?" He then tossed about again and fell back asleep only to wake and hear, "It is Lyme." He blinked a few times, thinking he was dreaming, and then he closed his eyes again. He heard something again, and strained his ears to make sense of it. He distinctly heard numerous times: "You need sleep—you need more sleep. Sleep." He then closed his eyes and smiled, knowing God had given him the answer. He sensed God's presence and relaxed momentarily in the comfort that God was looking out for him. "Lyme. Sleep. Lyme. Sleep" were two distinct messages.

After waking up, Jim excitedly told me of this experience, "Erica, it was as clear as any message you would leave me. I heard these two words and have been thinking I need more sleep. I am exhausted all the time."

I was completely impressed and floored simultaneously. "God just spoke to you? Like you heard an actual voice?"

Jim replied, "Not exactly. I could make out words somehow. They came to me. I could hear them, but I'm not sure they were another voice. It was like my voice saying these things, coming from somewhere else. God. I don't know how to explain it. It's hard to do so, but I did hear the words."

"That is amazing, Jim."

"I know," he confirmed, "I really do need to get more sleep." We hugged each other, knowing something miraculous had just happened.

Why we ignored the first message, "It is Lyme" is a mystery.

Perhaps the message was too close to the devastating ALS diagnosis for Jim and me to wrap our heads around it. This premonition was a gift that if acted upon may have saved Jim years of grief. Instead, the Dr. Wonka recording of "You have ALS" played over and over again in Jim's head. There was no room for another diagnosis at this time. *I will fight ALS with everything I have,* Jim thought. *No one knows what causes ALS, and therefore, it is possible to figure out some things that others don't know currently. I will figure out some things on my own and buy some time. I will beat this.*

**Miracle = Words from God**

✳ ✳ ✳

## CHAPTER 4

# Knowledge

*"The range of one's information or understanding"*

AFTER THE ALABAMA VISIT AND our renewed "we will beat ALS" attitude, Jim decided to see a chiropractor and acupuncturist to help calm the intense cramping and fasciculations that he was experiencing. During these early days, I could look at Jim sitting in a chair and see his body "jump" as neurons fired randomly in arms and legs and stomach. It was as if an alien was in Jim's body, running quickly back and forth along his arms and then jumping to his leg, where the alien would punch out as if to escape. Jim's body would respond in kind with his skin pulsing. At other times, Jim would just slightly move a body part, such as a leg, hand, or finger, and that part would cramp up so badly, it would lock. The pain was like a revved up "Charlie horse."

Another frustration that came during this time was intense headaches similar to sinus headaches. These headaches would intensify over the course of the next several months, leaving Jim completely debilitated. At its worst, Jim would have such a headache not only at night, but also during the day. He found that taking Excedrin migraine pills by the mouthful worked some of the time. Most of the time, however, the relief would only be temporary in nature. After a few hours, the pounding came back. He would then take Excedrin again by the mouthful. It was a vicious cycle.

The chiropractor helped to ease some of this pain, but mostly just at the beginning of the relationship. Eventually, the adjustments became very mechanical in nature and didn't seem to be targeting Jim's specific pains.

"I think I'm done seeing the chiropractor," he commented, "Today when I was waiting in the assembly line for my turn, I could see in the room occasionally that the doctor was doing the same thing to every person."

"That's too funny, Jim," I replied. "Are you being serious?"

When Jim shook his head "Yes," I pictured a scene from a bad movie with robot-like people moving obediently into the "fix-it" room and then promptly when the buzzer went off, out the robots came with a new look on their face, as they shook out their limbs in order to walk better. I realized that my view of the medical industry was just taken down yet another notch. This depressed me.

But my faith in healers was restored with the acupuncturist, who was genuinely very interested in Jim as an individual. Jim spoke at length with him about his ailments and how he was feeling now compared to the previous visit. The acupuncturist would make Jim a special tea remedy to take home and use until the next follow-up visit. The odor of this tea mix was quite intense. The smell was so powerful that I had to just walk into the pantry where it was located and back up. Jim never drank the tea as the acupuncturist intended. He was so busy trying to drink other protein shakes and supplements that the tea fell to the wayside. Regardless, the acupuncturist did help

Jim to relax. Eventually, however, it became too difficult to do everything; there was physically not enough time in the day to get it all done. It got to the point where Jim struggled so much physically just to get to work and make it through the day. He was so tired and weak that the idea of trying to add anything, like a visit to the acupuncturist, would have been too taxing.

Something of great significance did occur during this period of exploring and visiting various specialists. About a year after the initial symptoms, one of our neighbors saw me walking the dog one afternoon. "Erica," Lane spoke clearly and eagerly, "I have been wondering about you and Jim." I stopped to see how she was feeling. I hadn't seen Lane in quite some time. Lovely as always, with her gentle southern accent, blonde hair, and kind gestures, she asked again, "How is Jim doing? I hope you don't mind me asking, but my husband told me he was having some neurological problems."

I had to pause, trying to figure out when Jim would have had this discussion. He was still so private and closed, not sharing his health concerns with many people. I remembered a neighborhood party we had been to recently when Jim spoke to several men in the kitchen. The men were all talking about the woes of getting older. I didn't realize Jim had shared this with the neighbors, but I was glad he did. "Ah . . ." I replied. Then I decided to take a chance and tell her many details. "Actually, Jim is really struggling right now. We're really scared because his nerves are firing randomly and the muscles in his hands are so weak."

Lane gave me a nice smile, waiting for me to continue.

"We have actually seen so many specialists, and one says Jim has ALS." Lane's face changed instantly. Then she gave me a little pat on the arm. "But really, I feel like we still don't know anything. He's taking some supplements that seem to be helping."

Lane paused again, politely waiting to make sure I didn't want to say more. After this break, she stated, "You know, I have a movie you need to watch. I'm just warning you that it is an intense video, Erica. I cried a lot during the movie, but it helps to know that everyone in the movie turns out fine in the end."

I was confused, "What is the movie?"

Lane responded, "It is a documentary about Lyme disease. You know I have that, right?" I shook my head "Yes." "Well, my husband and I flew to New York to see the premiere of this movie, "Under Our Skin." It is so powerful. It is fantastic. I had to buy several copies of it. I know now that I am supposed to loan you one of them." We both looked at each other. "I'm serious, Erica," she continued. "This is an amazing movie. I don't know if Jim has Lyme, but there is so much about it that you don't know. I can promise you that. You and Jim need to watch this movie and decide if there is anything of value to you in it."

"Okay, thanks, Lane," I replied. "I would really appreciate it."

After Lane dropped off the movie, it sat on our coffee table for weeks. Perhaps because of the stress in general or perhaps because this wasn't a box-office thriller with a major movie star in it, Jim and I never found the time to sit down to watch the movie. One night, I said to Jim, "We have to watch this movie tonight, Jim. If I see Lane again, she is going to ask if we've seen it, and I will be so embarrassed."

"You're right," Jim replied.

Once the movie started, I knew there was something of major value we were learning. There were several people in the movie who had similar symptoms to Jim's. There was one man in particular who was told he had ALS and was to the point where he was struggling to physically get out of bed and needed help. He was destined for a wheelchair within weeks. A world-renowned ALS expert told him, "Don't even think you have Lyme disease. You have ALS." The man was preparing to die, but with the urging from his son, he decided to try intensive long-term IV antibiotic treatment for Lyme disease. His logic was that it couldn't hurt. After several months, the man could walk easily and eventually his fasiculations ceased as well. He had Lyme disease that was undiagnosed. This man could have been Jim.

From watching the movie, I was convinced that Jim had Lyme disease, but Jim remained skeptical. A well-respected physician told him he had ALS and that is what Jim believed. He told me time and time again, "I've been tested for Lyme already—I don't have it, Erica."

"I know this, Jim," was my reply. "But remember from the movie. We had no idea how unreliable the test for Lyme is. What if you really have Lyme and just don't have a physician who knows how to identify it?"

"Erica, let it alone. I'll fight this ALS thing to the end. Don't worry about that. Let's give the copper supplements a chance—they seem to be working. I want more time."

I collapsed in frustration. I didn't really know for sure if he had Lyme, but I knew there was something wrong with the ALS diagnosis. I didn't want to push too much. I needed to be supportive of my husband and nurturing to him. Jim was in such a delicate mental state that I worried that I could send him over the cliff if I continued what he perceived as badgering. It was a dance. One day, I would drop a hint of Lyme disease. The next day, I would cry and hug him and just try to be supportive and let him talk about his symptoms. The following day, I would get frustrated that he wouldn't at least entertain the idea of seeing a Lyme-literate doctor and would say something to try to push him along. The next day, I would again see the need to love Jim unconditionally and to let the day ride itself out. So it went for weeks and weeks and weeks. It was an emotionally draining rollercoaster that was eased by the kindness of my family and close friends. They would call to check on me or offer to stop by with dinner or offer to take the kids somewhere, so Jim and I could rest or talk.

*Miracle = Lane's Message of Lyme disease*

✳ ✳ ✳

## CHAPTER 5

APRIL 2008

# Villain

*"One blamed for a particular evil or difficulty"*

EARLY ONE FRIDAY MORNING, WHEN I was getting ready for work, Jim stepped into the shower as I was drying my hair. The mirrors in the bathroom were getting foggy, but I could still make out Jim in the shower paying attention to his hip more than one would expect. *"I wonder what he is doing in there?"* I thought to myself. A few minutes later, Jim stepped out of the shower with a concerned look on his face. "What is it, Jim?"

"Do you remember that tick I pulled off my hip the other day?"

"Yes, the one you got at the golf course?" I replied.

"Either there or in our backyard."

"You're right—you get so many ticks, Jim. Why is that?" I really wondered if some people were more attractive to ticks than others. Jim seemed to have ticks on him regularly, whereas I never had them biting me.

"I don't know, but look at this rash. What do you think of it?"

I looked at the streaky, blotchy red rash radiating up and

down his hip. I let out a sigh of relief, "I don't know, but it's not a bulls-eye rash, which is great."

"Oh yeah, you're right. It can't be Lyme if the rash is not a bulls-eye."

Jim and I were both thinking he was safe (at least from that particular bite). We learned after the fact that any rash is of concern, and it turns out with Lyme disease that often no rash presents itself at all. So any tick bite is of concern. Period. But we didn't know. I beat myself up often thinking about what grief might Jim have been spared if we had acted on this tick bite and its rash. Over the course of these years, Jim has done his own version of beating himself up, saying things like, "Why didn't we know?" or "I should have gone to the doctor sooner."

But really fault is to be found with the lack of an education campaign by the medical community itself. There is a controversy over whether Lyme can be chronic or not and how to best treat it. This certainly doesn't help the general physician who might be able to prevent many aggravated problems if he were only better informed. Still today, when I read short articles in the newspaper or see information on the Internet about Lyme disease, there is misinformation and/or vague information. Often it still states the bulls-eye rash is the telltale sign of Lyme and that Lyme can be reliably determined by a blood test. Both of these statements are misleading.

It turns out that Lyme disease is a strange beast. A tick transmits bacteria, and if caught early in the process, with a two-to-four-week course of oral antibiotics, there is usually no problem. In fact, when you talk to many people about it, they will comment, "Oh yeah, I had Lyme disease. I took antibiotics for a bit and it's gone. No big deal." I think for this reason, people have a hard time believing that the same bacteria, if left to multiply in your system, hiding out in protective cysts and protected from your immune system by biofilm, can ultimately harm you in a variety of ways. In fact, sometimes, Lyme disease can build and eventually kill a person. Even if the Lyme doesn't kill a person, there is a weird twist. Lyme (or specifically the bacteria that causes Lyme disease—*Borrelia burgdorferi*) hits every person slightly differently. In one person, it may look more like multiple sclerosis, and in others, more like Parkinson's disease. Some people have called Lyme the new "great imitator" [1] because it looks like so many different things. "Symptoms can be surprisingly variable, so that days of near normalcy can alternate with days of profound debility." [2]

Perhaps this is one of the reasons some physicians and researchers have a hard time believing that Lyme disease can cause such grief—it doesn't follow a set path for every victim and therefore treatment can be difficult—there is no set of "one size fits all" path of symptoms. When studying the scientific literature, there is ample evidence that *Borrelia burgdorferi* can cause neurological problems, including ALS symptoms[3, 4] and that it is much more prevalent than the average person is aware[5]. In fact, Lyme disease is considered to be four times more common than AIDS in the United States[6]. If you ask the average person what HIV/AIDS is, he will be able to tell you something. If you ask that same person about Lyme disease, he will likely look at you strangely. If he does know anything, he will say something about a bulls-eye rash.

This craziness in the medical community definitely influenced how Jim and I approached Jim's problems. We both mentally were going back and forth with whether or not Jim could have Lyme disease. Jim felt he could not have the disease because he already had the blood tests, showing negative results for Lyme. As Jim and I learned more about it over the course of several months, it turns out that the tests themselves were faulty.

There are four tests for Lyme (see appendix for more information), but the most reliable one is the Western Blot [see 7].
Unfortunately, it is typically only used if one of the other three
tests comes back positive. Historically, the test for Lyme disease
used by many physicians gives many false negatives, and therefore many doctors don't even use them. In general, the test is
unreliable. It aims to detect only one of three hundred potential
strains of Lyme bacteria by detecting whether a person is making the arbitrary set number of bands related to the antibodies
that he would be making against the bacteria. Additionally, the
quality of the lab conducting the test and the reading of the results varies too much for accuracy, with the tests we use today
being defined almost twenty years ago. These tests are missing
approximately 75 percent of the confirmed positive Lyme cases.[8]

If a person is given the Lyme test too early in the infection
process, he wouldn't be making antibodies against the bacteria and the test will read negative. If a person is already being
treated with antibiotics for something else over the course of
many weeks, and thus preventing the person from making antibodies against Lyme bacteria, as was the case with Jim, a person
may _never_ show a positive blood test for Lyme disease.[9] In Jim's
case, during the course of several weeks in the winter of 2007,
he had flu-like symptoms and couldn't shake the illness. He was
prescribed antibiotics after several more visits to the doctors.
The flu-like symptoms were deemed likely from some sort of
bug. Upon yet another trip to his general practitioner, with Jim
still not feeling well, a round of steroids was prescribed to try
to knock out whatever was causing him grief. We now think
the steroids are what "kicked off" the downward spiral in Jim's
body. These steroids, by suppressing the immune system, likely
jolted the bacteria into becoming more active and invading
more locations in Jim's body.

Physicians should look at all the symptoms of a person and come to a clinical diagnosis of Lyme disease. By studying the signs and symptoms of the patient and taking the totality of the case as one unit, a clinical diagnosis is a reliable diagnosis. The Center for Disease Control[10] reports that such a diagnosis is useful and some laboratory tests may be helpful if used correctly and performed with validated methods. It turns out that many people feel comfortable with a clinical diagnosis for some diseases, like Alzheimer's disease or ALS. These diseases do not have a blood test to identify it in a laboratory. They are clinical diagnoses calls by doctors. When we told some people Jim was diagnosed with ALS, they did not say, "Did a blood test prove this?" But when someone talks about having Lyme, the questions become, "How do you know? Did you get a positive blood test to confirm this?"

How many times have we had to justify that Lyme disease was "real," and that Lyme disease could cause such horrible symptoms as with Jim?

The other painful aspect to the Lyme debate is how to treat the disease and, therefore, how Jim and other Lyme victims get financially compensated from their health insurance companies. The Infectious Disease Society of America (IDSA) Board gives guidelines of two to four weeks of oral antibiotics to treat Lyme disease.[11] They argue that there is no such thing as chronic Lyme disease, and therefore long-term use of antibiotics is unwarranted. Another body of physicians, however, argues otherwise. The International Lyme and Associated Diseases Society (ILADS)[7] believes there is chronic Lyme and that the duration of treatments should be based on the patient's individual clinical response. They believe there is insufficient evidence to adopt standardized treatment protocols and argue against a "one size fits all" menu. With all the evidence in the literature and one major group of physicians (ILADS) stating that chronic Lyme is real and that treatment needs to take on all variations of Lyme, depending on the individual situation, you would not think that health insurance companies would not be able to deny treatment of chronic Lyme. But they do. Time and time again, health insurance companies deny payment of long-term antibiotic treatment of Lyme, citing the IDSA's guidelines. They ignore the ILADS and many peer-reviewed scientific journal articles.

The bulk of health care insurance companies, including ours, use the IDSA guidelines, stating that long-term antibiotic use to treat Lyme disease is "investigational" and thus refuse payment for treatment of chronic Lyme disease. I remain puzzled as to how this can be when there are much data to the contrary. There are articles (all peer-reviewed and in respectable scientific and medical journals) showing evidence that Lyme disease can be chronic, and that Lyme disease can cause major havoc with people's health, and that Lyme disease can be treated effectively with long-term antibiotics [e.g., see 12]. It is also puzzling that a physician, by default of what the insurance companies are doing, is unable to make a call for his patient whom he sees on a regular basis. As a professional, with years of medical training and practice, physicians are not allowed to choose the best course of action for their patients. With other illnesses, a physician is given leeway to try something unconventional without the fear of prosecution. Why is it so different in the Lyme world?

\*\*\*

1.  Pachner AR. 1989. Neurologic manifestations of Lyme disease, the new "Great Imitator." Rev Inf Dis 11(Suppl 6): S1482-6.

2.  Pachner AR. 1995. Early disseminated Lyme disease. *American Journal of Medicine* 98 (suppl): 4A-30S-43S.

3.  Hansel Y; Ackerl M; Stanek G. Wien Med Wochenschr. 1995. ALS-like sequelae in chronic neuroborreliosis 145(7-8): 186-8.

4.  Halperin JJ; Kaplan GP; Brazinsky S; Tsai TF; Cheng T; Ironside A; Wu P; Delfiner J; Golightly M; et al. 1990. Immunologic reactivity against *Borrelia burgdorferi* in patients with motor neuron disease. Arch Neurol, 47(5): 586-94.

5.  Louis Reik, Jr., M.D. 1993. *Lyme Disease and the Nervous System. New York: Thieme Medical Publishers.*

6.  Stricker, R.B. and L. Johnson. 2010. Lyme disease diagnosis and treatment: lessons from the AIDS epidemic. Minerva Med 101 (6): 419-425.

7.  International Lyme and Associated Diseases Society. 2012. Found at http://www.ilads. org/lyme_disease/about_lyme.html.

8.  Coulter, P,. Lema, C., Flavhart, D., Linhardt, AS., Aucott, JN., Auwaerter, PG., and JS Dumler. 2005. Two-year evaluation of *Borrelia burgdorferi* culture and supplemental tests for definitive diagnosis of Lyme disease. Journal of Clinical Microbiology 43 (10): 5080-5084.

9.  Weintraub, P. 2008. Cure Unknown: Inside the Lyme Epidemic. St. Martin's Press.

10. Centers for Disease Control. 2012. Found at http://www.cdc.gov/lyme/

11. IDSA Guidelines for Lyme Disease. 2007. Found at http://www.idsociety.org//Organism/# NervousSystemLymeDisease

12. Stricker, R.B. 2007. Counterpoint: Long-Term Antibiotic Therapy Improves Persistent Symptoms Associated with Lyme Disease. Available at http://www.ilads.org/files/ press_release_7_15_07.pdf

Reflection

**D**ATA, PATTERNS, LOGIC, PREDICTABILITY, ORDER. These are attractive to Jim and in part probably explain his attraction to computer science. When Jim finished college with a degree in computer science in the early 1980s, he started working for a large software company. This afforded him many opportunities to travel across the country as well as visit a few foreign countries. Jim valued these years, as he was able to see the world, meet new people, and contemplate life. As a general rule of thumb, Jim desires to see all that there is in the world, experience new cultures and food, consider new pieces of art, wonder about a provocative film, consider the arguments laid out in a documentary, and understand—truly understand something. He is the type that is not satisfied to just take a medication—he wants to know the contents and the chemicals and understand what they might be doing inside his body. He is the type that doesn't want to just get into a car and drive—he wants to understand how the engine works, how various components are coordinated to work with one another, and how to gauge a problem based on symptoms.

Jim has a curious nature about him when it comes to most things you would encounter in life, especially when it comes to people. He has a way of reading people, which is quite impressive. He will often tell me things about a person or a situation (based only upon picking up on clues from a person, not from any direct confessions) weeks before the event happens. As he tells me these things, I will reply, "No way—I can't imagine that to be true—you are being paranoid, etc, etc." Then exactly what he predicted to happen does, in fact, happen: A couple separates, a colleague is let go, or he is targeted at work. It was only after we had been married over a decade that I finally started to "get it." Once I begin thinking "no way," I remind myself that I am married to a very intuitive man. He is especially intuitive about people.

Jim is attracted to people. He is a people watcher and a student of human behavior. He is fascinated with them and thrives when conversing with his best buddies or a complete stranger. Just give him a smile or some small opening, and off he will go. He will talk about the weather, politics, or some local happening. As he talks to someone, you can see a mutual interest and consideration. Jim has that type of personality where people feel welcome and will open up during conversation. Whenever we would go out for an evening, it was always fun to wait for the conversation that was inevitable. Sometimes the discussion lasted for a while. And at the end, there were always handshakes given, smiles exchanged, and everyone's lives were a little better as a result of the encounter. Sometimes though, a cold shoulder was given to Jim.

Whether the interaction is invigorating or frustrating, Jim argues that there is typically something of relevance to glean from any situation. For example, early in Jim's career, when he was traveling a lot, he was in Iowa and got himself turned around on the way to the airport. There were no cell phones at this time, and there were no GPS units in the cars to easily provide Jim with vital information. Jim began to panic as the boarding time for his flight was closing in on him.

He stopped at a local store, and in an earnest voice asked, "Can you help me get to the airport?"

Overhearing the request, an older man responded, "Hey there. I'm headed that way. Follow me."

Jim was grateful and hopped into his car. Once he was in pursuit of his leader, he realized. *I have no idea how long we are out from the airport. I am at the total mercy of this man.* Five more minutes passed, and Jim could feel himself getting more anxious. *What am I supposed to be getting from this? I am supposed to learn a little about responding to stress* he thought to himself. Another five or so minutes passed. *Why is he driving so slowly?* Jim was feeling himself get impatient. *I can't even drive ahead—I have no idea where to go.* He looked at the clock in the car. He was cutting it so close. *I'm going to miss my plane. I'm going to miss my plane.* Jim then shook his head side to side and thought, *well, no need to get so upset. There's nothing I can do about it. If I miss the flight, I miss the flight. I can reschedule it and I'll figure something out.* With that realization, Jim's shoulders relaxed and his mood shifted. Once he remembered that he could look at a situation in any way he wanted, he choose the more positive path.

With this new mindset, Jim followed the stranger. He considered his surroundings and reflected on his upcoming day. This slight shift in attitude made all the difference in the world. Jim ended up at the airport with only a few minutes to spare, but he did make his flight. He, more importantly, decided a few things from this one experience. First, Jim reminded himself that having a complete conversation to fully understand the situation in question was paramount. "I knew I should have asked more questions. I knew I should have paused a bit more before jumping in the car," Jim said. "Even if it took one or two more minutes, having as much information at my disposal was important. Preparation is key. Period." Jim also realized that things just happen sometimes and you just have to go with the flow; at times there is nothing you can do and you have to be all right with that. You have to be confident enough and trusting enough and positive enough to say, "It's all right. It will work out. I trust that things will be fine."

This flexible mindset can serve you well in more serious situations, such as a major health crisis. Fortunately, I too have a trusting and relaxed nature to my personality. When I reflect on how I have been able to navigate this unforeseen new reality, I realize much is owed to my upbringing in general. My mother Wilma raised me and my two older sisters, Monique and Lisa, under some stressful situations, but she always managed to have fun and see the brighter side to life. When my sister Lisa was in high school, one of her friends was struggling with her family. Unfortunately, she swallowed a bottle of pills, and after her hospital stay, she did not want to return to her house. My mom welcomed her to our home with open arms, working with her parents so that healing could take place. On another occasion, when my mother's friend left her husband and had nowhere to turn, my mom offered our home. This friend lived with us for an extended period of time. She received lots of support and caring words from my mom that allowed her to heal.

Whenever someone asked for help, my mother was more than happy to answer the call. And it worked on the flip side, too. When my mother really needed help, her brothers came to the rescue. One of my uncles was fast to be at our house, sweeping up me and my sisters to take us back to his house for the weekend so my mother could have time to cry and figure things out. Another one of my uncles would take us school shopping to buy clothes for the fall season since money was tight. In general, family was always around for one another and family helped family. It was never something we talked about, with the exception that my mom would remind us girls often, "You are the only sisters you will ever have. You need to take care of one another." Other than this message, my mom's life lesson was by example. She helped family, neighbors, and our friends however she could.

This loving attitude wouldn't necessarily have been expected considering my mother was struggling financially after my father left. She was struggling emotionally, too, as she had never imagined she would be in the role of single mother. Still, with her brothers, sister, and her mother and father's support behind her, she was able to focus on the positive and move forward for her kids' sake.

At the time when my parents separated, I was only ten. My oldest sister Lisa was fifteen years old. Having three daughters in tween and teenage years could not have been easy for my mom. My dad moved to another state and was not an active participant in our lives. My sisters and I longed for a relationship with our father, but after years of trying, we all came to the same conclusion in our own ways: "A father-daughter relationship is not going to happen, so move on. It's all right." After my dad moved back to the state of Michigan, where the rest of us lived, we did interact on occasion. At that time, Monique and I were in high school and Lisa was living on her own. We would meet for lunch and talk about cars or school—nothing of real significance. My mom got worried we would be hurt again. With such vocal protesting, my mother inadvertently forced my sisters and me to evaluate the situation all over again. It forced us to grow up more quickly than perhaps we would have liked, but we did learn a valuable life lesson. The three of us all learned that you can forgive behaviors to preserve yourself and to move on with your life. We each will say in our own way, "We don't accept dad's actions, but we refuse to let them define us or our futures." We decided to take the relationship for what it was; there was interaction with our father, but it was not close. We took what we could from the relationship, focusing on the positives and learning along the way to deal with change and unpredictability.

CHAPTER 6

FEBRUARY 2008
# Miracle

*"An extraordinary event manifesting divine
intervention in human affairs"*

TWO MONTHS AFTER THE INITIAL ALS diagnosis, Jim went
skiing in Colorado with several of his college buddies. "I'm
not sure how I feel about this, Erica," Jim commented just before he left for the trip.

"Why? What do you mean?" I replied.

Jim sadly stated, "I think so many people are coming because they think I'm dying. I'm sure they think this is the last
time they will see me alive." He spoke so seriously and lifeless.

As I was trying to take all this in, I had the complete opposite
feeling. "You can't really be serious, Jim. Your friends arranged
this trip to support you, to encourage you, and to remind you
how much you mean to them and that you are loved." I smiled.
Jim smiled back, too, but it was not the normal genuine smile
he gives. This one was a forced smile—one to pacify me, one
that he was hoping might convince him that my words were
true. But they were in fact the reality. Jim's friends wanted to
motivate him to fight and remind him that he mattered.

Jim was happy to spend time with his buddies, but he was also sad that he was unable to ski as he had so easily done the prior year. Jim loves skiing and loves being outdoors in the snow surrounded by the beautiful mountains. He also likes the calmness of the slopes and the peace of being away from everything back home. On this particular trip, however, Jim was deflated and exhausted much of the time. His body was failing him and he was constantly reminded that he couldn't do things that only a few months before he could.

Speaking to him one night on the phone, I asked about his friends and the trip. Jim sighed, "I can't even hang out with them at night, Erica. You know how it goes here. You ski all day and then eat a big meal at night, drink beer, laugh and tell stories. By the time we get back to the house, I collapse. I am exhausted. My legs don't work. I can't even make it a half day because I am so tired."

I could hear his frustration and sadness over the phone line. "Jim," I replied, "tell me about the mountains. Is there a lot of snow this year?"

"Ah," Jim replied, "yes, there is a lot of snow. It is so pretty."

"Oh," I replied, "I am so glad. Those mountains are fantastic. I wish I could be there with you. We could take a sleigh ride together—something we've always wanted to do, but we never had the time. We were always so busy skiing."

I could sense a bit of a change in Jim's attitude. "You're right, that would be nice. I really wish you were here."

"Me, too," I said with a smile. "I am a bit jealous. How come the wives weren't invited on this trip?"

"You know why, Erica," Jim said. "This is a reminiscing trip."

"Oh yes," I stated, "then you better start doing that. Stop focusing on what you can't do and enjoy yourself."

The next day, Jim told me that he stopped on the slopes when his body was done and instead of getting upset about it, he embraced the opportunity to hang out in the lodge with a few of the guys and view the scenery . Maybe he couldn't make it to the night for the drinking and stories, but he could interact with his friends in the afternoon.

It was during this friendly hanging out session, that Jim's cell phone pinged. There was a voicemail message waiting for him. After dialing to retrieve the message, he heard an unexpected voice. It was Dr. Wonka: "Jim, I've been revisiting your file and something isn't quite right. The nerve conduction test results don't quite match what I might expect. How about coming into the office when you get a chance?"

Jim was taken aback and a bit surprised that this insensitive man would go out of his way to admit that perhaps he did over-look something. He sat pondering the message, the man, and what he should do. *Do I want to go there again?* he thought. *What will I gain from going there?*

After several more long seconds, his buddy broke the silence, "Jim," he asked, "are you all right?" Jim shook his head up and down. "What was that call? Is Erica all right?" Jim finally spoke and told Pat of the message.

"Okay," Pat replied, "you say this man is arrogant and not helpful, but does his expert status provide you with insight you can't get from some other physician who has a better bedside manner?"

Jim contemplated this. "You know, Pat," Jim said, "you bring up a good point. I don't know what I would get from meeting with him again, but I don't think anything."

Mike, who was also at the table sitting with the two, jumped in, "Jim, you have always been able to do amazing things with the power of your mind. Remember in high school when we would come up with all kinds of stunts that others thought were undoable?" Jim smiled, thinking back to some of the funnier moments these two men shared. "Really, Jim," Mike continued, "the power of positive thinking. I know it works and so do you. If you need this man's help, go see him. But if he is just going to negatively get after you and your ability to fight this battle, forget about him."

Jim, looked back and forth at these men, filled with love and gratitude for their friendship and words. "There is no way," Jim emphatically stated, "that I would ever go back to Dr. Wonka. The negatives far outweigh the positives." Mike gave Jim a quick pat on the back, and Pat for his part gave the thumb's up. Both men believed in Jim and knew he was capable of amazing things. Jim never returned the call. Dr. Wonka never followed through with another phone call on his end, either.

That night, Jim called and told me of the message from Dr. Wonka and his decision based on his interaction with his friends. "I think that is great, Jim," I stated in earnest. "See, we knew it. You don't have ALS, and there is something else going on." I continued, "Jim, you're going to be around for many, many years and your friends are right to remind you that amazing things are possible with belief and a positive mindset."

"Erica," Jim replied, "you sound different. Is Braxton all right? Anything I should know about on your end?"

"Everything is fine here, Jim. Braxton is good. He's sleeping right now. He was very sweet tonight after we got back from work. He kept wanting to sit in my lap, no matter where we were. I'm thinking maybe he's just in need of some more attention. He probably misses you, too, and is looking for some extra loving from me."

"Is that really all?" Jim asked again. "There's just something different in your voice."

I couldn't believe that my very intuitive husband was picking up on something. "There is nothing wrong. I promise. I'm so glad you are having fun now and really enjoying yourself. Please continue to do that and take some photos, so I can see some things. Braxton will like to see them, too, when you get back." I smiled big on my end, so happy that Jim genuinely seemed to be having fun and knowing that I had a secret that would help continue to lift his spirits.

My secret started with tacos. I like tacos, but they are not high on my list of "must haves" for a typical day. About the fourth day that Jim was on his ski trip, I got a major craving for a taco. *"Strange,"* I thought to myself and continued with my day. Later that afternoon, "tacos" was speaking to me again. I pushed the thought out of my mind, and then as I was driving off campus, "Taco Bell" came to my mind. *Are you kidding me?* I thought, but then drove straight to the restaurant and ordered a soft taco to go. I ate it as quickly as I got it in my car and continued my commute. After picking up Braxton at daycare, tacos came to me again. *I wish I had ordered two soft tacos instead of just one.* I thought. *Maybe I can swing through Taco Bell on the way home.*

I got Braxton into his car seat and we started for the house. *"Tacos, Erica. Tacos."* I couldn't believe that I could not stop thinking about tacos. It was at this time that it occurred to me, *the last time I craved tacos like this, I was pregnant with Braxton. There is no way I am pregnant now.* But after Braxton and I got home, ate our dinner, and Braxton was in the bed, I started thinking about tacos again, and then I got excited thinking about the improbable possibility that I could be pregnant again.

The next day, I rushed to the drug store and purchased what I needed for verification. Sure enough, I was pregnant and so excited. I thought to myself. *So this is what "normal" people feel like when they can easily conceive a baby?* I couldn't stop smiling. This baby was too "easy." There was a reason for this baby. I knew this was a miracle and that it was my sign—the sign I needed from God, telling me that miracles happen and that Jim would eventually be all right. My experience with conception prior to this event was trying, discouraging, and so frustrating. It took years to get pregnant with our son Braxton. Therefore, I was of the mindset that we would probably just be a one-child family. I was all right with that. I felt blessed to have Braxton and so happy to have a family. Still, with this new pregnancy, I was elated. The "miracle baby" was a sign that things would work out after all. The timing of this pregnancy was not a coincidence. The timing of this pregnancy was a gift.

This pregnancy and this baby would be my comfort for years to come. Every time I started to doubt that Jim could be healthy again, I'd look to this baby, now my daughter. She is all spunk, all determination, and all love. Her personality is one that reminds as well. Whenever Jim needs a reminder of how to fight and why to fight, he need only look to his children, and be reminded that his daughter was a gift and a message from God to fight, to believe, and that amazing things happen all the time.

*Miracle = Pregnancy and Gift from God*

\* \* \*

## CHAPTER 7

JANUARY—APRIL 2008

# Numbness

*"Devoid of emotion"*

WHEN JIM RETURNED FROM HIS ski trip and learned the wonderful news, he was motivated to work harder at beating his illness. Jim still believed he had ALS since that was what the expert had told him. His goal was to slow down or stop the progression and to prepare as much as possible for the inevitable decline.

His first order of business was to get finances in order and to continue excelling at work so that his job was not in jeopardy. "I do not want people at work treating me differently, Erica," Jim told me often.

"It's not that, Jim," I responded, "but don't you think they need to know what is happening? Don't your friends want to know?"

"Don't be naïve, Erica," Jim said. "I love you, but you never think about the realities of these types of situations. I can be discriminated against, not promoted, not given opportunities, or sidelined, if they think I can't do the job."

My heart sank, but I knew Jim was right. On the one hand,

I wanted Jim to have as much love and support surrounding him as possible, but on the other hand, I didn't want anyone to feel sorry for him or make him feel badly. So Jim and I moved silently along our path together. We tried to do everything as always, and since I was pregnant with a small child already, it was easy to turn down offers to go out with friends.

As the months went by, it became harder to keep silent. I wanted to tell neighbors why they never saw Jim anymore. I wanted to explain to friends that we really weren't trying to reject every kind offer they gave us, but that Jim was so sick and that he could barely keep his eyes open once he got home from work. I did talk with close friends and family, but only in sound bites. In addition to this balancing act of which people I could talk to about Jim and our uncertain future, I was also trying to help maintain Jim's spirits, care for our young son, and work full-time. I was balancing the roles of supportive wife, pushy friend, loving mom, and confidante. As a "single mom" at this point, I was juggling to raise Braxton, trying to stay as stress-free as possible for the health of the baby growing inside my belly, and conduct all the regular family business needs.

It was most important for Jim and me to keep things as "normal" for Braxton as possible. So while Braxton, the dog, and I would take neighborhood walks or attend friends' birthday parties or events, Jim was sleeping or resting on the couch. It was a sad time. I wanted so much for Jim to be able to spend time with Braxton and me. I wanted him to be healthy and happy, and Jim desperately wanted the same. It was so hard for him to see Braxton and me going out to the park or to an event without him. Jim was worried that Braxton wouldn't know his daddy and his feelings of being "stuck and abandoned" grew more and more over the weeks. It was during these days that Jim would watch so much television, it felt like it was on twenty-four hours a day. It was Jim's way of escaping. During these TV shows, he did not have to think about his troubles and what he was losing. It broke my heart.

Braxton, of course, knew that life was different, but adapted quite well, all things considered. "Daddy, why can't you play baseball with me?" or "Daddy needs to rest—he is sick" were common statements out of his mouth.

One day, I sat down with Braxton, knowing that I needed to try to explain things more fully than I had up to that point. "Braxton, sweetie," I started. "Mommy wants to talk to you about Daddy." Braxton ran to me and eagerly sat next to me on the couch. Since he was only two years old, I knew my time with him in this talking mode was limited. Soon, Braxton would jump up and want to play something. I acted quickly, "You know Daddy is very sick, don't you?" Braxton shook his head and looked at me like I was asking him the most silly, most obvious question. "Well, I need you to understand that what is happening to Daddy is not something that happens to everyone. When you or I get sick, we might have a cold for a few days. Unfortunately, what Daddy has is different."

Braxton stared at me. I continued, "He is trying to get well. He misses playing with you. He misses hanging out with us as a family. We have to believe he can do this and ask God to help him. Do you understand?" Braxton squeezed me slightly. I was proud and amazed that my two-year old son did seem to understand the basics and those basics were really the only things that mattered. Braxton's daddy was very ill, he was trying to get healthy, and he needed our help to make that happen. I finished it up with this, "Braxton, you know Daddy loves you. I love you, too. We both love you. We both want so much for Daddy to be well again, and I think he can get there. We have to be patient."

"Okay, Mommy," replied Braxton. "Can we go outside now?"

Braxton's attitude was refreshing in many ways. His daddy was his daddy and things were the way they were. Braxton fully expected that one day his daddy would be fine, playing ball with him again, and his behaviors followed suit. He relished in the times when Jim was able to interact and seemed to soak up the attention. One day when the three of us were on the deck, Braxton moved to get some bubbles. I could sense that Jim was struggling, and I'm sure Braxton got it as well. Braxton didn't even say a word. He simply got the bubbles, the bubble machine, and handed it to me. I understood what Braxton wanted. I started getting the machine hooked up. Braxton climbed on Jim's lap, and the smile that swept across Jim's face was lovely. Braxton adjusted himself, trying to get comfortable, and Jim tightened his grip and hug around him. I turned on the bubble machine and Braxton made some noises of glee. "Pop," went the bubbles and Braxton at the same time. Jim smiled. "More, Mommy," said Braxton when the machine needed refilling. I ran inside to grab my camera and snapped some photos—father and son, just hanging out, content with simple bubbles and each other's presence.

Still, there were those moments when I wasn't sure how Braxton was really doing. He struggled to go to bed at night, constantly wanting another story or reassurance. Other children his age could fall into this same trick mode as well, so I didn't know if this was "normal" behavior or something new as a result of Jim's illness. At other times, Braxton wasn't his typical sweet-natured self. "I want to go outside NOW!" was one outburst. "No! I don't want to get dressed for bed," or "I don't want to eat that for dinner tonight" were heard often. One time I was in the kitchen trying to get a meal on the table and I could hear Braxton in the other room, crying and holler-ing about a toy not working properly. "I can't make it work!" he screamed and threw the toy. This was so uncharacteristic of his normal style.

"Let me help you with that, Braxton," I said as I rushed to get the toy.

"NO!" Braxton screamed, "I don't want it anymore."

I fretted over this incident and called my mom as soon as I could, "Do you think I should take him to see a therapist, Mom?" I asked.

"You know, Erica. He really does seem like a typical two-year-old boy to me. He has his moments, but so do most kids. He does have more on his plate than some kids, but he seems to be fine to me. Still, if your gut tells you he is having problems, you should follow your gut."

I took my mom's advice and started to pay more attention to Braxton and how I felt at the moment he was doing things. I tried to pay attention to how often he was acting out and if the frequency was increasing over time. I tried to pay atten-tion to when the behaviors happened. Did they occur when Jim was tired and not around? Did they occur when we were all together? I didn't notice any patterns and didn't have a nagging gut feeling they were anything abnormal. So with my eyes ever open, we moved along as we had, trying to make sense of our new lives together.

In late April, I picked up Braxton from daycare. It was a typical day for us, as I was asking Braxton questions about his day on the way home from daycare and telling him about my day at work. Braxton quickly started rattling off events from the day and then stopped short. "What is it, Braxton?" I asked.

"My friend Bobby," replied Braxton, "is sick."

"Oh, I'm sorry to hear that," I responded.

Braxton shook his head around and then stated, "I hope he doesn't have what Daddy has—then it will really be a long, long, long time before he comes back to school."

My heart sank, but I managed to say, "Oh, sweetie, remember daddy is really ill with a disease that most people never get. Bobby likely has a cold or something temporary. I'm sure Bobby's body is working on healing itself and he'll be back at school in a few days."

A few weeks later, Braxton learned about a boy from our church who was in the hospital. The boy became paralyzed after a dive into a pool. We were all shocked and saddened to learn of this. Braxton responded, "I hope this boy doesn't get too tired too quickly." He was stating a fact. He was proud of his statement.

"What do you mean, Braxton?" I asked.

"Well, he just got sick. When you are really ill, like with daddy, you have to fight for a long time to get healthy. I hope the boy is able to fight for a long time."

"Me too, sweetie," I responded as I gave Braxton a hug.

Then he added, "People can get well."

"Yes," I stated, "they can, Braxton. But sometimes, bodies are so tired that complete healing can't come."

Braxton cut me off, "I know that, but it is possible."

I looked at Braxton so tenderly, wanting desperately to be able to wave a magic wand. The only thing I could mutter was my belief, "Yes, it is possible, son."

*Miracle = Braxton's Belief and Spirit*

✳ ✳ ✳

## CHAPTER 8

MAY 2008

# Action

*"An act of will"*

PRIOR TO JIM'S HEALTH PROBLEMS, our vet had diagnosed Lyme in her dogs and it was highly probable that she had the disease, too. Her quest to find a physician to take her seriously and her subsequent desire to help others in the same boat led to the formation of the North Carolina Lyme Foundation. I phoned her one afternoon, speaking to her about Jim and asking her advice about a specialist.

A few months later, my dog had an appointment with the vet. As a strong, kind, and confident woman, Dr. Vet is animated and likes to give her clients her full attention. She also likes to tell you how it is. She is quick to comment on something you should or should not be doing with your pet and she has no patience for ignorance. During this particular visit, after she examined the dog, she asked about Jim.

After listening politely, I wasn't surprised with her insistent tone. "Erica, do you know people can die from Lyme disease?"

"Yes," I replied.

Then she said, "I don't care if Jim hates you and you have to drag him to the appointment kicking and screaming. Do it. He won't do it and you have to do it for him."

She was so right. *Of course* I thought. *What am I waiting for? It seems so obvious.*

"What do you think, Erica?" Dr. Vet asked.

"I know you're right," I replied. "I think I've been so nervous to push Jim too far too fast. You know how that is. You have to balance support with nudging. It's tricky."

Dr. Vet gave me a stare like she didn't believe me. Finally, after several moments, she spoke, "Really? That's what you're telling me? Make the call. Make it now. Go to your car and dial this number." I shook my head up and down as she gave me a piece of paper with a phone number written on it. I was gaining the confidence I needed. The urgency of the matter was pressed onto me and my confidence quickly turned to panic. Dr. Vet sensed it, too. She smiled and then gently touched me on the arm. "You are doing the right thing. I'm glad you are moving on this, Erica." She paused for a brief second and continued, "And, I want you to give Jim a message for me. Okay?"

"Oh course. Sure," I replied.

"Make sure to tell him this precisely," she replied. "I want you to tell Jim to stop d***ing around and get on this. There is no time to waste." A little shocked, but not surprised, I smiled and knew I would definitely relay the message as told to Jim.

"Thank you so much," I said, shaking her hand. "I really do appreciate it."

"It's nothing. Get out of here." And then Dr. Vet added, "And really, you do have such a great dog."

I opened the door to leave and my neighbor Lane almost ran me over as she was briskly walking with purpose. As a member of the NC Lyme Foundation, she was there on business. "Oh, Erica," Lane said with a smile, "how great to see you. I hope you don't mind that I did something for Jim." I looked puzzled, so she continued, "I ordered a book for him. It is the best book I have ever read on Lyme disease and Jim needs to read it. It is called *Cure Unknown* by Pamela Weintraub and it should be arriving at your house in a few days."

I was astonished at the timing of all these events. I looked around at the dog hair on the floor, the files stacked in the lobby, and heard barking and meowing in the background. I thought to myself, *Weird. Surreal. Here in the vet's office, with all the activity, something really fantastic is happening.* My mind was racing. There were those dogs barking again. *What was it that I needed to do again?* Seconds ticked. Lane interrupted my thoughts, "Erica? Erica? Is that all right? Do you think it will make Jim mad?"

I was shaken from my thoughts, "Oh gosh, I'm so sorry, Lane. That is so kind of you. Jim will really appreciate it. Thank you so much. Really."

With that, I smiled, paid the bill, and rushed to the car. With my dog sniffing expectantly by my side and anxiously waiting for the car to start, I reached for my cell phone. After the receptionist answered, I explained who I was and that Dr. Vet had recommended Dr. Lyme. "Is there any way Jim can get an appointment in the next few weeks?"

The reply was disappointing, "I'm so sorry. Dr. Lyme is so busy and has patients coming to see him from around the world. The soonest we can get you in would be August."

I was a bit deflated at this announcement, "Oh, I understand. It's just that that is three months from now. My husband is so sick. I was just hoping."

The receptionist paused, and I could sense her kindness. "I really wish I could help. It's amazing how many people come here for Lyme help. It really is scary. I really can't do any sooner for you. I'm so sorry."

"That's all right, getting him to see you guys in the first place is a huge step. We'll see you soon." I hung up the phone and felt satisfied. I looked at my dog, that sweet panting smile and face looking back at me. "Okay, Annie Mae," I said, "we are making progress." The dog barked in reply. "And now, I just need to call Jim and tell him the news. Any advice?" After silence from the dog, I dialed Jim's number at work. The phone rang and rang and then the voicemail message began. I panicked. *Jim is going to be so mad,* I thought to myself. *Oh no, what have I done?* But then it was too late. Beep. I needed to leave the message. "Ah . . . Jim . . . Ah . . . just left the vet's. All is well with Annie Mae. Ah . . . She convinced me that I needed to get you to the Lyme doctor. So . . . ah . . . I made an appointment for you. It is in August. You need to go. We need to see someone who can help. I know you want to give the copper supplements more time, but . . . ah . . . you need to do this for me. Don't be mad." And then the beep sounded again. My message was too long, so I was cut off. Still, I said the important things. I waited for the return call.

I tortured myself throughout the rest of the day, considering how mad Jim was going to be, pondering what he would think when he heard the message. *What if I rambled so much that he doesn't even understand the urgency of the situation?* was my final thought before Jim did call. "Hey, Erica," he said. "I got your message." There was a pause—a long pause.

"And," I said, "what do you think?"

Surprisingly Jim stated, "Okay." He didn't follow up with any other thoughts. There was another long pause.

I broke the silence, "Okay then. Great."

"See you tonight, Erica," Jim said.

"Okay, have a good rest of the day."

***Miracle = Friendly Push Gets Jim the Help He Needed***

✳ ✳ ✳

## CHAPTER 9

AUGUST 2008

# Relief

*"Removal or lightening of something oppressive,*
*painful, or distressing"*

A S WE WAITED FOR THE Lyme appointment, we decided on a family vacation. First, we visited with my family in the Detroit area and then we headed west to Saugatuck, Michigan. There we met up with two dear friends from Texas, Bill and Linda. When we picked them up from the airport, they came bouncing out to the car, arms extended, hugs flying. "Jim," Bill started, "you look good. I thought you were supposed to be sick?"

Jim smiled. "Nice hair, Bill. What happened to it since the ski trip?"

Linda chimed it, rubbing the freshly shaved baldhead, "It looks good, doesn't it?"

"It really does suit you, Bill," I said. "It is so great to have you guys here." We got in the car and Linda talked with Braxton, telling him jokes and laughing it up. Once we got to the cottage and got settled in, I started thinking about all kinds of activities we could do. Even though I was very pregnant with the miracle baby, I was glad to be on vacation and with friends. "Let's have dinner on the beach tonight, guys." I suggested.

"Really?" asked Linda. "You can do that?"

"Yes. My mom does it all the time. We can grab a pizza and some beer and have dinner with the sunset."

"Sounds great, but of course no beer for you, Erica" replied Jim with a smile.

I looked at the two men. Bill was not too sure about the outing, sensing Jim's fatigue, but agreed to go along. Jim was excited for the outing, but really was exhausted. "Maybe I'll feel better after a nap," he said. So as Jim slept, I tried to fill in Bill and Linda with the latest news.

A few hours later, Jim emerged from the bedroom. "How was the nap?" I asked.

"It was all right, but I didn't sleep much."

We all looked confused until Jim held up the book he was reading, *Cure Unknown*.

"That's the book from Lane, right?" I asked.

"Yes, it is. This book is amazing. There is a man in this book who has my symptoms. He is me. He was told he had ALS and was preparing to die. Then, he chanced the IV antibiotic therapy and now, as a physician himself, he has switched specialties and he treats Lyme patients." Jim looked victorious. I hadn't seen him so upbeat in months. I smiled. Jim smiled.

"Well," Linda finally said, "let's go get beer and pizza!" And with that, we headed out the door.

After a quick stop at the pizza parlor and a five-minute drive to the beach, we all unloaded the vehicle. There were chairs to tote, kid toys to include, and the cooler and blankets. We set ourselves up in a fine location. Jim started toward the water with Braxton in tow while Bill, Linda, and I settled into our chairs. I wiggled my way down into the low-lying beach chair with my pregnant belly constantly getting in the way. But once I got there, I had the opportunity to enjoy the view and friendship. The sky was starting to turn different shades of pink and orange. I scanned the shore for my husband and son. There were other people frolicking around in the water and the sand, and as I continued to scan the shore, I spotted my family. Jim was holding Braxton's hand and the two were looking down at the footprints they were leaving in the sand. At that moment, Jim looked up and back at me. I waved and smiled. He followed suit. Another minute passed and Braxton ran back to me, "Come with me, Mommy," he stated excitedly. Again, I wobbled and awkwardly got out of the chair. I moved as fast as I could to catch up with Braxton and Jim. The three of us walked up and down the shore.

"Look at that, Braxton," I stated, pointing to the old wooden posts sticking out of the water.

"What are they?" he asked.

"What do you think they are? Do you have any idea?" I wanted to understand what his brain was thinking.

"Something from a pirate ship," Braxton replied with a smile.

"Ah," I said, "good guess. These are actually old posts from a pier that used to be here. You could walk out on the pier and look around. Pretty cool, eh?"

Braxton was considering this, "Yeah. Why don't they rebuild the pier?"

Jim replied, "I don't know. Seems like it would be a good idea. Good things sometimes get damaged and you have to rebuild them and make them stronger."

I shook my head up and down, wondering if Jim caught

the message he was giving himself. I replied, "So true. So true. Braxton, I hope you know how smart your daddy is." Jim squeezed my hand tightly.

We all returned to the blanket, chairs, pizza, and beer (and for Braxton and me, water) just in time for the sunset. It was beautiful. It happened too quickly. The sun almost instantly looked as if the lake engulfed it. "Do it again," screamed Braxton in delight. Linda and I chuckled. Then we all dug our feet in the sand, feeling the coolness and dampness sink into our skins. Finally a sweet little voice said, "I'm cold." I hugged Braxton, trying to warm him as Jim, Bill, and Linda worked to get our stuff loaded back into the car.

The next morning, Jim decided to stay behind at the cottage to rest and read his book while the rest of us went into town. Any possible moment that he could, Jim was reading the book. He couldn't put it down—he read all day and late into the night, becoming increasingly convinced that he did have Lyme disease. "Okay, Erica," he admitted one night. "I think you are right. I am sure I must have Lyme after all." What a gift to hear these words. Something clicked in Jim's brain, and we were now on a different path—a path of our own choosing.

"I am SO glad to hear you say that, Jim," I blurted out, struggling to hug him with my big pregnant belly.

From this moment on, both Jim and I were anxious to get to Dr. Lyme's office. The month from the vacation until our appointment was one of the longest months of our lives. Jim and I didn't quite know what to expect when we entered the office. We looked around and saw lots of impressive letters, memos, awards, and newspaper articles framed and hanging on the walls. The staff was all very courteous and kind. Fortunately, we didn't have to wait long in the reception area when Jim was called back.

Once inside the examination room, Dr. Lyme came in with hand extended and a smile. "Hi, Jim," he started. "I'm Dr. Lyme. I'm sorry to have to see you today since obviously you are coming to see me under less than ideal conditions. I know you are so sick." He looked at me as well, with a genuine smile. "Hi," he started and shook my hand. "Please have a seat and tell me everything you can."

Dr. Lyme had a friendly face, a confident stance, and a genuineness about him. He spoke low and even-paced, not skipping a beat. If Jim made one small remark in passing, Dr. Lyme picked up on it and probed Jim more. As he spoke, it was clear Dr. Lyme was very intelligent. He seemed to know something about everything. He was a modern renaissance man who definitely cared about his patients. Both Jim and I took to him immediately. After asking Jim question after question about his various symptoms and when they started and if they were still present, we filled him in on our experience with Dr. Wonka. "I'm so sorry that happened to you guys," Dr. Lyme commented. "It is obvious there are symptoms you have that have not been addressed. Tell me more about these headaches you get." Dr. Lyme seemed very interested when Jim commented they were primarily associated with red wine consumption.

After almost an hour of taking Jim's history and thoroughly asking us various questions, Dr. Lyme was ready to administer his own round of tests. "Please sit on the table for me, Jim," he kindly stated as he got out various metal instruments and probes. He had a tuning fork to check Jim's hearing, and he used another metal instrument to check reflexes. Dr. Lyme had Jim squeeze his hands and watched Jim walk—similar studying was occurring as it had months prior with Dr. Wonka. Another hour passed. I couldn't believe how long we were in this man's office and how much time he dedicated just to Jim.

Toward the end of our visit, Jim asked Dr. Lyme, "Have you ever heard or read the book *Cure Unknown?*" Dr. Lyme looked intrigued and waited for Jim to continue. Jim explained the premise of the book, where different people are profiled, each of whom have Lyme disease and each of whom looks very different from one another.

Then Jim mentioned the man in the book who was highlighted who had ALS symptoms. To this Dr. Lyme replied, "Oh yeah—I know him. He's one of my friends." What a strange, small world.

Next, we asked Dr. Lyme what his opinion was on copper supplements. Dr. Lyme replied, "I'm not too familiar with that—if you do have literature to share, that would be great. I always learn from my patients who tend to do a lot of research and in general are quite educated." He added, "If the copper is helping you, you should definitely keep taking it, Jim." Quite a different response from Dr. Wonka who belittled us when we told him of a hair analysis that had led us to this copper deficiency label and subsequent supplements.

As we were finishing up in the exam room, Dr. Lyme turned to face us. "Well, as I think you already know, Jim, you have too many symptoms that DON'T match ALS." I could feel my body relax in the chair. What a wonderful statement to hear. Dr. Lyme followed this statement with "But you also know, you do have some of the symptoms of ALS. When the motor neurons are involved, as with your case, you never know what to expect. But it is clear that you have chronic Lyme disease with overlap ALS symptoms."

A new diagnosis was delivered and a plan devised. Jim would get started with oral antibiotics right away and after a few weeks, he would begin intravenous antibiotics as well for at least six months. Jim had progressed far and Dr. Lyme wanted to hit the bacteria hard. We were thrilled to leave the office with hope, with a new diagnosis, one that didn't carry an automatic death sentence. We knew that Jim was in for a battle, and that tough days were in our future. Still, we had one doctor on our side and that was all we needed. We left the office that late summer day filled with warmth and enthusiasm, ready to fight the fight.

## CHAPTER 10

SEPTEMBER — NOVEMBER 2008

# Birth

*"The emergence of a new individual from the body of its parent"*

JIM'S IV ANTIBIOTICS STARTED IN September of 2008. Jim had a port inserted into his left arm that moved up the arm, across the shoulder and emptied down near the heart. Additionally, training was conducted, so that we could start the IV antibiotics at home and tend to dressing changes at the port site. During these "IV dosing times," Jim would hang out in a large overstuffed chair we have in the family room, watching TV until he passed out literally, so weak from the disease and the chemicals going into his body. Jim eventually found that the laptop computer helped him feel productive and by concentrating on work, he could ignore the bad feelings for a bit longer before the inevitable crash occurred. Regardless, at the end of the IV drip cycle, Jim was spent. He collapsed from exhaustion and took a nap in the chair. I usually gently nudged him to wake up and then Jim would drag himself upstairs and into the bed, crashing to sleep the rest of the night. His nights were not restful, however, with a co-infection of the Lyme bacteria called *Babesia*, which is a malaria-like parasitic disease. This bug gave Jim major night sweats and chills. Jim would toss and turn all night and in the morning, get out of the now wet sheets, drenched in perspiration.

Somehow Jim could pull it together in the mornings and make it to work. As long as he was concentrating on work, Jim could move through the pain and hold off the exhaustion. He was by all accounts on the outside, excelling at work. He was up for a promotion and wanted it badly. Jim loved his job, his company, and truly saw a path for his division to grow. A leader by nature, Jim had a vision and wanted the chance to implement it. With much experience under his belt, a winning personality, and a strong belief and drive to work hard and excel, Jim was sitting in a good place. "If I can just get through these antibiotics, Erica," Jim said, "I will be on the road to recovery and we can move forward." Jim was so excited for the new baby, to be well again, and for a potential promotion.

Things weren't this simple though. The Lyme bacteria had a time schedule of its own. Jim was experiencing an elevation of some of his symptoms, as a result of the treatment  and the die-off of the bacteria that came with it, which resulted in the massive headaches returning during the day and Jim popping Excedrin migraine pills to end some of the suffering. At work, he would skip eating lunch because he was so queasy from all the antibiotics.

By the time he returned home in the evenings, he would actually stumble into the door and collapse on the couch, where he would sleep and try to deal with the pain. "Are you sure you should be working, Jim?" I asked.

"How can I not, Erica," was the reply. "This will just last a few months. Remember what we know. It will get worse before it gets better, but I can work through this until that time." He tried to give me a reassuring smile, but he was so tired, so afraid, and so not himself.

"I just don't know if it is wise for you to work. Your body needs to heal. I don't want you to push yourself too much." Jim replied, "Don't worry. I'll listen to my body and if things do get bad, I'll take time off of work."

"You promise?" I asked.

"Yes, I promise." He stated, believing it himself. The problem was that Jim was too tired to pick up on the clues his body was giving him. I was too frazzled, being pregnant, working full-time, tending to our young son, and worrying about Jim to notice all the hints as well.

Because our medical bills were starting to accumulate wildly and quickly, I was fortunate to have been offered an adjunct teaching position at another university. After obtaining permission from my dean, I worked, not only at my full-time job, but also at the other university. I was thrilled for the chance to learn more, interact with new colleagues and students, and grow my connections. Still, it was exhausting. I was seven months pregnant when the job started, and it was a struggle to balance it all successfully. I would conduct a lot of business on my cell phone on the commute from one job to another and fortunately I had help at the university with grading. I put my all into both jobs, not wanting my students to suffer, and also hoping to impress people at the university. My friends during this time were unbelievable assets. Three buddies from graduate school days were ever-present and generous with their time and help.

Patty would bring us dinner regularly and help with logistics at the university (as she worked there as well). "Patty," I commented often, "I feel so badly. You don't need to make dinner for my family all the time."

"Don't be silly, Erica," she responded. "You know I love to cook and it's just me. Trust me, you are doing me a favor by allowing me to cook for you. It gives me food and then I don't have to waste the rest." I struggled during these days to ask for help. I knew everyone else had his or her own worries and I didn't want to be a burden.

One afternoon, another graduate school buddy, Patrick, finally stated quite firmly, "Erica. Really. Don't you think we want to do something for you? We don't know what to do unless you tell us. Please let us do something for you. It makes us feel good to help. Don't deny your friends that gift." Those words were so helpful and allowed me to stop worrying so much and to ask. Patrick was great to pick up Braxton if I had to stay late at the university or help with babysitting as Jim was too exhausted to do either.

My third graduate school buddy, Janet, would lend a hand whenever I asked for help. If she was able to do it, she would. It didn't matter what I was asking. She was also great to bring food to the house and to insist on occasion that I go out to see a movie or have a dinner out.

My routine when I got settled back at home after work was production mode. Not unlike any other mother, I needed to fix dinner, clean up after the meal, tend to Braxton, wash clothes, and do minor housecleaning tasks, write bills or deal with other logistical items, put Braxton to bed, and then perhaps do some other things not normally on the "typical" mother of young children list. I would grade papers, prepare for my classes the next day, and help Jim with some of his needs, primarily changing his IV port dressings.

This was the task I dreaded the most. It was very stressful and physically painful on my very pregnant back, as I had to lean over a table in a very uncomfortable position for twenty minutes to adequately help Jim. Any minor mistake could result in Jim needing to go to the emergency room. And, boy did Jim remind me of this. "Erica, be careful!" and "Erica, you have to make sure everything is sterile. You're not doing it right." Jim is very meticulous and he knew that if he were capable of doing the change himself, he would. And, of course, he would do a better job of it. Unfortunately, for both of us, that was not an option. I needed to change it. But oh, the stress.

First, I would pull out the instruction packet and reread it to ensure I knew what I was to do. Then I cleaned our kitchen table, which acted as our medical procedure station. Then out came the sterile kit. I washed my hands thoroughly, tied back my hair, and scratched every part of my face and nose that might get itchy. After I put on the gloves, I couldn't touch my face again. Then I went to the sink one more time for a final scrub. After putting on the sterile gloves, which never seemed to fit properly, I awkwardly would position myself against the table. My belly got in the way. Next, I would have to remove the sticky part off Jim's arm and undo a lock that never wanted to easily pop off. Then I applied the cleaning agent, used various sterile cotton swabs, and then had to reapply the lock, some dressing and the sticky overlap on top. By the time I was done, my back ached, sweat was dripping against my head, and Jim was very stressed.

About two months into this IV antibiotic treatment routine, the miracle baby was born. Jim's mom Patricia came to town in anticipation of the birth and to help out with Braxton when the time came. On the night of the baby's birth, we had all gone out for dinner. "I don't think I can go, guys," said Jim.

"Come on, Jim," I urged him. "You'll have time to work when we get home. It will be nice. The weather is great. We can sit outside. Besides, this way I don't have to cook and clean up. I'm too tired and I know you are, too."

Jim smiled. He loved going to restaurants and enjoyed the

experience of dining out and eating good food. We chose a casual restaurant, since Braxton was with us, and we sat outside
in the early November air. The night was beautiful. It was very
warm for the time of year with the moon shining brightly in
a cloudless sky. The tables outside had orange umbrellas over
them, each with their own sparkling outdoor lights inside. It
was a beautiful and tempting site for a two-and-a-half year old
boy. Braxton loved it. He ran around the patio, pointed at the
lights, chased a ball he had with him, and managed to eat a little
dinner, too. I could tell Jim was preoccupied at dinner. He was
concerned because he still had to prepare for a business meeting
the next day. I could see his energy level drain before my eyes,
too. "Are you all right, Jim?" I asked.

"I am so tired, I can't even think." He responded. "I don't
know how I am going to prepare for this meeting." Patricia
suggested that he take a nap when we got home and then work
after. We all thought this was a good idea.

After getting home from dinner, I got Braxton tucked in and
then readied myself for bed. Strange feelings started, so I came
downstairs and said to Jim, "I don't think you have to worry
about that meeting after all."

Jim looked up at me exasperated; he was not amused. "What
is that supposed to mean?" he said annoyed.

I repeated myself, "Don't worry about the meeting." Jim was
still confused. "I'm not sure," I tried to clarify, "but I think this
baby is coming out tonight. Let me go back upstairs and lay down
a bit and see what happens." I waddled back up the stairs, and
lay on the bed for about two minutes. I definitely knew this baby
was to be born. I found Patricia and let her know, got dressed
back into my clothes, and Jim and I left for the hospital.

When we got into the car, I said, "Jim, drive faster. I really think this baby is coming now." Jim took the quickest route and fortunately, the hospital is only a few miles away from the house. When we arrived at the hospital, I said immediately, "I need an epidural."

"Okay, honey, slow down," the nurse replied. "We need to see if this baby is even coming tonight." I had an urgent look on my face. I knew this baby was on the way. I moved as quickly as I could and got on the hospital bed.

I was so uncomfortable, barely able to move when another nurse popped into the room, saying, "Hello, Erica. You are far along! The other nurses and I couldn't believe your numbers when we saw your stats up on our board. How did you make it this long in labor?"

I tried to smile, saying, "The pain really just started, but it is intense. I need an epidural."

"Okay," she replied. "Let me see what I can do. But first, we need to get you hooked up to an IV and monitor what is happening to the baby. I'll put in the call and tell them you are priority." Within another few minutes, other nurses arrived, machines were hooked up, and IV lines started.

There were lots of beeps, monitors, and people moving in and out. "Jim," I said. "Where is the anesthesiologist? I need him." Jim looked at me with sympathy, but he was so tired and trying to hang on for me. More beeps, more people. Finally, the anesthesiologist.

"Erica," he started, "you are far along. There is not much I can do, but I can give you a partial epidural."

I just looked at him and thought, *is there really such a thing? Maybe this is a placebo thing they are going to do for me.* I said, "Please, sure, yes. Thank you." With that, he moved into action, and when I sat up on the side of the bed, I needed help. It was so painful. The baby was coming.

The anesthesiologist gave me something and what seemed to be ten minutes later at the most, a little girl was born. Jim and I were so excited that she was healthy and here. She was our miracle baby. Once things settled down, Jim looked at me with tears in his eyes and said, "Erica, she is all right. She doesn't seem to have anything wrong with her."

I kissed Jim and said, "Of course she is fine, Jim. She is our miracle baby. I knew she would be perfect."

On his end, Jim worried from the start of the pregnancy that something would be wrong with the baby. The bacteria that causes Lyme is related to syphilis, and therefore it may be sexually transmitted. Jim worried he may have given it to me and that the baby may have been infected. There are documented cases of maternal transfer of Lyme to fetuses, which can result in miscarriages. Jim was so relieved when he saw his daughter. He stared at her for a long time and then crashed in the chair to sleep for several hours.

✳ ✳ ✳

## CHAPTER 11

NOVEMBER 2008

# Annalise

*"Gift from God"*

THE BABY AND I BONDED in the hospital for several days. Because Jim was so tired, he took the opportunity with the days off of work to sleep. Patricia was watching Braxton, and we decided to wait a few days before bringing Braxton by to meet his new sister. I tried to focus on the positives of having this time alone with the baby. I got to know her differently than when Braxton was born. It was a calmer time, a more quiet time, with less visitors coming to the hospital, and I gained an appreciation for her personality. Still, it was lonely without Jim there. I felt badly for him and for my family in general during this time. Jim wasn't around, couldn't be around, and wanted desperately to be around, and I, too, wanted him to be able to enjoy our new baby.

This new child of ours was a determined girl with a strong personality. She would charm me one moment and then cry loudly and long until she could nurse. Even when she was nursing, if she wasn't getting what she wanted or as much as she wanted, she definitely let me know about it. In fact, when the lactation nurse paid a visit, she commented that the baby was like "a snake." She smiled while saying, "I have never seen a child go after a breast like that and I have been doing this many years."

"Interesting," was my only comment. As this baby has grown into a child, her persistence is still intact. She shows many of the same traits her daddy has: She is determined, demanding what she wants. She is also as sweet as anything, flashing a smile and look that melts your heart.

The baby didn't have a name for days. Jim and I had picked out two names that we liked very much, but we never decided which was preferred. Jim was so sick during the baby's birth that when I would ask him about it, a common reply would be, "I like both of them, so you choose." This didn't help me at all—the pressure felt so intense. I would study the baby and say both names to her. Both seemed all right at first, and I thought I would never be able to decide. Still, after a few days, I looked at her and did know absolutely—the correct name was Annalise.

I was satisfied and confident I had chosen the correct name for our daughter. I was excited to share the name with my mother in particular for a major reason we selected it was to honor my mom's Dutch heritage. My mom moved to the United States from the Netherlands as a teenager with her family. Being Dutch and being proud of being Dutch was a given for us. I grew up with my two sisters celebrating Dutch holidays and embracing our heritage. It seemed fitting to honor my mom for all she has done for me by giving my daughter a Dutch name. When mom and I spoke on the phone, I boldly made the announcement, "We decided to name her Annalise, Mom."

"Wow," she replied, "that's great. How will you spell it—the traditional Dutch way?"

Jim and I had contemplated this exact issue months before. The traditional Dutch spelling is Annelies. We knew on paper if anyone saw her name, he or she would not know how to pronounce it correctly. We decided on the English version for spelling the name—Annalise.

When my mom heard this, I could feel the drop in her enthusiasm "How can you give her a Dutch name and not spell it the proper Dutch way?" she asked. Mom seemed so frustrated.

I defended the selection, arguing that my sister Monique had a baby name book from Holland that had versions of the name in it and Annalise was one of those versions—therefore, technically, it was still Dutch. Deflated, Mom got off the phone. I wasn't quite sure what to make of the conversation.

Several hours later, the phone rang. "Erica," my mom stated, sounding very excited about something, "I've done some research on the name Annalise." Mom explained how she went to the computer to read about the name. There were various surveys conducted on whether people liked their names and for the most part, overwhelmingly, women did like their Annalise names (or any variations in the spelling). "The most interesting part though . . ." Mom continued "Well, let me ask you a question first, Erica."

"Okay, Mom, what?" I replied.

"Do you know what Annalise means?" Mom asked.

Interestingly, I didn't. When she asked the question, I remember thinking to myself, *how could I not know this? This is definitely something that I normally would investigate.*

"Well," Mom said, "let me tell you. The name Annalise means "Gift from God!"

I actually didn't know what to say. I knew this was the right name, but I had no idea that my miracle baby's name was so appropriate.

*Miracle = Healthy Annalise*

✳ ✳ ✳

## CHAPTER 12

NOVEMBER 2008 — JANUARY 2009

# Warrior

*"A man engaged or experienced in warfare; broadly: a person engaged in some struggle or conflict"*

JIM AND BRAXTON ARRIVED AT the hospital on a lovely fall afternoon. With the leaves almost all off the trees, and orange tints everywhere, it was time to bring Annalise home. When we rounded the corner to our house, there were balloons on the mailbox, and Braxton just grinned and laughed, saying, "For my baby sister!"

Braxton was excited to be a big brother, but he also had a tough time adjusting to the new demands placed on me. Jim was home for a few days, sleeping as much as possible. "I'm so excited you get two weeks at home, Jim," I said. "Now you can rest and don't have to feel pressure to work." Jim gave me a strange look. "What? You have two weeks for paternity leave."

Jim looked at me for a long time, "Erica," he finally said, "I feel like I need to get back to work. I really want that promotion and I don't want my boss thinking I'm not a hard worker."

"I don't understand you, Jim Young," I replied. "That is ridiculous. You have the perfect excuse for staying home. You should stay home and get to know your daughter. I think you are being foolish."

Jim paused, trying to figure out what to say. Finally, after many seconds, he stated calmly, "I know you are right, but I feel like I need to get back to work to prove that I am the right person for the job."

Frustrated with my husband, I just shrugged my shoulders and said, "You can't take the rest of your paternity leave six months from now. That's not how it works. I really am so mad at you."

Jim knew I was mad, but he felt so drawn to return to work. After one week at home, he started back.

My maternity break was spent driving Braxton to daycare in the mornings while the baby stayed at home with Patricia. Jim was struggling to get himself to work and asking him to help with Braxton seemed too taxing. Once I returned from the drop-off, it was usually nursing time with Annalise, followed by the infant routines that seem to never stop. Once there was a break, I would look at the clock and think, *time to get Braxton,* and off I would drive to retrieve him.

About four weeks into my maternity break, Annalise developed a rash all over her face and body. The rash behind her knees and on her arms was not completely unfamiliar to me. It looked like the eczema that Braxton had when he was a baby. But the rash on her face looked so raw and tender and it was obviously bothering her quite a bit. She would try to scratch at her face and would cry often to the point that we started putting those baby mittens on her to protect her face from scratches. After visiting my pediatrician and being referred to a general allergist, and then a pediatric allergist and a pediatric dermatologist, we tried everything. At first, we thought she had an allergy to eggs, so I cut out all eggs and dairy from my diet, so the breast milk would not cause Annalise grief. After a temporary reprieve, the rash was back and the doctors concluded she wasn't allergic and that it was just really bad eczema. All I could do was apply some lotion and wait. Eczema, in this extreme form, usually is present only the first couple of years of life. I didn't want to wait around until Annalise was two years old, but it seemed like we had no other recourse.

So my too brief a maternity leave was spent trying to figure out Annalise's rash and trying to bond and get to know my daughter better. During this same time, Jim was able to work, but when he would return home, he was spent. He would move through the routine of administering the IV antibiotics, crashing in the chair, and sleeping the weekends away to catch up on sleep and to be able to work another week. It was frustrating that Jim couldn't or wouldn't spend time with his new child. But it was evident that he was in no physical shape to do so. Every once in a while, as he was lying on the couch, I would place Annalise on his belly and he would talk to her. She seemed to respond quickly to her Daddy. Braxton, too, would shuffle over to the couch when he sensed that Jim was having a good day. They would throw a ball back and forth or look at a book together.

Over the course of the next many months, Jim increasingly struggled more and more. Trouble would start during the night when Jim would wake up with the worst sinus headache. Attempting to alleviate the pain, he would take all kinds of over-the-counter medications and then apply a rice pack to his face. The intense headaches never really went away, so Jim tossed and turned all night, only to discover at some point that it was morning and he had to gather up his strength to go to work. Once he physically got out of the bed, and because in general he was so weak from the treatments, a shower would wipe him out. Because I was busy nursing an infant, I couldn't devote the time to help Jim.

One morning, I was bouncing Annalise, trying to get her to go back to sleep, when we came into the bedroom. "Jim?" I asked, "What are you doing in the bed all wet?" Jim barely moved. I got a little nervous. Annalise started to cry again. Bounce, bounce, bounce. "Shhh, little girl." Bounce, bounce, bounce.

"Jim?" He moved just slightly. "Really, what are you doing? Are you okay?"

"Yes, I'm fine," Jim replied. "I just need a little time to recover."

"What do you mean?" I asked.

"The shower wiped me out. I could barely finish washing my hair. I am so tired."

I ached for him, but the baby was crying again. Bounce, bounce, bounce. "How long have you been laying here?"

Jim looked at the clock, "About twenty minutes."

This was the beginning of a trend of having trouble moving. When I looked at his hands, I could see the muscle wasting in between his fingers. "Erica," Jim said one morning, while staring down. "Look at my hands."

"I know, sweetie," I replied as gently as I could. "You can get it back. You can gain muscle back."

"I'm scared," Jim said. "It's getting harder to write and harder to do simple things."

"This is so awful," I replied. "I wish I could do something."

"I wish we could just make it stop. If I don't lose any more muscle, I could live with that."

I squeezed him, and then heard the crying in the background. "I'm so sorry, Jim. Annalise is crying."

"I know. Go to her. She needs you."

After tending to Annalise and getting Braxton out of bed, we all met up in the kitchen. Jim was shuffling, with his shoulders slumped over and back arched, toward the door. "Are you really going to work?" I asked, noting that he could barely walk. "Why don't you take a vacation day and tell people you want to spend time with the baby?"

Jim seemed so frail. "I need to go. Don't worry. I'll be all right."

I watched him get into his car and try to readjust himself in the seat. My urge was to run out to the car and help him, but I knew that would make him feel worse. I noticed he was struggling to turn the key in the ignition. But with all the will power he had, Jim got the car started and backed out of the driveway. As the kids and I turned to walk back inside, I said to them, "Your Daddy is one stubborn man. It is both a good trait and a bad trait. He is a hardworking person, too. I hope you guys know that." Braxton just grinned at me, while Annalise made a cooing noise.

A few weeks later, Jim had to go to Mexico for a business trip. He spoke to his doctor before the trip to ensure traveling was safe, and we arranged for transport of his medicines. The only logistical sticking point was what would happen if Jim needed help getting dressed in the mornings. It was sometimes difficult for him to zip his pants or get a button in place. "I think I have to ask Josh to help," Jim said when we were finalizing plans.

"Are you sure you want to do that?" I asked. "Can you trust him?"

Jim was still worried to tell his colleagues, afraid of discrimination. "I don't think I have a choice," Jim replied.

The short trip went well for Jim, and Josh did help a few

mornings. While Jim was gone, my sister Monique came to town to help and to meet her new niece. It was such a nice treat having my sister with me. She made food for the freezer, cleaned the house, and helped with childcare. The afternoon Monique and I picked up Jim at the airport, she said, "Are you feeling okay, Jim? You look horrible. I think maybe we should go to the hospital."

Jim just shook his head, saying, "No. I'm fine. Just tired. I need to sleep."

I was a bit concerned, too, but trusted that Jim wouldn't do anything silly. We returned home and Jim went straight to bed.

The next morning, Monique saw Jim again just after he woke up and came downstairs where I was with the kids. "Erica," she started, "have you seen Jim today? I think he looks worse than yesterday."

I considered this. I had seen him, but to me he seemed all right. "I think he's fine, Monique," I replied.

"Really? I think you are not seeing things clearly, little sister. I really think we should take him to the emergency room. Something could be really wrong. I mean, Erica, when I asked Jim a question, he could barely speak. I could hardly understand him."

Braxton then started fussing about his breakfast, and my attention was pulled from the conversation. Monique joined in to help with Annalise, and once things started settling back down again, Jim came down the stairs. He was dressed in his work clothes. They were casual clothes that he could put on himself. His hair was brushed, and he looked clean and professional. "Josh," Jim said into his cell phone, "I know what you mean." Jim laughed. "I should be to work in about twenty minutes. I think you're right in that we need to work on the plan for our next meeting and have that agenda in order before the day ends." Jim finished the conversation, laughing some more, speaking very eloquently and clearly.

Monique turned to me stunned. I knew what she must be thinking. I have seen Jim's magical transformation occur before. Monique then said, "How on Earth did he do that? He is a completely different person than he was thirty minutes ago. I honestly cannot believe it."

"I know what you mean," I stated. "I don't know how Jim does this, either."

"It can't be good for him, Erica," Monique said. "He is using a lot of energy to do this when he should be using it on healing."

"I know," I replied, "but there is the flip side, too. I remember reading an article in a magazine a few months ago about a woman who was convinced the reason she bounced back so quickly from her cancer was because she didn't let anyone know she was ill, with the exception of one assistant at work. This woman said she didn't want to be treated differently and didn't want to give into the illness. She commented that if she acted sick, she would get sicker. She acted as normal as she could and felt that this helped her. I kind of think this is what Jim is doing."

At that moment, Jim walked into the kitchen and gave his sister-in-law a gentle sideways hug. "I'm all right, Monique. I told you."

Monique, looking dumbfounded, replied, "How did you pull that off, Jim Young?"

Jim smiled and told the simple truth, "It is pure willpower." And with that, he went to the car—slowly, tentatively, but determined. We all waved. Monique quickly turned to me, with her eyes popping with expression and just stated, "Wow!"

The next day, Monique returned to Michigan, and for the first time since Annalise's birth, we were alone as a family. It was nice, but taxing, trying to care for everyone and worrying about Jim at the same time. Braxton seemed to be looking at Jim more often, studying his daddy's moves. "Daddy," Braxton pleaded one afternoon, "play knights and dragon with me. You can be the dragon." Jim smiled and tried his best, but it was evident his heart was not there. He was fighting off sleep and could barely move his arms, let alone his whole body to play a dragon. "Come on, Daddy! You need to blow fire on me!"

In the other room, I called after Braxton, "Hey, Braxton, why don't you come in the other room and we can play warrior. I have the swords."

"No, Mom," Braxton replied. "I want to play with Daddy."

"I know, sweetie, but Daddy needs to rest."

Braxton sulked and came into the other room. "You can't play. You have Annalise." He was so frustrated.

I tried to explain to him how Daddy was so sick and that the sleep allowed his body to fight the illness. I could see Braxton's body perk up slightly. "Do you understand, sweetie?" I asked.

"I do!" Braxton was so proud of himself. "Mom, it's good that Daddy has both warriors and knights inside his body."

Now, I was the one confused. "What do you mean, Braxton?"

Braxton gave me that look that said "What is wrong with you, Mom?" He had an "everyone knows why" look. After a pause, he replied, "Because warriors and knights fight differently. They have different things. The warriors use bows and arrows and the knights use swords and jousts. Then they can pweeh, pweeh, pweeh from all directions and get the Lyme. The warriors and the knights are attacking Daddy's Lyme. When

Daddy sleeps, they go crazy. Pweeh, pweeh, pweeh!" Braxton moved his body in combat mode, showing how the knights and warriors operate.

Several weeks went by and Braxton never mentioned the warriors and knights again. Then, out of the blue, when I was putting him to bed for the night, he made a declaration, "You know, the longer Daddy sleeps, the sooner the Lyme will go away. It is good there are knights and warriors in there going after the Lyme—the bad guys never win. They wear black—that's how you know they are bad."

"So they are killing the bacteria?" I asked.

"Yes, isn't that great?" Braxton asked.

"Absolutely," I replied. "We need all the warriors and knights we can get fighting for Daddy. Now time for bed." As I kissed Braxton goodnight, I prayed to the highest Warrior I knew, "Please, God, kill all the bad bacteria and cure Jim. My children need their Daddy."

A few days after this incident, Jim received great news. He got the promotion! Maybe the warriors were coming out in full force.

### *Miracle = Warrior Cells Attacking*

✳ ✳ ✳

## CHAPTER 13

JANUARY 2009

# Angel

*"An attendant spirit or guardian"*

MY FIRST DAY BACK TO work after maternity leave welcomed me with much mail. Stuck in the middle of it all, I noticed a large manila envelope hand addressed to me. I pulled it out and studied the return address noted with the name "David." *Could this be David from graduate school?* I thought. The city was one on the beach, and I remember my buddy from statistics class living there. Still, it had been over fifteen years since that class and graduate school.

Unable to put off my curiosity any longer, I tore the envelope open and a Bible fell out. On the cover were a surfer, the ocean, and the title, *A Surfer's Bible*. I smiled, now thinking this had to be David from graduate school. I thought back to our study sessions in the library. In the middle of discussing a statistics problem, David would pause and say something like, "Stop. Close your eyes. Do you hear them? The waves? Feel the light salt spray on your face. Oh, in the distance, I see something interesting. I think they are dolphins. About three of them jumping in and out of the waves. Feel the warmth of the sun on your face. I'm squinting in the glare of the moment."

If you dared to open your eyes during one of these "David moments," you would find him with an enormous smile on his face (which was commonplace regardless). You would see a man who was truly happy. It didn't matter how stressed he was, he could pause and live in that "happy place." He also had the ability to transfer that moment to the rest of us in the study group. Even though one of us might roll our eyes or comment that we didn't have time for this, in the end, we were always appreciative for the break and the reminder that statistics had its place, but that there were other things calling, other things that helped put things and life in perspective.

Jostling myself back to the present, I peered inside the envelope and saw a hand-written letter. I pulled it out and turned it over and over again. David wrote that he had googled me and found that I was a biology professor and it seemed like I was doing well. "I remember you said you wanted to teach at a small college," he wrote, "and obviously you are doing that. Good for you!" Then I read, "I wanted to let you know that I was praying for your family. I heard God telling me to pray for your family and so I am. I'm not sure what is happening with your family, but know that I am praying for you. I hope this gives you comfort and that whatever is happening in your life that you know God can help. He is there for you." David's letter was short, but to the point. The timing was remarkable. I was stunned, moved, and grateful. I was so excited to share this story with everyone I knew, again knowing that it was a way that God was speaking to us. Jim was going to be all right.

I kept the letter in my desk drawer at work and returned to it over and over again when I needed the uplift. It was comforting knowing the letter was there. It was my own connection to God. Sometimes, after a long afternoon, I would fold into my chair at work and touch the drawer. I didn't need to get the letter—that wasn't important. It was important, however, to be reminded that good things were possible and that kind, good people were all around us, helping us and encouraging us to believe and to fight. I was reminded that David found me for a reason. It was not a coincidence. I knew this letter and his friendship were gifts and ones that sustained me when doubts began to drift into my mind.

The most powerful sentence of David's letter was simply, "I was told to pray for your family." These words and this beautiful man helped me get through some horrible days. I wanted to let him know how much he helped my family and me and how much I appreciated his letter and his prayers. I wanted to tell him Jim's story. Still, every time I sat down to write David a letter, I found myself distracted, unable to put the time into the letter that was warranted. David's letter came in January. I finally answered him in May, when the semester was over, and I had the time to devote myself to telling him all these things.

Over the course of the next many months, David and I wrote each other and then eventually started emailing each other. Every time I was feeling a bit discouraged, an email "happened" to come from David. Every one had a message of hope and cheer. I would forward some of these on to Jim—they helped him a great deal, too. My angel David had amazing timing. His words, faith, and giving presence were always in love and always just what Jim and I needed.

Through our renewed friendship, I learned that David, too, had been struggling with his own health. He had been diagnosed with throat cancer, which came as a shock, since David never smoked and always took good care of his body. After he learned of his diagnosis, after much consideration, he decided to decline medical treatment. David and his wife put their faith in God and prayer. "Erica," David wrote in one email, "I am supposed to be dead. The doctors told me I only had a few months to live without medical treatment. That was last year. As a result of the diagnosis, my wife and I decided to move to Florida. I retired early and I spend my days praying, meditating, and connecting with other people. I am trying to focus on only things that are of importance to me. It is quite refreshing and liberating. I am confident I will be cured. I am waiting for my time and look forward to meeting Jim in person and celebrating with him."

David was inspiring and he was definitely helpful, connecting with so many people. I envied his connection with God and his unwavering faith. At times, he could hear God speak to him. I always wondered about stories such as this. Since nothing this powerful had ever happened to me, it made me question whether or not God was paying attention to me. Was I not faithful enough? Did I not pray often enough? Was I focused on the wrong things in life? When I really thought things through, I knew God was there for me. I knew He sent people at the times I needed them. I knew there were signs He put in place for me to see. David was both of these to me. David became my champion for healing, believing, and confidence.

My reliance on David grew. If I didn't hear from him for a while, I would start to panic. He was good about responding to emails. Then one week, he didn't reply. The week passed, and I didn't think much about it, but then another week passed. I began to worry about him. *Is he okay? I don't have his phone number to call his wife. I am being silly. David is fine. He is just probably caught up with a visit from his kids and grandkids.*

David finally emailed me that following week. "I'm so sorry, Erica," his email began. "I have been so sick. I am struggling to eat and to talk these days. I think you said Jim had this same problem. Please tell him I can relate and that this is awful. Still,

I'm praying daily and know we will both get through this. I'm so tired right now and losing weight, but we can do this. Keep the faith. Tell Jim to keep the faith." I had a sigh of relief. David was all right. This man of true faith, whom I felt had a direct connection to God, was alive.

A few days later, I started contemplating the connection that David and Jim seemed to share. When one was having some troubles, it seemed that the other would follow suit. Then I started panicking again, thinking, *if David does die, what does that mean for Jim?*

The next time this lapse of communication happened was several months later. My same panic returned with a slight twist. Something felt different this time, but I couldn't place the feeling. I waited and waited for an email. Just when I thought I would look up his phone number and call his wife, I received an email. At first I was so excited, thinking it was David. When I opened it and scanned it, I felt nauseous when I realized the email was from his wife. "I am sorry that you have to find out about David's passing from this email, Erica. He lived so much longer than his doctors said he would and he lived how he wanted to his last many months. He has helped so many people, including you and Jim, and I am so proud of him for this reason (and many others). It was a gift that he had so much time." She then proceeded to tell me about the memorial for him, which included many surfer friends riding out to catch a wave in David's honor.

My initial reaction was shock that David didn't make it. I thought, *if this man, this dear sweet person, and a man of unending faith couldn't make it, who could?* Then, my tears started flowing. It was so unfair, such an insult. The tears splashed against the computer screen. I cried a cry that I hadn't in months. I stared at the email and cried until I realized I needed to tell Jim.

When I walked into the bedroom, Jim looked up at me in his chair. His face was confused as he registered that I had been crying. He waited for me. "It's David," was all I could manage to say. Jim knew. After many minutes of Jim and I sitting in silence, I said, "You and David were supposed to meet one day."

"I know, Erica," Jim replied. "If David can't make it, what chance do I have?"

With that statement, a flood of doubt washed over me. Instant worry about Jim and our future started. I tried to push it back, smiled at Jim, and told him he was improving and doing well and there was nothing to consider with this. But my internal fears were there and they lasted several days. Every time I would think of David, I thought about the pain if Jim were to leave.

One afternoon when I again had a sick feeling in my stomach about Jim's health, I literally shook my body and said out loud, "Erica, stop it. You know Jim can do this. He has already proven so many naysayers wrong. David was sent to you for a reason—to remind you that people are out there pulling for us and that Jim can do this. Jim can do this." From that moment on, any time I thought of David, rather than tearing up, I smiled. I smiled for the man, I smiled for the promise, and I smiled for the gift.

*Miracle = David*

✳ ✳ ✳

## CHAPTER 14

# Crazy

*"Impractical, erratic, being out of the ordinary, unusual"*

THE SEMESTER AFTER MY MATERNITY break was a world-wind of craziness. Because Jim was so sick, I tackled everything with the kids, while also trying to help Jim get ready for work and out the door. Even though I woke up two to two-and-a-half hours before I needed to leave for work and dropping off the kids at daycare, it was always a hectic whirlwind.

After getting myself ready for work, I would wake Annalise, nurse her, and then move to Braxton. I would fix Braxton breakfast, work on getting Annalise dressed, and then run into Jim's room to help him with his dressing or to encourage him to wake up. Then I'd go back to Braxton, who was quietly watching a television cartoon. After that, I would quickly make my lunch and get all of the supplies together for the commute. Then I would run upstairs to check on Jim, back downstairs to a crying baby, and then run back upstairs to check on Jim. Finally, looking at the clock, realizing I was late, I would scramble and run out the door.

On the way to daycare, Annalise was usually screaming in the backseat. She had eczema so badly that we put those cloth "mittens" on her hands, so she wouldn't scratch her skin off. She had eczema in the typical places: behind her knees, behind her ears, and a random patch here or there on her thighs. But what caused the greatest stress was her face. She had a red rash all around her mouth, such that it looked like she had found a strawberry jam jar in the refrigerator and somehow smeared it across her lips, chin, and some of her cheeks. The skin looked so raw at times, it was painful to see, but at the end of this many-month process with various physicians, we were left with, "It's just really bad eczema, Erica. It looks bad, but it's okay. She will grow out of it probably by the time she is two years old." This prediction held true, but for years, Annalise's sweet face looked so tender and red. And when she was an infant, before I discovered various lotions and potions, it was especially sensitive.

So a typical short ten-minute drive to daycare was plagued with guilt on my part that I couldn't do more for my daughter, and sadness that my daughter was crying non-stop and there wasn't much I could do for her. Fortunately, once we got to daycare, her teachers greeted us with open arms, taking Annalise and trying to soothe her. After this drop-off, I would head across the street to drop off Braxton at his pre-school. The timing of this was tight. I couldn't drop off Annalise too early due to restrictions of the facility, and I had to nurse at home, and I had to drive an hour after this point to make it to work in order to teach my morning class on time. Jim felt horrible because he saw me scrambling around like a lunatic, but he, too, was so helpless. He was exhausted and barely able to function himself. The idea of Jim driving himself to work scared me; the idea of him trying to transport our children to daycare terrified me more.

After the drop-offs of children, I felt a little break when I could settle into listening to the morning news on my favorite radio station. The rest was short, though, for I needed to pump my breasts. And I needed to do this in a moving vehicle, while I was driving. Crazy indeed, but if my daughter was to get breast milk, which was something I valued highly, there was no option. If I waited until I got to work, I had no time. I needed to be in a classroom teaching. If I tried to do this before I left for work, there would be no milk ready to go since I had just nursed Annalise an hour prior. I was in a pickle, but one that was relatively easy to solve. I knew there must be some reason for the car adapter that came with the breast pump...

So the trick was really to make sure I wore the correct top before leaving the house. It needed to be loose fitting and not tucked into my pants. Since my commute is primarily on a relatively quiet highway, it was easy to pull up one side of my shirt while driving with my knee and get positioned correctly and then drive with one hand on the wheel and one hand on the breast pump.

One morning, after the rush of the crazy morning dulled and I began strategically placing the pump on the seat next to me, pulling out the various supplies, and working the car adapter into its socket (all while driving, of course), I realized I had made a mistake. I did not have on a typical blouse—loose and ready for easy pull up. Instead, I wore a dress. My heart sank, *what were you thinking, Erica?* I thought to myself. *How am I going to pull this off?* Then I realized it was okay, my dress was a crisscross low v-neck in the front, and I could easily wiggle out and all would be fine. There would be a second or two when I would be exposed, but the highway was sparsely travelled.

I looked in my rearview mirror. All was clear. I looked in all directions on the highway and saw no cars. It was time to make my move: knee on wheel, supplies on seat, breast being lifted out of dress, and then brrrmmm! Out of nowhere, a truck comes up behind me and then next to me. A flutter of panic raced over me, but then I reasoned, *the truck driver was driving too quickly, so there was no way he saw anything.* But then, there was the intense slow-down. My heart sank. *This can't be happening. There is no way this guy saw anything. It is just coincidence.* Just as I was starting to calm down, it happened. It was a shock. I could do nothing quickly. My hand was on my breast and the breast pump was doing its thing—back and forth, back and forth, machine running, and milk gently pouring into the bottle. There was nothing I could do. I saw the man's hands shoot up into the air, and then he gave me a "thumb's up" sign. I was so embarrassed, I wanted to crawl under my seat. But then I quickly thought *oh well, it could be worse. He'll just move on and I don't have to see him again.*

But the problem was he didn't move on. The next thing that happened was he rolled down his window and then started gesturing for me to pull over. *Oh my goodness, he thinks I flashed him!* I was mortified! *Stay calm, Erica. Stay calm. He will drive off in a moment.* But the moment turned into too many minutes. Back and forth, back and forth, machine running, and milk gently pouring into the bottle. There was nothing I could do. Panic started to rush over me again, and I decided to slow way down. The trucker followed suit. *Are you kidding me?* Then I sped up. The trucker followed suit. Then the lights of his vehicle started turning on and off quickly to grab my attention. *Look away, Erica. Don't look in his direction. Pretend you don't know what's going on. He will move on in a moment.* Back and forth, back and forth, machine running, and milk gently pouring into the bottle. There was nothing more I could do.

This cat and mouse chase lasted ten minutes. Back and forth, back and forth, machine running, and milk gently pouring into the bottle. My breast was starting to get sore. I needed to switch sides. I needed to turn off the pump, but I did not dare move in that way. I certainly did not want to give any more possible messages to this man. Then his hand came out of the window again, forefinger making a point toward the upcoming exit. *If he does not stop this, I need to call 9-1-1. This is going to get bad soon.* Back and forth, back and forth, machine running, and milk gently pouring into the bottle. Our vehicles were still following one another. I stopped trying to speed up or slow down, and my plan moved to "ignore" mode. *Give it one more minute, Erica, and if he doesn't stop or leave, call the police.* I looked at the clock. I waited my minute. When it was over and I was just about to flash him again, so that I could free up a hand and use my cell phone, he got off the highway. It was over just like that. No beeping, no hand gestures, no finger pointing.

As I watched the truck exit on the ramp, my body finally relaxed. Back and forth, back and forth, machine running, and milk gently pouring into the bottle. This time I reached over, exposed myself to the empty highway, and turned off the machine. I could feel sweat starting to form as if the shock of it all had just hit me finally. I could feel my heart racing. Then I could feel my nerves starting to calm. I continued to drive, and then was forced to switch to the other breast. It was heavy with milk and relief was necessary. Back and forth, back and forth, machine running, and milk gently pouring into the bottle. But this time, I was alone, and it was almost peaceful.

I looked at the clock again and realized the stress of the chase and the anxiety aftermath had lasted twenty minutes. I wished the stress of my life in general could be handled like this—super intense for a short period of time, but then peace. It was a lion threat that turned out to be a kitten in disguise. This twenty-minute "game" was a reflection of my life. I was stressed to the max, everything felt like it was out of my control, I had no clue how things would end, and instincts of survival took over.

✳ ✳ ✳

CHAPTER 15

JUNE 2009

# Tick

*"Any ...bloodsucking arachnids that are larger than the related mites, attach themselves to warm-blooded vertebrates to feed, and include important vectors of infectious diseases"*

COULDN'T BELIEVE IT. THE TICK was there. Tiny, hardly visible, but there on Braxton's back. After an afternoon of play in our backyard, it was there. A tick. An awful, bacteria-filled tick, representing all that had caused my family grief and pain over the past several years. A tick from our home—just to add insult to injury. A tick from our suburban backyard—our suburban backyard with a small patch of trees, our suburban backyard with pesticide sprayed on the lawn and no visible signs recently of deer, who often harbor ticks, our suburban backyard with all its concrete, busy streets, and no real threat of "tick land."

I was shocked this tiny, barely able to see tick, came from our "safe" backyard. I couldn't believe with how careful we were about ticks, with how much we had curtailed our once "let's go hiking" attitude, that Braxton had a tick on his back. After my initial shock wore off, I was scared to remove this tiny creature. I worried I might not remove the head properly and could envision more and more bacteria leaking into my son's body from this tick. But of course I removed it and of course I fretted about his health.

A few days after this incident, Jim had an appointment with Dr. Lyme. Jim told him of the story and Dr. Lyme said, "Definitely get him some antibiotics if you can. If he were my patient, I wouldn't think twice about it. But of course, as you already know, you are going to have a heck of a time finding a pediatrician to write you a prescription."

Jim knew this would be a battle, but kept after me, saying, "Erica, take him to the doctor. Braxton needs antibiotics." Another day would pass and he would ask, "Erica, did you make an appointment yet for Braxton? He needs antibiotics."

"I know he does, Jim, but I don't think the doctors will give us anything. Remember what Weintraub wrote in her book, *Cure Unknown*? Doctors will write prescriptions for ear infections like candy, but try to get a pediatrician to give you antibiotics for a tick bite? Forget it."

"Erica," Jim replied, "really? That's what you are going to tell me after all we've been through? I want my son to have antibiotics."

"Okay," I said, "you're right. I'll try. I'll call tomorrow."

When I told the pediatrician about the incident, we were given the expected answer: "Don't worry about it—keep your eye on him, but Lyme is extremely rare in North Carolina." No luck—the pediatrician would not give me antibiotics. Jim stayed on this; it bothered him so much. He wanted to be sure Braxton would not get Lyme.

With this in mind, after several more days, I went back to the pediatrician's office, but requested another doctor in the hopes that things would go differently. I have learned over the years to not mention Jim's condition—this would make me suspect for being oversensitive. "I'm back because I am worried about my son's tick bite," I started.

"I see that in his file. You were just here the other day. Did something change?" the doctor asked.

"Well, not really, except that I keep thinking about all the people that live in our neighborhood that have had Lyme. It bothers me."

"What do you mean? How many people are we talking about?"

I continued, "Well, we know for sure that five people in our neighborhood have been treated for Lyme. And, we don't live in a very big neighborhood."

"Here?" the doctor asked, "Where do you live?"

"I live just around the corner," I replied.

"Really?" he said. "Remind me to never buy a house in your neighborhood." The doctor still didn't budge.

I finally said, "Look—check out Braxton's file—I don't bring him in here often for anything other than his wellness checkups and immunizations. I'm not paranoid. I would rather be safe than sorry."

With that, he wrote me a prescription for antibiotics. As he was tearing it off from his pad, he looked me directly in the eyes and said, "You know, these antibiotics are to be given everyday for three weeks. Are you up for that?"

I smiled, so grateful, and said, "Of course. Not a problem at all."

*Miracle = Treatment for Braxton's Tick Bite*

✳ ✳ ✳

CHAPTER 16

SEPTEMBER — DECEMBER 2009

# Decline

*"To tend toward an inferior state or weaker condition"*

IN THE FALL OF 2009, Jim's mom came to stay with us for several months, as I was returning after the summer months to my teaching faculty position at the college. As Jim was unable to help with the children, Patricia thought it would be nice to stay with us for a while. Since she was retired, she could afford the time. She was thrilled to be able to help and to spend time with her grandkids. As Patricia and I got used to each other's roles, ultimately it worked out that Patricia worked on making meals for Jim. She was diligently researching foods that would serve him well, wanting to be sure he had lots of protein and nutritious food to help him fight. She was also kind to do laundry and was great to stay with the kids when they were sick, so that I could still go to work for the day.

As these fall months went by, people at Jim's work were starting to realize that something was wrong with him. He was losing weight. He was coming into work later than he normally did. He was not interacting with colleagues over lunch. "Jim," one colleague, Deb, said, "Stop losing weight. You look good. There is no need to diet anymore." Another colleague, after seeing Jim walk across the parking lot asked, "Did you injure yourself, Jim? I find that now that I am older, I can hit a tennis ball just so and I can limp like you are for days. So what did you do on the court?"

Jim realized that he couldn't hide his symptoms anymore, so he began to tell a few people. "Well," Jim responded to his buddy in the parking lot, "actually, I'm struggling to walk in general. I wish it was from a sports injury, but unfortunately I have Lyme disease."

When Jim told another colleague, Shelly, about this, she replied, "Really? Lyme can do that? That is crazy. Are you sure you have Lyme disease and not something else?"

Even though Jim had to explain a lot and justify his symptoms as Lyme, he did start to feel a burden of silence come off his shoulders. This seemed to offset the sick feeling that would follow, his gut instinct telling him he would become a target at work.

Jim became obsessed with his symptoms and how his body was responding. He wanted to understand what his body was capable of for the day before he started to work. So every morning, without fail, Jim would wake and before getting out of the bed, he would go through a routine of moving various body parts. First the right foot would circle around and move up and down. Then the left foot. Jim then moved to his legs—first the right, then the left. Arms came next. Jim would gauge his progression by how well he could move his limbs.

At times, one of his feet would drop, so he was unable to lift it up easily on his own. This is probably what was causing the limp. Typically if a foot drops, it doesn't recover. And, unfortunately, the rest of the body will follow, resulting in the inability to move permanently. In Jim's case, his foot would recover sometimes weeks later, sometimes only days later. Even the best of the skeptical doctors commented, "Wow, that is good. The neurons may not be damaged after all." At other times over these fall weeks, Jim could not move his arm to place it behind his head. But as with his foot, his mobility would return as well.

The biggest problem that was occurring at this time was weight loss. Even though Jim's mom was making nutritious meals for him, he wasn't eating. Things didn't settle with his stomach—he was too weak. The IV antibiotics became his food, and Jim often rejected real food with the idea that he needed to just get through the IV antibiotic cycle and then things would get better for him. I never realized how little he was eating during this time as I was focused on the kids and making things run as smoothly as I could with their care while working full-time. Still, it was evident that Jim's body was changing shape as the weight continued to fall off his once-healthy and vibrant frame.

My first clue came when we all went to a friend's house for a gathering. The kids and I were dressed in shorts and skirts—appropriate attire for the early fall in North Carolina. Jim was wearing jeans. "Jim," I said, "you are going to be so hot. The party is outside. Why aren't you wearing shorts?"

"I don't want anyone to see my skinny legs," he replied.

"Really?" I asked. "Your legs have always been skinny, Jim. They are not that bad."

Then Jim raised his jeans. I don't know how I missed it all those weeks. His legs were very skinny—just sticks poking out from under his jeans. His lower body looked more like a cartoon stick person that our son would have drawn. I tried to hold back my surprise. "Okay," I said. "I get it. But what's going on? Are you not eating enough?"

Jim reflected on this briefly and then commented, "I feel like I'm eating as much as I can. I can't get the food down that my mom is giving me. But now that I think about it, I'm not eating very much. It's so hard. I don't have any appetite and I can't breathe well. So if I try to eat, my breathing gets even harder."

"What do you mean your breathing is difficult?" I asked. "I haven't noticed this."

"I know," Jim said. "It's not really anything you can see. I just feel like I can't breathe well." As Jim was speaking, I was getting more and more nervous. I also started feeling guilty. Shouldn't I have noticed that my husband couldn't breathe well? What was my problem?

Even though we knew he was struggling and we tried all kinds of supplements added to his diet and tried pushing in high-calorie, healthy food, the weight kept coming off. Over the course of that fall season, Jim lost about sixty pounds. Coupled with the massive weight loss was the continued problem with breathing. By the late fall, Jim's chest would heave up and down as he would try to get air. His shoulders slumped over and he shuffled along rather than walking with his normal confident, erect, and determined gait. Jim had gone from a man most people would say looked a whole lot younger than his birth years to someone who aged leaps and bounds over a few short months.

Jim visited his general practitioner for help. He mostly saw his assistant, Ms. PA, a fit woman who had a nice smile and a warm place in her heart for Jim. She grew more and more concerned about his health as well. At the visit, she noted, "I think it is time for you to see a pulmonologist. I know when we check your oxygen levels in the office, they are always fine, but obviously something is wrong. Can I make an appointment for you to see a specialist? There is a pulmonologist just around the corner here. He's very good." Jim agreed. He was fully aware of his status, reminding himself that not only could he not breathe well, but he was also struggling to walk, and if allowed, he was staying in the bed all day. He was exhausted all the time. He knew he was becoming more and more isolated in the bedroom, away from friends and the family. He wanted to hang out with the kids, but the chaos that comes with little children always got after him and he couldn't handle it. Jim knew he needed some additional help. Both he and I would think, *this will turn around soon*, but it didn't seem to be moving in that direction.

Christmas day came again—another year with Jim terribly ill. It was another year that we both thought would be the turn-around year, but it wasn't. It was troubling that in this season of great celebration, I hardly felt like celebrating. Jim was becoming more and more secluded in the bedroom when he was home. If the kids and I tried to spend any time with him, he would grow agitated. The noise, particularly any crying from the baby, would really get to him. He spent the holidays in bed, holding on until the week between Christmas and New Years. This week was a holiday for everyone at his company, so Jim could rest and store up some energy. The holidays for me were again spent in routine mode, trying to do everything I could to make things special for the kids and everything I could to take my mind off my sincere sadness. There was a void that was growing larger by the minute. My husband was living in the house, but he was not present. My children had a father, but they couldn't interact with him. The void was partially filled with hanging ornaments on the tree, visits from family, and seeing the joy on Braxton's face as he was playing with toys that Santa brought.

On Christmas day, Annalise slept while Braxton and I built Legos and strategized on what we would play for the rest of the day. Janet came over after lunch to celebrate with us, bringing a movie that we could all watch together. "Has Jim made it downstairs, Erica?" she asked after looking around for him.

"No," I replied, "not yet. He can barely keep his eyes open."

The look of disappointment on my face was intense, and Janet simply and kindly said, "I'm so sorry, Erica." She helped fill the gap of joy and attention that she lathered on the kids.

A few hours later, Jim was able to come downstairs. As he descended the stairs, Braxton shrieked with delight, "Daddy, Daddy!" We all smiled. Jim eased his way to the large olive green chair that had become his, and we gave him presents to open. Jim seemed happy for the attention and to be up from the bed, but I could tell he was truly miserable. He shifted back and forth in the chair, unable to get comfortable. His face tensed up when the kids started getting rowdy. He tried to make small talk with Janet and me, but his voice would fade off.

Finally, I said, "Do you need to go back upstairs, Jim?" He could only shake his head up and down. I moved to help him up, as Braxton protested, "No! I don't want Daddy to go back upstairs." Janet soothed Braxton and occupied his attention by helping to build a pirate ship. I helped settle Jim into the bed. That was the last time he got up from the bed, other than trying to use the bathroom, for many, many days.

A few mornings after Christmas, the kids and I were downstairs, when Jim called me up to the bedroom. I walked quickly, sensing in his voice that something was terribly wrong. "Erica," he started, "call poison control."

"What?" I was terrified. "What did you do, Jim?" I was thinking the worst, unable to believe he would do something crazy. He loved his family too much and he was a fighter.

Jim just stared at me. I repeated again, "What did you do?"

Jim realized why I was so upset and calmly said, "No, no. It's not that. But I am worried. I have been using my inhaler all morning and I'm starting to feel very strange. I know you are not supposed to use it all the time, but I can't breathe. I need you to call them and find out if I'm in trouble."

Trying to get my bearings, I ran back downstairs and tore open the phonebook. I dialed the number. The voice on the other end asked all kinds of logistical questions—our address, Jim's name and age, and some others—before I could ask if my husband overdosed on inhaler puffs.

Once I was able to explain the situation, she said, "Now explain to me again why he is taking so many hits from the inhaler?"

I tried to explain, but it was so strange. She asked again, "Are you sure he is getting enough oxygen?" and I replied as honestly as I could, telling her about Jim's normal oxygen readings when we had doctor's appointments.

Finally, she replied, "The inhaler should really not be used in this fashion." Of course we knew that, but she was missing the point.

We got off the phone and I returned to the bedroom to report what I hadn't learned from poison control. "Jim," I tentatively said, "maybe we should go to the emergency room. I think someone needs to check you all over."

"Erica," Jim replied "the pulmonology appointment is in a few days. We should be able to find out more from that appointment than from the emergency room." I agreed and tried to not worry so much. But it was tough. I looked at my husband in the bed. He couldn't breathe or get out of the bed, he was so exhausted. His head was in constant pain and he was withering away—he was all bones, with muscles now wasting away along with any fat he had. On top of this, Jim's digestive system became impacted—he hadn't had a bowel movement in days. He didn't want to eat and all I could convince him to eat during these days was a bowl of grits. He was so ill and too stubborn to go to the hospital.

After Christmas, Jim's sister Priscilla came for a visit. "Oh my, Erica," she commented after seeing her brother. "You were not exaggerating. Jim is in really bad shape."

"I know, Prissy. Maybe you can convince him to go to the hospital."

"I'll try my best."

It didn't work. Prissy and I bothered Jim day after day, as we grew more and more anxious. The only thing Jim would consider was something over the counter to help move his digestive system along. "Jim," I said after many days of trying, "this is crazy. You need help."

"Leave it alone, Erica. I feel like something is happening. I just need to have a BM and then things will start working again. I think I am close. Just give me one more day."

"I will give you two more days, Jim. If it doesn't start working again, your digestive system and you are going to the hospital. This is crazy." I busied myself over the next few days with the kids. It was still winter break for me, and it was nice to have the free time playing with them. I found myself growing more and more distracted, though. I was bouncing Annalise on my lap and listening for any sort of noise coming out of the bedroom. I was playing pirate with Braxton and waiting for a thump of Jim falling out of his bed. I could hear the clock ticking in the back-ground. Time was going so slowly. Annalise was crying again. Braxton needed attention again. I kept checking on Jim. The day finally was over and Prissy left to head back to Alabama.

Finally, the pulmonology appointment was at hand. I phoned Ms. PA before we went to the pulmonologist appointment to give her an update. "Erica," she said, "I want you to be very prepared. I am sure that after seeing Jim, the pulmonologist will send him to the hospital."

"I know, thank you." I replied. "I know he needs the help. I think this will be good."

I phoned our parents and close friends, alerting them to this likely outcome and had Patty, Patrick, and Janet in the wings as backup help for the kids if the need arose. Jim and I headed to the pulmonologist. I drove because it was difficult for Jim to do anything, let alone drive. I parked as close as I could and noted that Jim could have used a walker or cane to help him get inside the building. Once we were inside, I thought to myself, *why didn't I drop him at the door? How silly of me.* I realized I hadn't thought of this because I couldn't believe that my husband could really be as sick as he was. Still, when I watched him struggle to breathe and walk a short distance, it was undeniable. I fought back tears and went into production mode.

Once we got ourselves into the office, the receptionist greeted us with a strange look. We sat down and other patients in the office also seemed to be staring at us in a most uncomfortable way. Minutes later, the nurse called Jim's name. We slowly made our way to an office and Jim dropped into a chair. His whole body folded as his relief to get to the chair of rest was evident. The nurse looked at me with concern. I glanced back to her with a plea of help. The next words out of her mouth, directed at Jim, were, "Honey, you're not going to pass out on me, are you?" I couldn't figure out if she was concerned or annoyed that a patient might cause her "grief." Her voice did not ring of sympathy, empathy, or kindness, but I figured since she was a nurse, she must be concerned about the patients. Jim tried to smile. She then placed a pulse oxygen meter on Jim's finger, and the oxygen levels registered as normal. I was stunned. Once again, Jim was heaving for oxygen and the instrument was telling us all was fine.

After a few logistical questions and the normal blood pressure check and weigh-in from the nurse, the pulmonologist arrived and sat across from us in his chair. A very calm, short man, who had been practicing medicine for a while, asked the "usual" questions, such as "What brings you in today?" Eventually, he asked in a surprised fashion, "Why are you breathing so heavily?" The confusion was apparently over the pulse oxygen reading in the high nineties.

"Well, that's why we are here," I said with a smile. "Could you please help my husband?"

The pulmonologist studied us. He looked from Jim to me and then back again. I did my own assessment of the man. He seemed too casual for the state of my husband. He seemed a bit annoyed that we were in his office. He seemed the type who liked predictability and order, not surprises and questions. My gut instinct told me this man was not going to be very helpful.

Dr. Pulmonologist then asked Jim a few more questions, eventually getting to the Chronic Lyme disease diagnosis, and expressed serious doubts that Jim had Lyme. "But have you had a blood test that says you have Lyme?" he protested. He continued on some more after we answered that question with another, "Yes, I realize that, but you have not had a blood test confirming Lyme." Again, I tried to explain. Jim did, too, but it was difficult for him to talk as well as breathe. He was so weak in general that the act of speaking itself could wipe him out.

I tried to explain the way that I thought Jim might if he had his voice, "Doctor, from what Jim and I have learned since this whole crazy situation started is that Lyme disease is tricky. It looks different in different people. It acts differently in different people. The bacteria can hide in different forms and evade the immune system. The testing for Lyme bacteria is highly unreliable. It only targets one of the hundreds of strains of the bacteria and even if you have this one strain, but you don't have all the markers, say you only have five out of the six markers, you would still get back a negative test result. It is for all these reasons that people who study Lyme argue that the diagnosis of Lyme disease needs to be clinical. It should not be based on a blood test." I felt proud of myself. I thought I had summarized the overall situation nicely.

Dr. Pulmonologist looked at me directly in the eyes and coldly stated, "Yes, this might be all true, but the only thing we have to go on is the blood test. This is what the medical community looks to for confirmation."

I was annoyed at his stress of the medical community. I guess his point was that Jim and I didn't know anything since we weren't physicians.

As if he really needed to make his point, he paused for a brief second and then said again, "Jim's test for Lyme came back negative!" His thick accent could not hide his disdain for us and his lack of patience. We all stared at each other. I did not dare say another thing, and Jim was unable to do so. Eventually, the pulmonologist stated, "I want you to get a chest x-ray next door this afternoon and then I want you to have some atrial blood drawn at the hospital." He scribbled off a script that we would need to take to the hospital with us. "I will then see you for a breathing test when the technician comes to our office," he continued.

"When will that be?" I asked.

"She comes every two weeks," was the reply. "And she was just here, so we can set up the follow-up for two weeks from today."

I was surprised. "Our GP thought you would probably send us to the hospital today. We are prepared to go now."

The pulmonologist waved his hand in the air and said, "No, no, your husband is fine. I need all the test results in hand to know what I'm dealing with. There is no need to go to the hospital." My shock increased, but as good little soldiers, we complied.

Poor Jim moved so slowly to the next office for his chest x-ray. People in the waiting rooms at both places looked at us as if they, too, were in pain. Some people looked sympathetic and others looked confused, but all of them stared at Jim for much longer than they should have. Jim was too ill to notice. He was just concentrating on making it to the next room. He felt like his body was going to crumble underneath him at any moment. He got his chest x-ray and it was normal. According to all tests, Jim was fine. But he obviously was not.

The next day, I went to work and Patty drove Jim to his follow-up GP appointment. Ms. PA was shocked when she saw Jim, saying, "I thought you were headed to the hospital." Patty explained what happened. "We need to get him to the hospital," replied Ms. PA. "Can you wait with Jim? Let me call ahead to the hospital and get things set up, so you don't have to wait when you get there."

While Patty waited, she phoned me. I was in a meeting, but knew to keep my cell phone handy. When I saw it was her on the phone, my heart sank. I stepped outside and Patty told me they were on their way to the hospital. "Did anything happen, Patty?" I asked.

"No, it was nothing like that. Jim is obviously struggling and Ms. PA really thought the pulmonologist should have sent him to the hospital. She was very disappointed in the pulmonologist and shocked when we got to her office. She's arranged every-thing. We'll meet you there."

I hung up and felt instantly guilty. I should have been with Jim at the doctor's office. I should be taking him to the hospi-tal. He was probably scared and I was an hour away. When I returned to the meeting, I must have had quite the look on my face. Fortunately, the meeting was wrapping up, so my dean took me aside and asked if everything was all right. I told him about Jim being on the way to the hospital. "Please, Erica," he replied. "Go. You don't need to stick around here. We'll take care of things. Good luck." With that, I frantically gathered my belongings and made the long commute back to town.

Once Jim got settled into his room, the physicians on call—the hospitalists as I soon learned they were called—began the question and answer session all over again. The attending phy-sician seemed a kind and young soul who was conducting a thorough medical history. "Okay, so Mr. Young," he started, "tell me when your symptoms started." Jim was frustrated. He was so tired of telling physicians the same story over and over again only to be discounted. I could sense his hesitation. So could Patty. We gave each other a quick glance, which gave me the courage to take over for Jim. I answered the questions. Another hospitalist joined us with more questions. I answered as politely as I could. I kept the faith that someone would have the puzzle piece we needed for Jim to get over this Lyme. The hospitalists were polite as well, but I could tell there was confu-sion and disbelief. One hospitalist finally said, "Lyme doesn't do this." Again, we would have to argue our case. It was ex-hausting and infuriating.

✳ ✳ ✳

## CHAPTER 17

JANUARY 2010

# Square One

*"The initial stage or starting point"*

THE HOSPITALISTS ON STAFF THAT first day were trying to do their own assessment. I learned that these physicians were the newly hired, I'm guessing they were paying their dues going around the hospital helping patients in all areas. They were eager to prove themselves, and I rationalized with a fresh medical school perspective, they would be interested in learning more about Lyme and Jim's strange case. By thinking this, all the questions and starting from the beginning again didn't seem so bad. Still, I did wonder if all patients get asked the unbelievable amount of questions to justify your diagnosis that we seemed to be getting. For example, if someone with known kidney disease came to the hospital, would the staff disregard the diagnosis and start from the beginning until they came to the same consensus?

I learned later that Jim's admission papers listed "labored breathing" as the major cause for admission. This made sense, but it would have been helpful to have this put in context with the "chronic Lyme disease" diagnosis. I never was privy to Jim's charts, but I don't think it was clearly stated that he had

Lyme, since Lyme was so rare in North Carolina. The other label on Jim's hospital admission paper was "failure to thrive." I thought this term was strange since I had only heard it in reference to babies. When newborns were struggling and the physicians didn't know what was happening, they would get this label. This again made me realize that the doctors did not believe Jim had Lyme disease. Or, if they did believe he had Lyme disease, they thought it was inconsequential to what was currently happening. Regardless, his diagnosis was disregarded and we started from the beginning.

After the medical background questions, one hospitalist said, "Are you sure of the diagnosis, Mr. Young? It looks like from what we can gather that no real diagnosis has been given yet."

"Well . . ." another physician continued, "Lyme disease in North Carolina is extremely rare. Have you traveled to New England at all?" Yet another opinion was, "Lyme disease doesn't look like this in a person. Mr. Young. Did you get a confirmation with a blood test?"

As we learned over the eventually weeks-long stay in the hospital, the overall feeling from the staff there was that Jim did have ALS, or some sort of neuromuscular disorder. This term started being used first by a pulmonologist who came to visit Jim in the hospital, but then it became the word of choice.

Initially, the doctors would all say things like, "Your husband has ALS," or "It looks like ALS is what we are seeing here." And my favorite, as a doctor was going over Jim's case with an intern, was, "You can see here classic ALS symptoms with the muscle wasting. As an ALS patient continues to decline, the ALS kicks in aggressively."

Every time I would hear such a statement, I would cut off the physician at the appropriate time or wait for the end of the thought and then as politely as I could, which became more and more difficult over time, say, "Jim has ALS symptoms, but he does not have ALS. Jim has chronic Lyme disease."

In all cases, the physicians stared at me, unable to think of something to say. After the pulmonologist said something about ALS again, and when I said my standard, "Jim does not have ALS," he replied, "Okay, Erica, we can call it neuromuscular disease if you would like, but the result is the same. Jim's muscles are being attacked and his nervous system is being attacked."

I felt like I had won a very small, but meaningful battle. I agreed, "Yes, we can call it neuromuscular disease, but it is caused by the Lyme bacteria and we can figure this out—unlike with ALS."

After Jim's initial check-in, Patty left, and Jim and I were alone to discuss the stay. A nurse came in to tell me visiting hours were over. "I really do need to get back to the kids, Jim," I said. "I hate to leave, but Patrick is with the kids and I'm sure he needs to get home, too." Jim looked terrified. He was sweating and nervous. He didn't want to be left alone in the hospital. The nurse jumped in, sensing the problem, "How about taking an anti-anxiety pill?" It was the same pill that Jim used at home on occasion.

"Maybe," Jim said. "At home I just take a half pill. Could you do that for me?"

The nurse thought about it and replied, "I really think you should just take the whole pill. You are really nervous and this will help you sleep and get the rest you need to get healthy."

Jim looked at the nurse and at me for reassurance. I wasn't sure if he should take the pill or not. He so rarely took them at home and when he did, he commented that he didn't like the way it made him feel. "It's up to you, Jim," I finally said. "What do you think?"

The nurse jumped in there again, saying, "I do think it's a good idea, Mr. Young." With that, Jim agreed. After he got resettled, I kissed him goodbye and returned home.

Once home, I updated Patrick and off he went. My house seemed extra quiet. It was late enough that Patrick had already gotten the kids into bed for me. I snuck into their rooms, kissed them softly, thinking things would be turning for the better. Their daddy was in the hospital getting help and soon we would have some answers.

After sitting alone in the dark for a bit, I turned into bed as well. I slept a deep sleep, and in the morning after having breakfast with the kids, I was starting to get things in order to head back to the hospital when I received a phone call.

"Is this Mrs. Young?" said the voice on the other end of the phone.

"Yes, this is Erica Kosal, Jim Young's wife."

"This is the doctor from the hospital. I'm sorry to tell you that when the nurses came to check on your husband the morning, he didn't wake up. They shook him and called his name loudly, but there was nothing. After rushing him to the Intensive Care Unit, they were able to wake him and he seemed stabilized."

I was numb, trying to make sense of all this. I realized quickly that it was likely due to the anti-anxiety pill. It can slow everything down, including your breathing and Jim was already having trouble breathing. I was frustrated and scared. "What do you mean?" was my only reply.

"Listen, I need you to give me permission to intubate your husband," she replied earnestly.

*What?* I thought to myself. *What is intubate?* I didn't even understand the words she was using with me. Again, I spoke, "What do you mean?"

The doctor continued, "Mrs. Young, I don't think your husband understands—we need your permission to intubate him—to put a tube down his throat to help him breathe. He is not breathing well and he seems to not understand what is happening to him."

Getting my bearings again, I replied, "I'm actually sure Jim did understand you. He said he doesn't want to be intubated. He doesn't want a tube down his throat. Don't do anything." I couldn't believe my confidence and assertion, but I knew Jim well and knew that if he were talking, he was understanding what was being said.

The doctor protested, "You don't understand how labored his breathing is. It is really important that you give me permission to do this."

I replied, "Don't do anything. I only live five minutes from the hospital. I will be there as soon as I can." I hung up the phone. Still unsure of what I heard and what was happening to Jim, I moved into production mode. I needed to get someone to the house to watch the kids. And I needed to get my head screwed on correctly if things were as awful as the physician made them sound. Most of all, I needed to calm myself down, so I could think clearly. Check, check, check as I went through the motions. I was off on my way quickly enough, as all our friends and neighbors were kind to spring into action.

It turns out that over the course of that day, many kind souls came to the house. Many friends came over to play with my children. Others cleaned my bed sheets and clothes. Others vacuumed and cleaned the bathrooms. Their acts of kindness were so welcoming when I did return home, exhaustive, deflated, and feeling so alone. I just needed to look around to be reminded that there were good people in the world and that Jim and I were fortunate to have such nice friends.

Before I did get to return home to this welcomed kindness, I stayed at the hospital for days. When I initially arrived in the ICU, Jim was in the bed with a mask on his face pumping oxygen in through his nose and mouth. I was shocked. I didn't prepare myself for what I might find when I got to the hospital. My preparation was all on the front end of just getting to the hospital. I paused at the door. All the machines, the noises. Little hisses of various instruments. The heart monitor and the vital stats were bouncing around on the monitor. Then there were the harsh florescent lights, making Jim's color look strange. I glanced around the room again. Hiss, pop, and movement on the monitor. I looked at Jim. He was angled in the bed, with many blankets over his body. The mask covered almost his whole face. He glanced my way weakly, barely able to move his head. I wondered if he did understand. He was so different from just the previous night. He looked nothing like my sweet husband.

Then the voice from the phone met me in the room. The doctor was a young hospitalist, with long dark hair, bouncing eyes, and an impatient body. She spoke quickly, ready to move on to her next rounds, and already seemed to have lost her patience for Jim and me. "Mrs. Young?" she asked.

"Yes," I replied. "I got here as soon as I could."

She seemed impressed, "Yes, you were fast. I wasn't sure if you really did live just around the corner." She continued, "You can see what I mean. Your husband doesn't understand and I need to intubate him."

I asked a very obvious question that hadn't been addressed

up to this point, "Why does he need to have a tube stuck down his throat? What will that do to his breathing? And is this tube permanent? I don't really know what intubation is."

The doctor studied me. She quickly looked me up and down. She straightened herself ever so slightly and then calmly replied, "Oh, I see. Well, the intubation is a temporary tube that is inserted into a patient's throat to help him breathe easily. Sometimes, it turns into a more permanent structure—no one will know until we can figure out why your husband crashed. The tube will instantly help your husband breathe, and you can clearly see he needs help. So again, Mrs. Young, I need to intubate your husband. If you give me permission, I can do it quickly and it will bring much relief to your husband."

I looked at Jim. I went to his side, held his hand, and tried to process all the doctor was telling me. With the beeps, the monitor, and the surreal nature of the room, my thoughts were interrupted, "Mrs. Young, you don't understand how serious this is. This must happen." She looked at me with her piercing brown eyes, obviously so frustrated that I was slowing down her day and obviously so incensed that I would not listen to her.

"Let me explain what is happening with Jim," I started.

She interrupted me, "It doesn't matter what happened. Your husband needs to be intubated. His carbon dioxide levels are increasing to the point that they are very dangerous. Jim's carbon dioxide levels are at ninety-eight. Normally, the numbers would be in the thirties."

Finally, I received some information that I could work with to explain what happened over night, but why was the carbon dioxide so high? I couldn't understand why this particular doctor didn't want to hear more about Jim's illness, so I said, "Don't you want to understand the totality of Jim's illness? It could make a difference in how you treat him. The whole story is important for how to proceed. It might explain why the carbon dioxide levels are up."

"I have other rounds to make, Mrs. Young," she replied, with her leg pumping up and down with impatience.

I tried a different strategy, "How about we give it some time and see if we can get his carbon dioxide levels down?" She didn't like this idea, either. I continued, "When do you absolutely need to intubate him? Can we see what happens over the next few hours? Why is it so critical to do it this instant—can't we at least wait one hour?"

I think she finally decided I was an idiot and didn't want to deal with me anymore—she had those other rounds to make and I was hindering her progress. She agreed to come back in a few hours, but told the nurse to stay in touch with her if Jim's vitals worsened.

I returned to Jim's side and tried to get him to see me or answer me. He was in another place. He was unable to really communicate, and the only responses to my questions were the beeps and hisses of all the machines and monitors. I squeezed Jim's hand again, and he moved his head a little. I knew he was in there, but off in some high carbon dioxide place. It turned out that when Jim was awake, he was able to void the carbon dioxide from his system, but if he went to sleep, and if he went into a deep sleep (say caused from a drug), his body couldn't keep up. The carbon dioxide would build in his system. With this information in hand, the logic was that if Jim could stay awake so that his breathing was better, he could void the carbon dioxide that was toxic to his cells, and therefore avoid intubation.

So the plan was struck: Keep Jim awake and see what happens to his carbon dioxide levels. He seemed to understand this, so I paused talking to him to find some food. It was very late in the morning and Jim hadn't eaten yet. He couldn't afford to skip any meals, and I was desperately trying to get some help. The nurse replied, "I'm so sorry. We can't give your husband food right now."

"Why not?" I asked. "He is sixty pounds underweight—he needs food."

The nurse looked at me with sympathy. "Ma'am, right now the breathing issue is the bigger problem and we need to take care of that first. If the doctor does intubate him, it is better to do so on an empty stomach. That way the tube doesn't stimulate vomiting."

I was confident he would not need to get intubated and therefore food in his body was fine, but it was obvious I was not going to win that battle. I returned to the room to help keep Jim awake.

A few minutes later, Patty arrived at the hospital. Patty, a dear friend, who always has the knack to identify the need, showed up with a smile and some food. Her kind gesture was just to hang out with us, so we had the support and she was present to do whatever was needed. It turned out that Patty became my "keep Jim awake" partner in crime. We told him stories. We talked to each other. We read him magazines—silly articles that no one was interested in, but the words were out there and helping to keep Jim with us. But most often, we yelled his name to get him back into the room rather than drifting off. The nurses would come in every once in a while to check Jim and most importantly, his carbon dioxide numbers. I was thrilled with the news that the levels were going down. They were moving in the right direction. Upon learning this, I asked Patty, "Do you mind if I step out to phone Dr. Lyme? I know he can help us more than these physicians here."

Patty smiled, "Of course, Erica. I'll keep reading to Jim, so he stays awake."

Dr. Lyme is a busy man, but he always makes time for his patients in true need. I did not know if I would be able to contact him immediately, but I knew he would try his best to be there for Jim if the need arose. I made the call and left a message with his nurse. I had no idea if and when he might call, but I certainly expressed the seriousness of the situation to the nurse. Fortunately, only twenty or so minutes later, he returned my call. I told Dr. Lyme Jim was in the hospital with high carbon dioxide levels and the inability to breathe. I told him that the hospitalist wanted to intubate Jim. The first words out of his mouth were "I am so sorry this happened, Erica. Tell me everything you can." He listened as I relayed the events, trying to make sense of the last few days. I told him of the rounds of physicians coming in to see Jim: a pulmonologist, a neurologist, a nutritionist, and an epidemiologist. When I asked if the Lyme doctor would talk with the hospital staff, he replied in a serious and deflated tone, "I am happy to do what you want, Erica. I will help you however I can; however, just to let you know, the infectious disease people in particular won't listen to what I have to say. Probably none of them will, but I will try." This was in reference to the attitude of "Lyme doesn't exist" that many physicians have. Instead, the two of us talked at length about different ideas and strategies. Based on what I was telling him, he suggested several tests that he would like to run if he could.

I tried to convey this to the hospitalists and nurses in the hospital to the best of my ability, but, unfortunately, I don't think they really listened or put much credence into these comments and ideas. Dr. Lyme was right. He was discounted just because he studies and knows Lyme. "Could you please call Dr. Lyme?" I asked. Nods were given and false assurances made, but I could tell behind the words was an insincerity. The hospitalists were starting their own case, and as far as they were concerned, there was no need to talk to outside physicians.

As Jim was able to get the carbon dioxide out of his system more and more throughout that afternoon, he started to act more like himself. He went from acting dopey and drugged to being more alert and smiling. I started to feel like things were going to be all right. The day flew. It was now dinnertime. "I think I'm going to head out, Erica," Patty told me. "I think I'm leaving you in good hands."

Unable to fully understand what she meant, I turned around to see my sister Lisa outside the door, her arms extended in a big hug to me. "Wow, Lisa," I said, "You didn't need to fly here all the way from Michigan."

"Yes, I did," she said, "Don't worry about it. Brian is fine and Mom is helping with the kids, too." She gave me a big smile and added she could stay as long as we needed her. With that, she came into the room and said hello to Jim. We looked at the clock and realized it made sense for her to go to the house and help with my kids, get them to bed, and start making phone calls. This allowed me to spend the night at the hospital with Jim and to be on call in case any other emergency popped up.

Lisa loves her family and is the type that would do anything for them. She will shower love easily and work to ensure her kids are happy. Always quick with a new idea or plan, she shows support to her kids and encourages them to follow their dreams. By showing up to my house, unannounced, she was passing along this same unconditional love. "Don't worry about anything right now, Erica, except Jim. I've got everything taken care of at home." And she truly did. She made phone calls to out of town family, she came up with the idea of starting a website to keep people up-to-date on Jim's health, she got things in order at the house for Jim's return, and took care of the kids. I was so much more at ease, knowing my big sister was at home with the kids. She was obviously sleeping there and thus able to tend to any of their needs that might occur in the middle of the night. On their end, the kids were so excited that their aunt was in town. I think this helps ease the pain of their daddy being in the hospital and their mom being away for blocks of time. Additionally, other friends came over to visit with the kids. Braxton was getting all sorts of attention, going to movies, having play dates, watching soccer games, and the like. He didn't have time to truly miss either Jim or me.

My life during this hospital stay was hectic. My time was spent battling physicians, answering questions, filling out forms, getting Jim's needs met, and trying to keep up his spirits. The days in the hospital flew by because there was always someone from the hospital in Jim's room doing something—a test, a series of questions, a checkup, a follow-up, a new assistant to meet, etc. etc. It was unusual for Jim and me to be alone in his room for ten minutes. The days seemed to start and end within a blink of an eye. Even after I left for the night, poor Jim would be subjected to poking, prodding, and the like over the night hours, so he never truly got a good night's sleep.

About a week after his admittance into the hospital, Jim was discharged. Everybody, myself included, thought it was premature. "I'm not comfortable with Jim going home," I said. "I thought we were trying to figure out what was wrong."

The response was, "Well, we know the headaches Jim has been experiencing were due to the carbon dioxide buildup in his body."

"Oh yes," I said to the hospitalist on staff that day, "that's right. We knew that Lyme can cause headaches, so we figured the bacteria was causing them. This is good to know." As I was processing this, I continued, "So Jim's big problem is at night when he sleeps. His body has a harder time getting the carbon dioxide out of his system effectively. So just like here in the hospital, can we have a mask to use at night?"

"Unfortunately," the hospitalist answered, "Jim needs to have a sleep study done at the hospital before he can get a mask."

"Great. He is here. Can we have the test done tonight?" I asked eagerly.

"Unfortunately, no. The test has to be done as an out-patient study and since Jim is here, he is in-patient."

I was confused, "This makes no sense. Jim is here. It would be so easy."

"I know Erica, but everyone agrees that Jim needs to be in his normal routine at home before the test is administered in order to get the benefit of the test."

I was so frustrated, "But he needs the mask now. This isn't a normal type of situation. Certainly there can be an exception made?" Sensing the reluctance, I continued, "Besides, what does normal routine mean anyway? Jim is so sick, I don't think he has a normal right now."

To this, I received a smile and nod, "I'm sorry, but I can't do anything about that. These are the hospital rules."

A bit frustrated, I decided to turn to the next big concern, "How can my husband be released from the hospital when one of the two reasons he was admitted—"failure to thrive"—wasn't even touched. He is sixty pounds lighter than he was just months ago and obviously in trouble with nutrition and weight."

The hospitalist countered, "Well, because Jim's breathing became so critical, the weight issue was placed on the back burner.

We needed to get Jim's breathing under control before we could focus on the weight."

"I know," I replied, "that is my point. Now that we understand why Jim was struggling to breathe, can't we focus on the weight problem?"

After a brief pause, the reply was, "Well . . . that is really up to your husband at this point. We have prescribed a medication that will help with appetite. It is the same medicine used with our cancer patients and it works really well. We've done all we can do for him now."

## CHAPTER 18

# Return

*"The act of coming back to or from a place or condition"*

THE RETURN HOME WAS BITTERSWEET. Lisa left to return to her own family, and Jim was at home, but scared and trying his hardest to eat and concentrate on breathing deeply. Days were spent focusing on Jim and the kids. Braxton was back at daycare, so most of the time, it was Annalise, Jim, and I at home. Now, instead of letting Jim sleep all the time, I worked to keep him awake during the day. Annalise and I hung out with Jim and talked about past trips and the future. "I thought things were as bad as they were going to be, Erica," Jim sadly said. "I really did."

"I know, Jim. I, too, thought that once you were on the IV antibiotics, it would get worse—but not hospital worse—and then things would start improving."

"They don't feel like they are improving," Jim sadly reflected.

"I know, but we always knew things would get worse before they got better," I stated.

"Yes," Jim countered, "but how much worse and when better?"

I squeezed him as tightly as I could. "I wish I knew. I really wish I knew."

"I want that mask to sleep with," Jim stated.

"I don't understand why you couldn't get one. That still makes no sense to me. You obviously have a sleep problem. You don't need a sleep study for that."

Jim reflected on this, "Well, I guess in a week, we can get that done and then get the mask."

During this waiting week, Jim's dad Harold and his wife Peggy came for a visit and to help as I started back at work for the semester. Making a great team at our house, they would divide up roles and gladly moved into production mode. Harold was quick to work on projects around the house that Jim couldn't tend to anymore, and Peggy was quick to make meals and provide all sorts of love to the kids. And because they stayed at our house whenever they visited, if any emergency popped up in the middle of the night, they would be right there to help.

When they first arrived at the house after their car trip from Alabama, they stretched and we exchanged small talk. Then Harold said, "Where is he? How is he doing?"

"He's upstairs right now in the bonus room. He's trying to watch some TV to keep his mind distracted. He's afraid to sleep." I tried to explain more about the carbon dioxide levels and how they are related to sleeping, and then I continued, "Jim is really having a tough time. I know you haven't seen him in a while. He's really skinny. He's lost a lot of weight."

Peggy then jumped in, "How are you handling all this with the kids and with going back to work?"

I smiled, "I don't know. I get a lot of help. That's why it's great you guys are here." I continued, "The goals are to fatten Jim up and to keep him awake during the day."

Peggy laughed, "I can handle both of those. I'll make him all kinds of good southern food and I'll talk his ears off."

"Excellent!" I replied. Then we all went inside to see Jim.

That next day was the first day of classes for me. I didn't like leaving Jim alone even though Harold and Peggy were there and I knew Jim was in good hands. The drive in the morning to work was a struggle with my mind racing and bouncing from topic to topic. I kept thinking about Jim and the strange night he had the night before. Jim had gone to sleep and I was in the other room with Braxton. After hearing Jim cry out, I rushed into the bedroom and found a frazzled Jim. "Do you see Oma's dog, Erica?" I looked at him puzzled. He was talking about my deceased grandmother's dog, Petey. "What is Oma's dog's name?" Jim called out.

I was shocked. "Jim you are scaring me. What are you talking about?" Looking around wide-eyed and crazed, he replied again, "Don't you see him, Erica? Why don't you see him? He's right here. What is his name? What is that dog's name?"

I started getting very concerned, moving close to Jim and waving my hands in front of him. I kept thinking, *what does this mean? Why is Jim talking nonsense?* I tried to snap Jim out of his dream-state, "Jim! Jim! Stop it. There is nothing going on here. Wake up. Look at me!"

Jim continued his protest, insisting that he could see the dog jumping up and down on the bed. "Why is the dog here, Erica? Why is it here?"

I thought at the time that he was so stressed out and scared to go to sleep that his mind was playing tricks on him. "Jim, stop that," I urged. "You are scaring me. Are you all right? Tell me exactly what is happening."

Jim just waved me away, seemingly confused, a little embarrassed, and unsure of what to do next. I, too, was unsure of what to do. After staying with him several more minutes, he was acting more like himself. "Go to bed, Erica. I'm fine," he said.

"No way, Jim. I'm hanging out here for a while longer."

Jim looked at me again, his face cocked to one side. His eyes were back to normal and his crazed look was removed from his face. After many more minutes, Jim said again, "Erica, really I think I'm fine. You have to work in the morning. Go to bed." Jim convinced me to leave the bedroom. I returned to the office where Braxton and I had been sleeping. Jim did better when he had the bed to himself, and it made sense for him to be as comfortable as possible. I reluctantly lay down on the bed, but turned on the baby monitor. I left the other part in Jim's room as my security blanket. If Jim started breathing heavily or talking crazy again, I would know it.

On that morning commute, upon reflection, I decided to call Ms. PA and talk to her about this incident. She became instantly concerned, "Erica, listen to me carefully." The insistence in her voice made me nervous. She continued, "If this happens again, you get Jim to the hospital. Right away. Don't wait." She waited for this to sink in and then after a few moments continued, "Jim was likely not getting enough oxygen last night or too much carbon dioxide was building up again."

"Are you sure?" I asked, "I thought maybe he was so tired because we're not letting him sleep much in the day anymore."

"Erica," she replied without hesitation, "I am sure."

As I hung up my cell phone, I felt numb. I felt dumb. I felt deflated. What was to become of my husband?

I made it through all my classes for the day, but had a sick feeling the entire time. I decided to call the house before heading back on the commute. "Harold," I asked, "how is Jim doing?"

"He's fine. I just helped to feed him lunch, and I'm headed outside to cut down that dying tree of yours in the backyard."

"Is he really all right?" I asked again.

"Yes," Harold replied, "don't worry about that. Just drive home safely. Jim is fine."

We hung up and I started the drive back. A nagging feeling kept after me, so I decided to call Dr. Lyme again. After Jim returned from the hospital, he asked me to phone him to update him on Jim's progress. We had been playing phone tag for days, but I hoped to speak with him that day.

Fortunately, this turned out to be the case. "So tell me what's been happening since you've been home, Erica," Dr. Lyme kindly asked. I summarized the past few days and my frustration over the lack of a mask to use at night. After hearing all the news, Dr. Lyme insistently said, "You can feed him until he pops, Erica, and it won't make a difference if you don't get his breathing under control. Every bit of energy he is getting from food is going to help him breathe—he's not going to gain weight." This made sense, but I just hadn't ever thought of it. Dr. Lyme hit at the heart of the problem, and I found myself slipping into depression. "Erica, this is important, too." I braced myself for what was going to follow. "If Jim's breathing doesn't get solved, vital organs will start to shut down. There will not be enough oxygen to support all the organs and Jim will shut down." I got it. The bluntness of this statement was needed. We needed to be more proactive and get after the physicians for help with the breathing mask.

When I walked in the door, Jim's dad was upstairs feeding

Jim dinner. His dad was literally holding a fork to Jim's mouth and putting the food in as if Jim was an infant. Jim didn't seem to take notice of this strange setup, and in general he just didn't look right. I told him about the conversation with the Dr. Lyme. "Jim," I asked, "are you hearing this? Do you understand?"

Jim just didn't seem like himself. He was unresponsive and in another place again. I looked at Harold. He looked at me. We were both trying to make sense of what was happening. Jim broke the silence and stated bluntly, "I think what the doctor says is true."

I was trying to figure out what doctor he meant when I noticed Jim grabbing his chest area. "Are you trying to tell us something, Jim?" He just looked at me. I figure he was referring to Dr. Lyme and his heart feeling like it was shutting down. I looked at my husband. He began to sweat, and I ran around trying to get things in order to go to the hospital. "We need to go to the hospital," I screamed with urgency.

Harold stepped up and commented, "Okay, okay. What needs to be done?"

I ran around, changing from work clothes to more casual clothes, I called Ms. PA, who called ahead to the emergency room to let them know we were on our way, and then ran into the kitchen screaming to Peggy, "We need to get Jim to the hospital."

Then I saw Braxton. He rounded the corner, looking so innocent and confused. "Oh, Braxton," I said, gathering composure. "Listen, something is wrong with Daddy. We need to get him back to the hospital, so they can help him. Okay?" I tried to give him a smile. "It's all right. It will all be all right." Peggy moved toward Braxton and took him under her arms and into the other room. I ran back upstairs, called Patrick quickly to come over and help us, and then Harold and I moved into production mode moving Jim down the stairs.

Within a matter a minutes, Jim was fading fast. Harold and I were talking to him, telling him to stay with us. We got him down the stairs and into the car when Patrick pulled up. He joined us trying to move Jim's body into the car when Jim started talking about his wedding band, "Take it off. Get it off." He was struggling to breathe and still mumbling, "Get it off, why can't you guys get it off?" Harold was desperately trying to remove the band, so Jim would calm down.

Within a few more minutes, the ring slipped off and onto the floor. "Okay, Jim," Harold said, "it's off. Don't worry, it's safe." With that, we drove to the emergency room. Patrick stayed behind to help Peggy with the kids.

On the five-minute ride to the hospital, Jim kept on about the ring, "Where is my ring? I need that ring. We can't lose that ring."

"Don't worry about the ring Jim," I said, "we'll find it. Just stay with us. Fight."

Then we pulled up to the hospital and three people came running outside to meet us. Their swift response was very welcoming and lifesaving for Jim. After getting Jim into a wheelchair and placing an oxygen mask on him, the vitals checks started. Jim's oxygen levels, which should be in the high nineties or ideally at 100 percent, registered at sixty. Vital organs, such as the brain, the ones that Dr. Lyme warned me about, can start to shut down when the numbers are in the high fifties. Jim truly could have died that night.

Within minutes, Jim was rushed to a back area as I was giving his medical history in a nutshell. A kind physician gently told me she needed to intubate and I knew this was required. This time there was no discussion. It had to be done. Jim's life was dependant on it. Harold and I were directed into a family waiting room. We settled into the room quietly, both of us in shock. I called the house to make sure the kids were all right. Peggy assured me Braxton was fine, the baby was sleeping, and not to worry about the kids. "I have it all under control, Erica. Don't worry about anything here. Take care of Jim."

My second call was to Patrick, "I can't talk to people, Patrick. I will start to cry. Could you please call one of my sisters? Then she can call everyone else."

Patrick kindly said, "Of course. I've got you covered. How are you doing, all things considered?"

"I have no idea," I responded.

"Remember, Erica, you are strong. You'll get through this."

I sighed, "I know that whole 'God doesn't give you more than you can handle' thing. Well, I'm tired of handling. I'm tired of being strong. If I fold, does that mean things will get better faster?"

Patrick gave a faint giggle, "Not sure. But hang in there."

After the brief intubation, Harold and I were allowed to see Jim. There was that tube, which we worked so hard to avoid, now shoved down my husband's mouth and throat. The hissing, beeps, and monitors were all back. But this time, Jim did look more at peace. He was on all kinds of drugs, which obviously helped, but his breathing was more normal. Even though Jim's face had tape on it and various braces and lines coming to and from his body in various places, he was alive and breathing normally. As I heard the hisses, beeps, and footsteps of nurses and physicians coming and going, I took the time to look around at all the cubbies of people. Each family was separated by a curtain in the emergency room, each with their emergencies of different levels.

After many hours, Jim finally had a room waiting for him in ICU. We all transferred up to his new home. It turned out to be the exact same room we had just left not even a week prior. One familiar face said, "So sorry to see you guys back so soon." I smiled, trying to focus on the no-coincidence nature of this.

***Miracle = Jim's Life Saved***

✳ ✳ ✳

# Battle

*"An extended contest, struggle, or controversy"*

THE NEXT WEEK OR TWO were bizarre, unreal, blurry, frustrating—you name any bad feeling—and I experienced it. There was Jim, my husband, lying in a bed with tubes all over the place, with nurses, hospitalists, specialists, social workers, case workers, and insurance case workers all coming and going, constantly. The day would start and be over within an hour it seemed. When there was a brief reprieve of a hospital staff visit, someone else would come in—it was as if they were hovering at the door, waiting for that brief instant when they could breeze in ahead of the next person who was in line. Harold and I were there together during these initial horrible days, trying to process everything and make decisions without Jim's input. Doctors would consult with us, and when Jim was "awake," most of them tried to include him somewhat, but it was difficult due to his medicated state. "Mr. Young," they would shout. Jim would respond by giving them a funny look. I'm not sure if they are trained to speak loudly to patients lying in hospital beds, or if they are used to elderly patients, or if they think the patient can't hear over all the machines and their noises, but scream they do. Inevitably, I would smile and sometimes laugh quietly because Jim has some of the best ears around. Ironically, I am the one who often times strains to catch something. So there was Jim with his eagle ears, grimacing when a doctor would holler at him, and me being spoken to so quietly by another physician who was trying to avoid disturbing Jim. It was the one of the few things during this hospital stay that would bring a smile to my face; maybe that was the point: God's way of helping the tension and stress in the room.

This was sorely needed given that the overall feeling I sensed from the hospital staff was that Jim was on his deathbed and it was just a matter of time. One visit from a neurologist summed up the overall feeling and approach toward Jim. I happened to be down the hall using the restroom when a nurse came to find me. "Oh, Erica, Dr. Wonder Neurologist is coming to see Jim. You are so lucky. She is so nice and great. You'll really like her."

*Well, all right,* I thought to myself with a smile coming to my face. *This is finally a turning point then. Someone who will have an optimist attitude.*

I rounded the corner, entered Jim's room, and found Dr. Wonder Neurologist. I was confused by her overall presence because I had been expecting a smile and genuine nature. Instead, I was greeted with a nod, a tight mouth, and an overall body posture that said, "Do not come near me." Dr. Wonder Neurologist shook my hand and told me she was the neurologist on call and she came to check on Jim.

She began, "I see from the records that you visited Dr. Wonka and turned down his offer."

I was confused and tried to get some clarity, "Yes, we met with Dr. Wonka a few times, but I don't know what offer you mean."

Very abruptly, she sternly replied, "He offered you a clinical trial and you turned it down."

I paused and tried to figure out what she could mean, and then replied, "I honestly don't remember anything about a clinical trial. When we last spoke to him, he told Jim not to take any supplements because if there were a trial, he would not be eligible. But he didn't tell us there was a trial to start."

She gave me the once-over glance. I felt uncomfortable and bounced nervously from foot to foot. She then bluntly stated, "I don't have anything for you."

I couldn't believe what I heard. I was completely blindsided. "Okay, I'm not sure what that means," I said. "Jim had been diagnosed with chronic Lyme disease with ALS symptoms. He does not have ALS."

Again, she stared at me for a long time. Dr. Wonder Neurologist finally spoke, "I want you to know that I did a fellowship in the Midwest at an institution that treats and sees a lot of Lyme patients. Trust me, I know Lyme. I also know neurological diseases—obviously that is my area, my specialty. Dr. Wonka is the best of the best in this area. If he says that your husband has ALS, that is what I will go with. You turned down a clinical trial that might have bought your husband some more time, some more years. Because you did that, I cannot help you anymore. You blew your one chance."

I was dumbfounded. "Dr. Wonder Neurologist," I replied, trying to stay as calm as I could. I looked over at Jim who was awake now, but not really appearing himself, and fortunately unaware of our exchange. I continued, "Again, we did not know of any clinical trial offer. Dr. Wonka phoned Jim and left a message to call back, but never said anything of a trial. I just want to clarify that. I disagree with you on many counts, but you are right about one thing. You don't have anything to offer us."

With that, Dr. Wonder Neurologist gave me a contemptuous glare, flipped her hair ever so slightly, and with an upright jolt, repositioned her jacket and did an about face move that reminded me of a soldier following orders. Off she went.

Shortly after this encounter, Jim came to fully. He looked at me with a confused look on his face. He struggled to talk since he still had a tube stuck down his mouth and throat. He grimaced in pain. "Don't try to talk, Jim. It's all right," I reminded him. Then he shrugged his shoulders. "Do you want to know what happened?" I asked. Jim shook his head "Yes." "Okay," I started the story. "This is why you are here." I began with the phone conversation I had had with Dr. Lyme about eating only to fuel his breathing, told about the emergency run to the hospital and the necessary intubation to save his life. Jim then nodded as if to say he understood. Then he slept again. The next time he would wake, he would question again how he got to the hospital and again, I would repeat the story. Regardless of how many times I told him of the events, I would also remind him that he could beat this. "Jim," I said often, "you are doing great. This is temporary." Jim would shake his head up and down and flash me a look of both determination and pain all in one instant. Then, he would look off and fade, the heavy medication taking him away back to sleep.

I stayed with Jim for as long as I could. Peggy was at home to take care of the kids, and friends and neighbors came out in full force. We had friends getting the kids from daycare, friends walking our dog, friends dropping off food, friends stopping by to visit Jim in the hospital, and friends sending notes and cards of encouragement. It was powerful and helpful. Still, the stress got to me, and when I would return home at night, I would be mentally drained. The house was always silent with Harold, Peggy, and the children sleeping. I typically would wander around rooms as if I were looking for something, but of course, I had no idea what I was really doing. I tried to eat some food, but usually I was never hungry. I would sit in Jim's chair and reflect on things and then, feeling overwhelmed, I would usually decide to go to bed. That was usually a process, too.

Falling asleep when you have so much on your mind is almost impossible. I would read parts of a book to try to take my mind off things, but as soon as the book closed, my mind started racing again. One night, it was almost unbearable. I found myself tossing back and forth in my temporary bed, which was housed in the office. I chose to sleep there rather than my own bed, where Jim had been sleeping alone for weeks, because it felt better. I would sleep next to Braxton and being able to see his sweet face when I would wake throughout the night brought comfort. On this particular night, my brain started its usual routine, trying to process things that happened over the day. Shortly into this process, I started to pray and talk to God. I said, "I really need something right now, God. I don't know what, but some sort of sign, some sort of reassurance would be so nice." Ideally, I desired actual words, similar to what Jim and David had experienced in the past. I was hoping for an absolute definite signal that Jim was going to make it.

About two or three minutes later, I started to hear a noise. It was a buzzing noise of sorts that I assumed was coming from the computer. I sat up in bed, trying to focus on the sound. Before I could really make sense of it, silence came again. I lay back down, and the noise started again. I sat up and the noise stopped. I lay down and the noise returned. It became a comedy of sorts. Over and over again this happened. Finally, I thought to myself: *This is my sign. You are always here—You are with me. I get it.* The next time I laid back down, it was silent. The buzzing never returned. I collapsed into sleep.

This event and sign helped to keep me strong in the hospital. It gave me the confidence I needed to believe Jim could get his health back and that physicians don't necessarily have all the answers. This attitude was necessary when major decisions needed to be made. The pulmonologist approached Harold and me and said, "It doesn't look like Jim is going to be able to come off the ventilator on his own."

I asked, "What do you mean?"

"Well," the pulmonologist continued, "we just tried to turn off the ventilator so that pressure is not pushing oxygen into your husband through all the tubes in his mouth and throat. When we did this, his body went into shock. He didn't last long before we had to turn on the ventilator again."

"Okay," I said, trying to process everything. "But how do you know he can't get stronger to be able to tolerate coming off the ventilator?"

"Typically, Mrs. Young," the pulmonologist gently continued, "we can tell over the course of several days. We've been trying this with Jim over several days and every time it is unfortunately the same. I'm so sorry."

I looked to Harold. He looked as dumbfounded as I felt. "Help me understand something," I asked the pulmonologist. "We were sent away from the hospital a week ago without a mask for Jim to sleep with at night."

"Do you mean the masks that force oxygen into someone's body through the use of pressure? The type they use if a person has sleep apnea?"

I replied, "Yes, exactly. We were told Jim couldn't have one and this frustrated me. I feel like maybe this would have been avoided, if Jim had the mask."

The pulmonologist reflected on this, and then said, "To be honest, we don't like giving people masks because we find they misuse them." I felt my anger start to boil, but waited for him to continue. "You see, Erica, what I find in my practice is that when people are told to use the mask only at night, they will sneak and use it during the day, too, when they shouldn't be. We need to see the patients in our office to figure out what's wrong rather than them relying on the masks."

I needed to choose my words carefully. I knew that. Finally I said, "So basically what you are telling me is that because you didn't trust my husband to use the mask properly, you denied him the opportunity to use something that could have made a major difference in his life?"

The pulmonologist looked hurt and a little shocked. He finally shook his head and said, "Where we are now is that your husband is in need of a tracheostomy. This will extend his life some. We can also insert a feeding tube. This will help, too. The quality of Jim's life will be altered, but his life will be extended. The second option is to let Jim run his course and not do the surgeries. We let things go and maybe Jim would have a shorter time here, but he could really immerse himself into his family, spend time with his kids, and give them memories, so later in life the kids would have that."

Harold and I again looked at each other, each one of us fighting back tears. "But why isn't Jim breathing well?" I asked.

The pulmonologist started, "This is not unusual for neuro-muscular disease."

I protested, "But again, the Lyme disease could be doing this."

The pulmonologist conceded, "You're right in that with ALS,

we normally see foot drop, followed by paralysis up the body, finally working its way up to the lungs and diaphragm. With your husband, it is strange that his problems happened quickly and went straight to the breathing."

I smiled a bit and commented, "That's because Jim doesn't have ALS."

The pulmonologist smiled back, "I'll tell you what, Erica. Let's try to figure out what's going on with his diaphragm. I'll schedule a test and we'll take it from there."

That afternoon, Jim was wheeled away to have his diaphragm studied. Upon return to the ICU, we were informed that the right side of Jim's diaphragm was not working well at all. Now at least we had an answer to the breathing issue. The pulmonologist returned, saying, "I'm sorry we don't have better news." He waited and then continued, "We do need to make some decisions about where to go from here."

"Okay," I replied, "we need to do the surgeries." Harold shook his head. To us, it was a no-brainer. Jim would get the tracheostomy, get stronger, wean himself from the ventilator, and we could all move forward.

Later that night, we had another pulmonologist visit—a kind man, who looked different every time we saw him, like a chameleon who changed with the scenery. He was younger, with a sweet smile and a caring manner about him, and seemed to understand that things weren't always the way they appeared at a quick glance at a patient's chart. He came very late into Jim's room. "I'm so sorry to be so late," he started. "I was at another hospital and got caught up. How are things going here? I learned you are going to do the tracheostomy."

Jim was awake and much more coherent. He listened closely as I talked with the pulmonologist. "Listen," I said. "Do you know the television show House?" The pulmonologist shook his head, unable to understand why I would ask such a strange question. I continued, "Good. This is the thing. We need a Dr. House. I need you to be Dr. House. I need you to be open to possibilities and to think outside the box. I know there is something we are missing with Jim. He has a great Lyme doctor, but he is out-of-state and it's difficult to see him. I imagine after the tracheostomy it will be very difficult to drive to DC to see him." The pulmonologist was waiting for me. I continued, "Do you have children?"

"I do," he replied, "my youngest is three years old."

"Our oldest son, Braxton, is about that age, too. We also have a daughter. My kids need their dad. I need you to believe there is something we can do to get Jim over this hump. I need you to be Dr. House."

The pulmonologist sat for a long bit. The three of us just looked back and forth at each other in the dark with the beeps, hisses, and monitor moving along. I waited. Dr. House then replied, "You know what. I would do exactly what you guys are doing. You have nothing to lose and everything to gain. I will work with you and help however I can, and we can get as aggressive as we can to get you off the ventilator." Dr. House moved his body slightly up and down. I was amazed at how much energy this man had at 11 p.m. I was confident Dr. House was our visiting pulmonologist for a reason. He would become Jim's main pulmonologist from that point on and a physician who gave us the confidence to keep on fighting, when others would have said, "You need to stop."

*Miracle = God Is Here for Our Whole Family*

✳ ✳ ✳

*Reflection*

THE NAME GAME. ONE OF my favorites. You and friends are al-lowed only one word to describe every other person in the group. This can be very tricky because often there are so many words to describe your friends. But only allowing for one word, you are forced to fine-tune and really capture the essence of your friend. I have found I can learn a lot about someone from the words they choose, but also from the words others choose to say about that person. Years ago, I chose to write down everyone's words for each other on a small piece of paper. I had tucked the paper in a drawer and lost track of it. Recently, I found that piece of paper with everyone's names and words written on it. I smiled thinking about these friends and these fun times. I looked to Jim's words: "insightful, deliberate, gentleman." I smiled again, thinking that our friends really did nail Jim's essence.

Jim is a true southern gentleman. He opens doors for people, he makes sure that he walks on the correct side of the road while walking with a lady, he pays for things just to be kind, offers to help strangers, takes time to talk to people, and is most considerate if someone is distressed. Jim doesn't cuss (or at least very, very rarely), and he will always say something kind about someone, even if it means he really has to think long and hard about it. Once when Jim and I were dating, he found himself at a garden center, there to pick up something for me, and ended up in a conversation with an elderly woman. Jim offered to help her tend to some outdoor fix she needed. He followed her to her house, helped her hang a bird feeder, spent some time talking with her, and then came to my apartment. Days later, he received such a nice thank you note from her. He obviously touched her deeply, and she returned the favor with this sincere gesture.

Talking comes very easily to Jim. Unfortunately, he can get caught up in a conversation and forget about time. Because he has so many interests, he usually has something appealing to discuss. He also has a welcoming presence, which usually allows people to open up to him, and then the conversation flows. Jim does a fine job at small talk. Using it to always try to connect with a person or bring a smile to her face, Jim will often just say, "Hello," followed by a sincere, "How is your day going? Anything good happening?" And he means it. He'll wait for a reply and if none comes, he wishes the person well. And he means it. Other times, Jim's small talk wins him favors.

For example, it was not an unusual occurrence to hear Jim say to someone working at a tollbooth, a restaurant, or a store, "Are you giving the good guy discount today?"

Most of the time, the worker would smile or say something like, "I can't do that," but every once in a while, the person would laugh and say "Sure—I'll give you 20 percent off."

This unlikely event happened just enough that Jim remained motivated to ask the question as much as he can. He figures, "Why not ask? You never know what might happen." He does like to see how people operate. He studies the human interaction and is eager to make the world a better place by just being nice to strangers. One summer evening, Jim and I went to dinner with some friends. We didn't have

Reservations, and were directed to wait ten or so minutes outside. Jim lingered behind, while the rest of us chit-chattered among ourselves. One of our friends seemed to be getting nervous. Kevin looked into the restaurant several times, trying to find Jim. Many minutes went by. Kevin again seemed uneasy that Jim was inside with the very attractive hostess, while the rest of us were outside. Again many more minutes went by and finally Kevin chuckled and said, "Doesn't that drive you crazy, Erica? Aren't you jealous?"

I had to pause to consider this. "No, it's just Jim. He likes to talk to people. I think the fact that she is pretty is an extra bonus. Can't blame him there. Jim is Jim. Isn't it great?"

Regardless of age, Jim has always had a way with people. He can connect with his elders, peers, and on the opposite spectrum, with children. He is goofy enough that kids are charmed, especially since he can do some coin magic tricks, making him popular at gatherings. "The magic man is here! The magic man is here!" kids call out when we arrived at a party. Jim loved the kids' sense of awe and his ability to make them laugh. In addition to magic tricks, Jim loves to dance and can entertain children with his MC Hammer imitation, tell jokes and funny stories, and give a pretty good flying chair ride to toddlers.

## CHAPTER 20

FEBRUARY 2010

# Anomalies

*"Things [that are] different, abnormal, peculiar,
or not easily classified"*

"THE DOCTORS THERE THINK JIM will be lucky to make it to July." These are the words I heard from Ms. PA as we were speaking on the phone.

"What?" I replied. "Are you serious?" I couldn't believe what I was hearing.

Ms. PA continued, "I contemplated telling you this, but I decided you should know. The hospitalist I spoke to said you were in denial and he thinks you need to face the circumstances as they are. He thinks Jim needs to go to a group home when he leaves the hospital. It's too much work for you to do all this on your own."

I was speechless for a while. "So you're telling me that this man who has a blip of Jim's history—a man who has studied Jim's story by focusing on a computer screen of data for twenty minutes has things figured out? That is insulting. And," I continued, "I don't think I'm delusional."

Ms. PA tried to reassure me, "Right now we don't know a whole lot and there is no reason to give up on Jim at this point."

I hung up the phone, frustrated that the medical community was willing to write off Jim so quickly. I tried to stay positive and focus on Jim. It didn't help when later that afternoon, a nurse pulled me aside. "Erica, can I speak to you in the hallway?" A bit confused, I complied and met her outside Jim's room. "You know," she started, "I see you here every day with Jim. I hear the things you say to him." I didn't know where she was going with this, so I just waited. She seemed reluctant to talk, but she finally continued, "Well, it's just that sometimes cheerleading is not what is needed. Sometimes there is peace in acceptance."

I said nothing. This nurse was kind. She brought me my favorite soda when I was down, went out of her way to say nice things to Jim and me, and seemed to be competent in her job. I knew she was not trying to be mean, but her words hurt deeply. After a few moments of silence, she continued, "I just want you to think about yourself, too. Maybe you could get a pedicure or a massage sometime. A break for you, just you."

Still unable to find any words, I simply replied, "Okay" and walked back into Jim's room. I considered Jim's condition. His ALS symptoms were so much better than they had been months earlier. The fasiculations were minimized, the cramping was gone, and he could move body parts he couldn't before. Although he lay in a hospital bed, with things looking grim, I couldn't shake the gut feeling I had that he was making progress. I rationalized that the tracheostomy would force him to take the break he needed from work to heal. I considered the trach would allow him the opportunity to get oxygen more freely, have an easier time breathing, and thus his body could rest and build up the reserves to actually fight the bacteria.

The next night, I had another encounter with a nurse—another kind nurse, who seemed to like Jim and connected with us instantly. I liked this nurse, too. She had a head of beautiful silver gray hair, a kind face, and an ease about her that was telling of her competence. Her best quality of all, though, was the fact that she was a go-getter for Jim. She truly wanted to help him, push him to improve, not just tend to his immediate needs of suctioning, feeding, and bathing. The nurse would move Jim's legs up and down and rub them in specific areas to stimulate the muscles. She gave him advice—both medical and personal. She spoke to him like a person, rather than speaking over him like a sick patient, and she really cleaned him. "So, Erica, really, how are things going?" Her question was so sincere, I knew she was opening up the floor to listen to my woes.

I answered as honestly as I could, "I don't know. I really can't tell yet. Everything is either on autopilot or I am so busy answering questions, returning phone calls, or filling out forms, that I can't process anything."

"On top of that," she asked, "you are also working, right?"

"Yes. Fortunately Harold is here. Jim's dad stays at the hospital during the day, so I can run to work to teach classes." The nurse shook her head in an "I understand" way. It made me pause. I gave her a look. "You know what I'm going through, don't you?" She smiled. It was one of those comforting motherly smiles.

"Unfortunately I do," she started. "Many years ago, just after my fourth child was born, my husband was on his way to work. It was his first day on the new job. He was so excited. I remember waving goodbye to him with our baby in my arms and my other three kids around my legs. 'Have a great first day' I remember saying. He kissed me and drove away. On the way to work, a drunk driver hit my husband's car, and he died before help could reach him."

I was speechless. I wanted to hug this woman, but I didn't dare move. "Wow. I can't imagine."

She continued, "I had all those great people around me, too. Just like you have. It makes all the difference in the world. The point of me telling you this, Erica, is that you can do this. You have no choice. Your kids need you and that is that." We stared at one another for a while. I was now part of a club I didn't want to belong in, but a member by default. "Erica, you are not allowed to fall apart for the sake of those sweet children of yours. Oh course, you can do this. I did it, and you can, too. I can tell."

The next day, she smiled at me and winked, "Keep your focus on what really matters, Erica. The rest will follow, and you won't need to worry about it."

A few days later, another older nurse with much experience asked me if I was going to bring the kids to see Jim. It had been several weeks since the kids had seen their daddy. I replied, "I didn't think I could bring the kids—the visiting policy states that kids have to be twelve years old."

The nurse said, "Ah, we can work around that if you want. I think it is crazy when people try to keep things from children. It's not fair to "protect" them as such. Your children need to know what is happening to their father and to their family." With a twangy Australian accent and fire red hair, you could tell this woman had some stories under her belt as well. She was deliberate. She was passionate. And what she said definitely resonated with me. I agreed that the kids needed to know the reality of the situation. We decided to start first with Braxton and allow him to come for a short visit. "Don't worry about a thing on this end, Erica," she reassured me, "I'll handle it here. Just bring in your son."

On the way to work the next morning, I was speaking to a friend on the phone. "You are going to do what, Erica?" she yelled.

"I think it will be good for Braxton to see Jim in the hospital."

She replied in earnest, "That's crazy. Just tell him that Daddy is out of town for a while."

I couldn't believe what I was hearing. That sounded crazy to me. Lie to my son? What if something suddenly turned for the worse? How could I live with not letting Jim or Braxton see one another? "Do you really think it would be bad for Braxton to see Jim?" I asked.

"Yeah, I do," she replied. "Hospitals are scary places. Braxton is too little to understand what is going on. I think he will be freaked out."

I considered this very briefly and then thought better of it. "I think it is the right thing to do."

"Okay," my friend replied, "I hope you know what you're doing."

I did feel like I knew what I was doing. The Australian nurse spoke to me, and from that moment on, I had no doubts the visit would be good for all parties. I prepared Braxton by explaining what he would see in the hospital and why Daddy would have a tube connected to his throat. I started first at home, "Hey, Braxton, you know how it becomes difficult for you to breathe in the spring sometimes?"

He shook his head and said, "And then I have to do a breathing treatment."

I replied, "Yes, exactly. Well, daddy has something like that going on in the hospital. And he'll need help for a while, too, when he gets home."

Braxton seemed excited, "We can do breathing treatments together?"

I smiled, "Sorta. Daddy is hooked up to a constant breathing treatment, so that he can breathe easier. He has tubes connected to his throat to help with this."

"Okay" was Braxton's reply. He didn't seem fazed at all.

On the way to the hospital, I continued, "Remember when your friend, Joshua, got in a car accident with his mommy?"

Braxton shook his head up and down and said, "And he got hurt."

"Well," I continued, "do you remember he had to wear a cast on his leg for a long time, so that his body could heal?" Again Braxton shook his head "Yes."

"When we get to the hospital, you are going to see some things on Daddy that are like the cast that Joshua had. He'll have tubes connected to his breathing machine that are helping Daddy to heal. Just like Joshua's cast, these tubes can be removed when Daddy's body works better. Do you understand?"

Braxton seemed fine with the idea. "Also, Braxton," I continued, "hospitals are kinda strange places sometimes because there are people running around with masks on their faces to keep away germs, and there are lots of noises and bright lights. In Daddy's room, there are lots of beeps and hisses of the instruments they are using to help Daddy. But they are only there to help. They won't hurt Daddy or you."

I waited. Nothing from Braxton. "Are you all right with that?" Braxton shrugged his shoulders.

Once we parked and walked into the hospital, we were greeted by the large Jesus sculpture. With arms wide open, Jesus was saying, "I will help you. I will comfort you." I looked at the statue and smiled. I looked at Braxton and smiled. "Please help us with the visit, Jesus. Please help Braxton deal with this." On the short walk to ICU, I prayed I was doing the right thing and not damaging my son.

I questioned my judgment when the ICU doors automatically opened up into a world of beeps, lights, and nurses walking to and fro. Braxton's eyes grew wide as he took it all in. My heart started to sink, but then I heard, "Oh, wow. Look at all this stuff, Mom!"

"Okay," I thought, "this is going to be okay."

We rounded the corner and entered Jim's room. Jim smiled as best he could and straightened up in the bed. Braxton was a bit tentative. I'm positive he must have had the same reaction that I did when I first saw Jim in the hospital for the first time. He just looked different. It was strange. "Hi, Daddy," I said. "We were just getting excited about all the cool stuff here to help people."

Jim pointed weakly at his monitor. I helped, "Oh, yeah, Braxton, look at this. See the first blip—that is checking Daddy's heart rate. Then see all these other numbers? They are checking on oxygen levels in Daddy's body and making sure things are good inside there."

Braxton smiled a very big smile. I placed him on Jim's bed. Jim tried to touch him, and initially Braxton pulled back. There were cords, tags, clips, and various things coming at him, too, not just his Daddy's hand. "It's all right, Braxton," I said. "Those are all the cords to register this cool stuff we were talking about. Hey, can you tell Daddy what you've been doing lately. Tell him about your baby sister."

Braxton didn't say much. "She's good." I made some

additional small talk that was of no significance, and then it was time to go. The visit lasted ten minutes.

"Jim," I said, "I'll be right back. Your dad is waiting in the hallway to take Braxton back home." I kissed Braxton goodbye. "What did you think, Braxton?"

"Fine," he replied. He really did seem all right.

After they left, I returned to Jim's room. He looked at peace. The visit was good. There were tears in his eyes. He was grateful. He was relieved. He was happy.

About a week later, we decided both kids should return for a visit. It was a bit trickier because Annalise had to be held the entire time. The nurses didn't want a baby touching things and potentially being exposed to nasty things on the floors and germs in general. Annalise, however, didn't understand this. All those cool things Braxton saw, she wanted to touch. The idea of interacting with her daddy given all these new "toys" was not on her radar. She also seemed a little scared of all the beeps and hisses. When she looked at Jim, she didn't register that this was her daddy—there were too many tubes and extra parts to this man. I sensed a bit of disappointment on Jim's face.

"Hey, Braxton," I tried, "tell Daddy about playing outside with your friends today. Didn't you say you played a new game?" Fortunately, Braxton took over and told about red rover. It helped, but I know Jim was still sad about Annalise. A few minutes later, it was time to leave.

"But Mom," Braxton protested, "I need to tell Annalise about the room." He then strutted around on the area, letting his sister know some things. He told her about different instruments and equipment and what they did to help Daddy. He pointed out the monitor. He seemed to love this role of helping and being the big brother. This gave me hope that the transition back home would be okay for the kids.

My other reassurance came from a hospital staff child therapist who offered to speak to me about the children. The therapist phoned me and we spoke for about twenty-five minutes. She started the conversation by asking how I was handling things with the children.

"We talk about Daddy being sick and needing to get help from doctors. We talk about Jim having an illness that is a difficult one to beat and that it's not like catching a cold. I heard recently that I needed to label the disease and not make it generic or it can confuse the kids. So I've started calling it what it is: Daddy has Lyme disease."

"I see," she said, "that is all really good, Erica. Very healthy. How do the kids respond?"

I thought about this a few moments before I spoke. "Well, they seem to take things in stride. On the outside, they seem quite normal, but since they are so little, it is hard to really know what they are thinking and how this is all really affecting them. I did bring them both to the hospital last week to see Jim."

"Really?" the therapist seemed surprised, "Did that work out all right?"

"Yes," I said confidently, "it did. Braxton did well and I think it helped him understand where I was all the time and how people really are trying to help his daddy. Annalise is so little. I don't think it really registered with her."

There was a pause. "You know, Erica. You really are doing a lot of things well. I feel like you are interacting with your children at an age appropriate level and this will help them greatly. Let me offer a suggestion that has helped other patients and their families in the past."

"Oh," I replied, "that would be great. I would be most appreciative." I smiled to myself with the reassurance this woman had just given me.

"If you can find something small, something to buy the kids, like a small stuffed animal, they can hold it when they miss their daddy. It could even be something small around the house that represents Jim, as long as it is "huggable." The thrill of a new stuffed animal can go a long way. If Jim gives the kids the animals in the hospital, you can tell them the animals represent Daddy and they will be with them when Daddy can't."

I thought this was a great idea, "Thank you. I will definitely try that."

The therapist added, "For what it's worth, you could do the same for Jim. Have the kids give him something small he can look at or hold onto when he is sad."

"Yes, absolutely," I replied. I hung up with gratitude and confidence that the kids were adjusting well.

The next day, I found two cute stuffed animals in the hospital gift shop and brought them home, telling the kids about Daddy's gift. Braxton seemed excited. Annalise didn't seem to register anything, since she was just so little. At bedtime, I asked Braxton, "Do you want to sleep with Daddy's stuffed animal?"

He looked at me and then seriously said, "No, it's all right. I don't sleep with stuffed animals." Then he added, "but you can put him on that table for me." I smiled and put the monkey on his bedside table. Every once in a while, Braxton would ask about the monkey, but he never really clung to it.

I recalled the last message the therapist told me, "If your kids don't seem to want the stuffed animals, I wouldn't be surprised.

You really seem to know what you are doing, Erica. It sounds like you've made some good choices and that the kids are doing well under the circumstances."

*Miracle = The Transformative Power of a Child's Love*

✳ ✳ ✳

## CHAPTER 21

FEBRUARY — MARCH 2010

# Milestones

*"A significant point in development"*

OVER THE NEXT SEVERAL WEEKS in the hospital, it was constant with trying to get Jim physically up walking, to get him off the ventilator for short periods of times, to get him breathing room air and not needing supplemental oxygen, and trying to get him to swallow and eat solid foods through the mouth. There was a lot going on constantly in Jim's cubicle of a room. Two solid walls, one with a large window and one with a glass door with a curtain that you could move for "privacy." Jim was tired most the time, and anxious. He wanted to run, but was told by so many people, "Remember this is a marathon, not a race. Take it one step at a time." This advice was good in principle, but after hearing it for the dozen plus time, it rang a little empty. Did these people really know what Jim was capable of? Did anyone really understand his battle? Did they realize Jim was a fighter and someone who was used to working hard and achieving his goals? If Jim had the energy to express some of this, I am confident he would have; however, it was difficult for him to even take a twenty-minute nap with all the commotion. Just making it through a day was a major victory.

Positive milestones came. About four days after the tracheostomy, Jim was able to talk a little when a finger covered the
hole in his neck. The first word he was asked to say was my
name. It was fantastic to hear! It sounded just like Jim. Prior to
the tracheostomy, we didn't know what to expect. We weren't
quite sure if his voice would sound different, mechanical, or
like a robot. Days prior to this, before the tracheostomy surgery, Jim's dad and I were asked to watch a videotape on the
procedure and care. We were escorted to the hallway of the
ICU, and a TV was wheeled to us. In went an ancient videotape
and up came an elderly man showing us how he tends to his
trach and how he cleans his metal tube and static diagrams,
showing how it lays in the neck and what happens when it is
inflated and what to expect when it is deflated. I was numb the
whole time. After the surgery, we learned that they don't use
metal trachs anymore and that the plastic ones can be thrown
away, so there is no need to clean them. I wondered why we
were made to watch the outdated video. As I would find out
constantly over the next months and years of my life, there is
much that happens with the medical field that is strange. People
often seem to go through the motions because this is what has
been done. It seems like more people need to start thinking
about why things are done and if they should be done like that,
and most importantly, given all the advancements in technology
(including animations and video), what can be done to help the
patient and his family.

Over this same short time period, Jim's ventilator was reduced
from 28 percent oxygen to 21 percent oxygen, ambient room
air. To get him stronger, Jim would be taken off the ventilator
machine for longer and longer extended periods of time. He
would have good days where he could do physical therapy (and
other days when he was simply too tired to do any exercises). His

heart rate was going down, indicating to us that his heart wasn't having to work so hard, down from the starting one hundred and twenties range to the nineties and then the eighties.

Seven days after the tracheostomy, Jim was eating for "pleasure and to practice swallowing." After a swallowing study in the hospital, the speech therapist gave Jim the green light to start slow and boy, was it ever! The instructions were to take a very small piece of solid food, chew thoroughly, double-swallow, then sip a syrupy-liquid (nectar consistency), then double-swallow, then cough, and then swallow again. Then another very small piece of food and go through this routine all over again from the beginning. Just eating one small piece of chicken could take twenty minutes. The process of eating itself was exhausting. Therefore, I often held the fork or spoon for Jim, and he would open his mouth and chew as directed. At other times, the process was so long and labor-intensive that we knew to stop because Jim was burning up too much energy in the act—precious energy that he couldn't afford to waste. Over time, Jim "graduated" and was directed to just double-swallow after chewing—this cut down on the process dramatically and was a very welcomed event. The next step, which didn't occur until weeks later when we were back home, was that Jim was allowed to eat normally and drink thickened liquids. Several weeks after that, the nectar consistency liquids were removed completely as a requirement from Jim's diet.

Jim was recovering well—faster than some expected. This presented another problem of sorts. My gut instinct told me that Jim needed a bit more time in the hospital, specifically at a "step-down facility" where he could get constant care and attention and work on getting even stronger. Because Jim was progressing so well, our insurance company said Jim didn't need the step-down facility. The caseworker at the hospital really went to battle for us.

She was a busy person, very capable at her job, and commanded the stage whenever she was present. One afternoon she indicated, "You know, Jim is the nicest sick person I have seen in a while. I've told him he might as well learn something while he's here, so he is taking up learning a new Spanish word a day." With that "can-do" attitude, the case manager called many people on our behalf, arguing Jim's situation and the presence of small children at home. This finally won over the insurers and an agreement was struck, so that Jim could transfer to a facility for five days before returning home. When we learned of the news, the case manager said, "I was considering changing my insurance from what I currently have to your company. This situation is making me think twice about that. I don't think I will change companies after all." I, too, was shocked at our treatment. Jim's company had "Cadillac coverage" for their employees, Jim included, and other people would comment how lucky we were to have such a plan. If this was truly the case, what do other people get?

I continued to visit Jim at the step-down facility, while Harold and Peggy stayed at the house, working to get things ready for Jim's return. Both Harold and Peggy moved furniture around from room to room and performed some major feats with arrangement, including disassembling and reassembling furniture pieces. We decided it made the most sense to make my and Jim's bedroom into Jim's room where all the equipment would be, including the hospital bed. There is a bathroom attached to the room, so the nurses, who would be present with us 24 hours a day, 7 days a week, would have easy access to what they needed for Jim's care. In light of this, our queen-size bed needed to be removed. It went into Braxton's room where he and I would sleep. Braxton's bed would be moved to our bonus room, which could house long-term visitors. A large recliner and another large oversized chair were to be moved into our bedroom. Harold and Peggy moved tables, lamps, sheets, comforters, rugs, and various decorations and photos to try to make the new arrangements as nice as possible. When Jim was ready to come home, the house would be welcoming for him.

✳ ✳ ✳

## CHAPTER 22

MARCH 2010

# Wishes

*"Expressed wills or desires"*

WHAT STRANGENESS TO COME HOME one night to find the new arrangements. I left with my house and my life set in one way, and just like that, it was completely different. My sleeping arrangement had already been with Braxton in his bed, but now it was permanent. This was my new bedroom. The bedroom that Jim and I shared was sterile and empty. Even though the house was mine, there was no longer any personal room or space for me. My bedroom would become a hospital room, my bathroom would become taken over by equipment, supplies, and "stuff," and nurses would invade my closet constantly. I had no privacy, and I had nothing of my own anymore. This seemed so ironic. The house was ours. My physical items and personality were everywhere, yet, it seemed like there was nothing that was truly mine. I was sleeping in my three year old's room, and although I was using my bathroom and closet, it felt as though someone would come in at any moment. I began to feel like I was part of some warped reality show.

The bedroom that Jim and I used to share was transformed. An antique hospital bed was brought in—it looked and sounded like one that you would see in a 1920s movie. Jim insisted that I find some colored sheets over the sterile white ones. This was an excellent idea for it does help to make the room feel cozier. In addition to the antique hospital bed, the room was accessorized with a large silver medical pole and a feeding pump attached to it, a ventilator, a back-up ventilator, a giant oxygen tank (for emergencies), a compressor to help make oxygen (for emergencies), back-up batteries for ventilators (the size of a car battery), a humidifier, multiple small oxygen tanks (for emergencies), tubing for the machines, extra supplies stuffed in the bathroom closet and then attractively arranged in boxes on boxes in the bonus room, and a large plastic organizer station that contained various medicines and supplies. Our bedroom that had once been a warm, inviting place that I loved, had become a strange, surreal home for Jim. We tried to make it less institutionalized and more cozy by hanging drawings from the kids, arranging photos to inspire Jim, and trying to be present as much as possible.

But before the return home, many things needed to occur before Jim would be released. On his end, Jim wanted me to know several things "just in case." He was still so weak and talking was difficult, but he said in a raspy voice one afternoon, "We need to talk about the kids."

I looked at him confused. *What do you mean?* I wondered.

"Listen. If something happens to me, I know you will want to sell the house and move into something smaller," Jim started.

I smiled, "Yes, you do know me well. We can have a smaller mortgage and live somewhere else."

"Yes, Erica, but our neighborhood is good. Our neighbors are great."

"I don't disagree, Jim. But as I've said before, if we need to move, we can handle it."

He paused, trying to get some energy before continuing, "That's just it, Erica. I don't want you to move even if it frees up more money. We've worked too hard to get here and the neighborhood is good for the kids. Don't do this. It's important to me that the kids are raised here. If I die, I want my kids to stay in the neighborhood."

Tears began welling up in my eyes. "Okay," was all I could manage to say.

"Let's talk about how you could stay in the house without stressing about money," Jim continued.

"Jim, you seem so tired. How about we continue this later?" I asked.

"No, we need to talk about it now. You never know what might happen." I waited. Jim gathered some energy, but seemed to be fading quickly. I grew more anxious. "I want you to think about applying to my company. They pay a whole lot more than your college and the kids will have daycare."

I began to think Jim was losing it, "Jim, you work for a computer company. Who would hire me?"

He gave me the look of "think about it" and then replied, "We have an education division and you would be perfect for it. Stop selling yourself short. You always do that."

I thought about this. I loved my job, but obviously there were more important considerations on the table. "Do you really think they would hire me?" Jim shook his head "Yes" and added, "I'll ask Tim to help you."

As it turned out, upon talking with Tim, a friend who happened to also work for the same company, I decided not to apply to Jim's company. I wasn't convinced that I actually had the qualifications they would seek. I also realized that my job and its flexibility and blocks of time off were benefits that would serve my family well in the future.

As Jim and I continued our conversation in the hospital room, Jim's face suddenly changed. Sadness washed over him, and he was present, but not really present. "Jim?" I asked, "Are you all right?"

He shook his head "Yes," but didn't speak for many minutes. I could see the sadness and the tears in his eyes. Jim was thinking about something, but I didn't want to press him. I waited for him to speak.

When he finally did, he said, "If I die, there are some things I want you to promise me you will do."

"Jim," I protested, "you are not going anywhere. Stop talking like this." Jim then looked frustrated, and I realized he needed to get some things off his chest. Even though it pained me greatly to hear his words and to consider life without a husband or a father to my children, I sat waiting.

Jim insisted, "Please, Erica. Just listen. Just write these things down. I need you to know these things." So fighting back tears, I pulled out the small notebook in my purse. Jim started by telling him he wanted the kids to know their daddy, and he wanted them to grow up strong and confident. The pain expressed in his voice as he was telling me these things was almost unbearable. I was trying to concentrate, but my mind was racing with thoughts like, *this can't be happening—this can't be true*. I didn't want Jim to say these things; I didn't want to hear the words because if the words didn't come out, this new future wouldn't happen. At the same time, I worried that there was some small part of Jim that was giving in to the bad vibes and thoughts and that he may have been starting to give up.

"Jim," I said. "Stop. You are going to be raising your kids. We are going to do this together. You can tell me all these things later."

Jim shook his head firmly "No." He wanted to speak his peace. "Write these down, Erica," he pleaded. "Please. For me."

"All right," I replied as gently as I could.

"Okay, they are simple and sweet. Nothing magical, but important." Jim started, "Number one, the kids need to have good manners. They need to be raised in the church and finally, number three, the kids need to hang out with the right crowd."

I wrote them down in my shaky handwriting, unable to believe I was writing these things down and that my husband could be gone in months. We both just looked at one another when Jim finished. I shook my head up and down and blotted my eyes with a tissue. "These will happen, Jim," I said, "and I expect that you will be part of this with me." Jim just shook his head.

That night when I went to leave, Jim said, "Tomorrow bring in the large burgundy notebook from the office."

"Okay, Jim. How about you stop talking now, your voice sounds so strained." We kissed each other good night, and I drove home in silence, wondering what the future held.

The next day, I brought in the large burgundy binder full of our financial logistics. "Do you really want to do this again, Jim?" I asked. "I am mentally exhausted from yesterday."

Jim smiled and said in a strained raspy voice, "Don't worry, this is just logistics, stuff you should know anyway. Yesterday was the hard one."

I knew he was probably right, and I felt my body relax a bit.

I sat down next to him and opened the binder. It was neatly arranged with tabs, clearly labeled, and in each section an appropriate sample, highlighting account numbers, locations, phone numbers, and any other important piece of information. Jim went over each section with me and fortunately it was a short activity. I did already know much of this. It was more of a reminder for me, and it helped to put Jim's mind at ease.

Now, with his mind at ease and a move to the step-down facility, Jim could put all energies into healing and getting stronger. From when Jim entered the hospital, through the surgeries, and step-down transition, a month had passed. He was ready to come home.

✳ ✳ ✳

## CHAPTER 23

MARCH 2010

# Training

*"The skill, knowledge, or experience*
*acquired by one that trains"*

B EFORE JIM COULD BE RELEASED, I had to be trained and "certified" in several areas as the primary caregiver. For the most part, care was relatively minor and things went smoothly enough. I learned trach care (removing and replacing the inner cannula tube inside the more permanent hard plastic hardware tube), cleaning around the site, feeding tube care, priming the food pump, operating the ventilator, suctioning (to help get secretions out of his trach), and how to emergency "bag" Jim (manually pumping air into his trach/lungs with a balloon apparatus—the ambubag). Learning these skills was straight-forward, and I was anxious to get the process completed, so Jim could return home.

There was one issue, however, that wasn't teachable in the sense that I could watch nurses perform this activity and learn from them. There was no demonstration. No video to watch. The in-home health care company that would be providing nurses at home for us wanted me to change his actual, more permanent, trach in the event of an emergency at home. The trach hadn't been replaced yet—a doctor was to do this. Jim was so afraid to have the trach removed in general, but to have his wife do it without any experience or practice was daunting. He knew by removing the trach, there would likely be pain and that when removed, a giant hole in his neck would be revealed. He wanted it done by a pulmonologist in a doctor's office. He certainly didn't want his wife to do it and I certainly didn't want to do it, either.

The nurses said I needed to be qualified to replace a trach in the event that Jim's fell out. I kept thinking, *how could the trach accidentally fall out?* It seemed so unlikely to me, but apparently, I was told, this has happened. If the trach did come out, there was only a thirty-minute window before the hole would start to close. I found this truly fascinating and remained in awe that the body would respond so quickly. If the trach closed, Jim would obviously, not only be in trouble for the short-term, but he would also have to have surgery again.

So this blockade remained: All that kept Jim from leaving the step-down facility was my ability to change his trach. Jim had been in the step-down facility for five days. He was tired of it and the hospital stay in general. After being away from home for a month, Jim wanted to be with the kids again, in his own home. Jim was also worried that the staff might hold him at the step-down facility indefinitely if we didn't comply, so after intense conversation for many minutes, Jim finally said, "Just do it, Erica. If this has to happen, so I can go home, let's just do it."

So that is exactly what happened. The respiratory therapist came down and told me what to do and then said, "Okay— your turn—I'm here to help if you need it."

I was horrified. I looked at her so tentatively. She was kind and patient and gave me a warm smile, "You can do this, Erica. It really isn't as hard or bad as you are thinking. You can do this."

Still, I was so tense while getting the different parts out on the table. I was so worried about maintaining sterility—this contraption after all was about to go into my husband's neck. While I was going through the motions and concentrating on what to do, it occurred to me that if someone came over and touched me, I would crack in half. I could feel my back tighten. I could feel my body getting hotter. I knew Jim was so anxious that I decided to not even look at him. This somehow made it easier. I looked at the respiratory therapist. Time was moving so slowly. The look on her face was sympathetic, and she was non-verbally encouraging me to "move on it already." We all paused.

The respiratory therapist then said, "Are you sure you have to do this, Erica? I've never heard of such a strange requirement." Still, we all knew I had to do it.

More time went on. "Come on, Erica. Just do it." One final deep breathe and boom! I moved quickly. I was going through the checklist in my head, "Trach out, place on tray, pull out new trach—sterile. Check. Replace in neck. Don't think about what you are doing, Erica. Breathe, Erica. Don't forget to breathe." I did it and it was truly one of the most horrible experiences of my life.

Added to this overall terrible experience was the realness of it all. It is one thing seeing a plastic tube coming out of your husband's neck. It is tidy enough with a collar around it, appearing almost like a strange kind of necklace. Seeing the large hole that appeared after removing this "necklace" was reality. I could see the tissue inside his body, the rawness of the wound site, the swollen cells and the liquid body juice. It was strange and upsetting to see, but also interesting and wonderful at the same time. Where would Jim be without it? I knew that if he didn't have that hole in his neck, that tracheostomy, my husband would be dead.

✳ ✳ ✳

## CHAPTER 24

MARCH 2010

# Home

*"One's place of residence"*

MISSION ACCOMPLISHED, AND JIM READY to return home, Harold and Peggy headed back to their home in Alabama. My mom arrived a day or two before Jim returned home, and she did a nice job preparing the kids. They made some pictures for him, and she hung them on a bulletin board in his room. She cleaned some things and tried to tend to my emotional needs. I remember seeing her that afternoon when we arrived in the ambulance. My mom was waiting for me, for Jim, and for the crew of medical people. She opened the door with a welcoming smile and introduced me to my new life.

Over the course of the next few hours, I was shocked at the number of people coming and going in and out of my home: nurses, home-health care specialists, administrators, and ambulance EMTs. At one point, I counted thirteen strangers in my home. It was overnight crazy in the house. From here on out, we would never be alone. This is obviously both good and bad. It is wonderful care for Jim, but having people in your house all the time is difficult. You get used to the constant invasion and are grateful for the help, but I never felt like I could truly do

what I wanted to do in my own home. One afternoon, several
weeks after getting used to this new life, the reality show analog
popped in my head. I considered some of the shows I had seen
on TV in the past, shows where parents are filmed with their
multiple babies. Years prior to this point in my life, I remember
watching such shows and thinking to myself, how funny that
this mom is yelling like that at her husband. It seems like you
would always be on your "best" behavior since you know the
cameras are on. Now, I understood. Eventually, I got to the
point where I didn't care what nurse thought what. At first, I
was tentative about disciplining the kids, thinking to myself,
*what will the nurse think if I scold Braxton?* Then, it became,
*whatever I need to do is what I need to do. I don't care what the
nurse thinks of my parenting style.*

At other times, when things were tense between Jim and me
with the "typical" couple type of arguments—"Why did you
let Braxton do X?" or "I can't believe you just said that" kind
of stuff—I realized that I had to do as I would always do. Jim
and I had said many kind, loving, and supportive things to one
another during these dark days, but we've also had stress bring
out some strange behavior and hurtful comments. Still, after
any flare-up, we knew what it was really. It was just stress, sadness, anxiety, and frustration coming out—it truly didn't mean
anything. We were both quick to forgive, forget, and move
on. We were glad to have the emotional release, glad the other
spouse "got it," and glad that when all was considered, we were
lucky and life was good.

Initially, upon the return home, Jim was really concerned
about how this all would affect the kids. Jim asked, "Do you
think Braxton and Annalise will think I am weak? I don't think
they will understand what's going on, Erica." He desperately

wanted the kids' lives to be "normal" or at least as normal as they could be.

"Jim," I would reassure him often, "the kids will be fine. They will see kindness and learn how to be compassionate. It will be good for the kids to see that people help each other and are kind to each other."

Jim just felt guilty. No matter what I would say, it would not help him. He felt like it was his fault and that he was hurting his children. It also didn't help that often Jim was so exhausted that he couldn't interact with his kids. At other times, when the kids were in his room, the hustle and bustle that comes with small children overwhelmed Jim. I could see a wave of anxiety come over Jim's face, with more labored breathing following. Sensing these cues, we would make our exit. I spent my time dancing a delicate dance between nurturing Jim, nurturing the kids, pushing Jim gently, and disciplining the kids gently. I felt like I was pulled in all directions and that no one ever had enough of my time.

Fortunately, we had help at all times. After my mom left from her visit of a few weeks, Jim's mom came for several months. There was typically someone in the house to help in general (usually Harold, Patricia, or Wilma) and then a nurse to help with Jim. The nurses were present to help Jim and this was vital. Without their help, it would have been extremely difficult to raise kids, work full-time, and help Jim. In general, we were fortunate to have nurses who not only cared about Jim and took good care of him, but also nurses who cared about the children.

On the other side of that coin, we also had our fair share of frustration with nurses. We had a nurse who smelled so badly of cigarettes that Jim would instantly begin a coughing fit when she walked in the room (she was only there one night). We had another nurse who wore so much perfume that you couldn't be around her, either. I almost sent her home the second time she was at our home (this is after asking her the first time to please not wear perfume for obvious reasons), but we decided if she just stayed in the other room and only came into Jim's room for an emergency, we would be all right. We then asked that she not return. We had some nurses who didn't seem quite competent, either—in some cases, to the point that I couldn't understand how they had a nursing license. And then there was the case of the missing wallet . . .

Prior to Jim's return home, Jim's dad convinced me to hide Jim's wallet. Thinking this a reasonable idea, I hid it in our bedroom closet. However, it became evident that this location was not going to work since the nurses were in the closet often. With this in mind, I moved it to another location, told Jim about it, who agreed that this was a good hiding place, and I never thought about it again for weeks. Jim wasn't using his wallet, so there was no need to get it out of the hiding place. After several weeks, Jim was able to stay off the ventilator for many hours at a time, gaining weight, and feeling much better. He still had trouble talking at times and was still tired, but he was getting stronger. In anticipation of his return to work, Jim found something online to help him at work. Jim's good buddy, Bill, was visiting from Texas, and Jim asked Bill to get the wallet so he could retrieve a credit card. Bill went to the location, but could not find the wallet, so Jim asked him to phone me at work. After telling me the story, Bill asked, "Erica, where's Jim's wallet? Jim figured you moved it again and didn't tell him."

"Did you check the spot?" I tried to clarify.

"Yes, there is no wallet there," Bill told me.

My heart sank. "What do you mean, it's not there? It has to be. I didn't move it. I haven't thought about it for weeks," I said, starting to panic.

"Okay, don't worry, Erica. Let me go check again. Maybe I made a mistake." After a few moments, Bill returned, "Sorry, it is not there. Jim is freaking out. He's sure you moved it."

I was frustrated now. "Why would I move it? I didn't move it," I said. Dumbfounded, I promised to think through things and figure out where I had moved the wallet. Certainly, the wallet must be in our home somewhere. I had been so tired lately. Maybe they were right and I had moved the wallet and forgot I did so.

I drove home thinking about that wallet, *Erica, where did you put it? Think . . . Where could that wallet be?*

When I got home, Jim and I talked through various scenarios about strategic hiding places. Patricia popped in during our conversation and said, "You know what? I remember you saying something about moving the wallet into the laundry room, Erica."

I was so confused. None of this made sense to me. I have no recollection of a statement about the laundry room. "Are you sure, Patricia?" I asked. "I don't remember saying that, and it would be a very strange place for me to hide something. That would not be one of my usual rooms."

She looked confident in her reply, "Yes, you did say this." I was still confused, but if she thought I had said this, then maybe I did put the wallet in the laundry room. I went downstairs and looked in every box and nook and cranny in the laundry room. Still no wallet.

After days and weeks of searching the house, the wallet was still missing. Jim was in a frenzy over this, voicing his frustration at me that I lost his wallet. His driver's license, various credit cards, and $200 cash were in the wallet. I finally told other people about the incident and various friends offered the idea that the kids found the wallet and moved it. Finally, an idea that made sense was presented. So I started thinking differently about hiding places for a wallet. Asking Braxton about it, he looked at me like I was crazy, so my bet was on Annalise. Where would a little girl hide a wallet? Days went by again and I could still never find the wallet. The only remaining hypothesis left was that the wallet was physically not in the house. Someone had taken it. The only logical person who would have taken it was a nurse, maybe one who was only with us for one night—we had several of these at first until we settled into a working team. My search continued, but the wallet was never found. Eventually, Jim cancelled and ordered new credit cards. Our hope is that the person was only after the cash and nothing else.

Still, during these initial trying times at home, we had support from family, overall good care from nurses, and kindness from neighbors and friends. It kept us all going. We had the balance of physical care from the nursing/physician side of the coin and the mental care from the family/friends side of the coin. Overall, we were in a good place and counted our blessings.

✳ ✳ ✳

## CHAPTER 25

EARLY APRIL — MAY 2010

# Steps

*"A stage in a process"*

"HI" I SAID TO THE case manager from the hospital "It's Erica Kosal, Jim Young's wife."

It took a moment for this to register with the case manager, and then I heard the recognition in her voice, "Ah, Erica. How is Jim? Is he learning his Spanish?"

I laughed and said, "Actually, he has been too busy trying to get stronger and working."

I waited and the surprise came, "What?" she exclaimed, "That is fantastic, Erica. Jim is working again?"

"Yes, he is. I wanted to wait to call you until things were moving more in the direction we wanted."

The case manager paused and then said, "Well, to be honest with you, Erica, we didn't know how it was going to go for Jim. I knew it could go either way. This is honestly the best call I've had in weeks. What fantastic news!"

I smiled, proud that my husband was able to do something some thought impossible.

Then the case manager added, "When was he here again? Oh yes." She paused again, reflecting on the time, and added, "Jim was here over seven months ago. When did he start back at work?"

"Well," I answered, "sooner than he should have for sure. I was really begging him to give himself more time and to stay home to recover, but he was worried about his job. So when the family medical leave act time ended, Jim had to go back. There were some logistics to get through with doctors signing off, so he actually got a little more time, but he was back after being off just over three months."

"How is he doing at work?" the case manager asked.

"He's doing all right. It's tough and the days wipe him out, but he seems to be gaining some strength from the interactions with colleagues and getting his mind active again."

"That's great, really great, Erica. Please send my regards to Jim."

"Oh course," I replied.

Then she added, "And again, Erica, this is the best news I've heard in a while. I typically never find out what happens to patients when they leave. Thank you so much for calling."

"I knew I had to," I replied. "You really were so kind and helpful. I really appreciate it."

"It was my pleasure," she commented. And with that, we hung up the phone.

About a week later, Jim had a checkup at his general practioner's office. Although he was working, Jim was still recovering, and any major activity could really stress him. Such was the case with the visit. I could see the anxiety on his face, the sweat starting to drip down his face, and his labored breathing as we made our way down the hallway to the office. Both Ms. PA and the GP were present today. When we saw Dr. GP, he shook Jim's hand, smiled widely, and then said, "Well, I've been signing off on all your documents from Ms. PA. I knew I needed to come see you today personally and see you for myself." Jim smiled and we all sat down.

The appointment started with the typical measurements, such as temperature, weight, blood pressure, and the questions about how work was going, how Jim was feeling in general, and how the logistics of the trach were going. Then Dr. GP said something that was so unexpected that I almost fell out of my chair. "Jim," he started, "I'm not sure if anyone at the hospital talked with you about hospice or not. They are really a great organization and are available for you if you choose to take advantage of their services."

Because I was so shocked, my voice didn't come. It was as if I was frozen and unable to move or speak or communicate in any way. The doctor continued, "Really, when you're ready, just let me know. I'll be happy to help."

Jim was also silent. He was already taxed from answering the other questions, but he was stunned that after all the progress he had made, the physician was talking hospice.

Dr. GP continued, "You know the organization just finished a new building, or maybe they are just finishing it up, but regardless, it is just down from your house. I'm sure someone could come speak to you easily if you would like."

At this comment, I finally found the strength to speak, "Dr. GP, Jim is working right now. He's doing well. We fully expect that he will continue to do well."

"I know, Erica," Dr. GP commented, "but I'm not sure what we are working with here. On the one hand, we have ALS, an

incurable and fatal disease and on the other hand, we potentially have Lyme disease, which is treatable. I just don't know
which one it is."

I could feel my blood starting to boil and my body started
shaking. I looked at Jim. Poor Jim, unable to speak loudly in
his own voice, so deflated from having to defend his illness. I
gathered some more strength looking at Jim. I started, "Dr. GP,
we are not delusional. We know Jim has ALS symptoms, but he
does not have ALS. He is getting stronger all the time."

"Don't get me wrong," the physician replied, "but it's my
obligation to let you know about your options."

"I understand that if Jim was declining and doing poorly,
but he's not. We have no reason to believe he is on the way out.
In fact, it is just the opposite. He is moving forward. I'll admit
it is slower than we would like and there are back steps that he
has encountered that have not been foreseen, but he is moving
forward."

I sensed that my voice was shaking a bit and the physician
stared at me like I was crazy. He waited. It felt like five minutes
had passed, but I'm sure it was only a few moments. Finally,
he said, "I just think we need to be clear about whether Jim is
backsliding or not."

I paused before I responded, trying to catch some composure.
Then I stated, "I feel like you think Jim and I are working based
on hope alone. We have done lots of research on the disease,
and we don't think we are being delusional. We're not idiots,
and we're trying to be realistic. I have my Ph.D. in biology, so I
feel like I know a little something about science and literature."
I stopped. I looked at Jim. His eyes looked sad, but he also had
a bit of a perk to his body that told me he was glad I said what
I did. He even gave a little smirk.

The doctor looked at me and then tilted his head toward Jim. "Well, then," he said. "Okay." Our conversation had ended as abruptly as it started.

At work Jim was eager to get back into his role as manager. He had such big plans for the group and a vision that was as optimistic as his person in general. He was excited, but also apprehensive. Jim needed to work because he needed to see if he could do it. He needed to try. He needed to show his kids that you work hard—even when you are down. He felt this over-whelming "duty" to go to work, even though I would beg him to reconsider. Just days before the scheduled return to work, I said again, "Jim, you really don't have to go back to work. We can figure something out with daycare for the kids. Your health is much more important."

Jim sighed and looked so disappointed in me. "Erica, haven't we already had this conversation? If I don't go back to work, how are we going to make it? Who is going to hire me when I do get better if I still have a hole punched in my neck?"

I found myself on the verge of screaming, wanting to walk over to him, so I could shake some sense into him. Instead, I took a deep breath and said, "Seriously, Jim, you can't think about that—things will work out somehow. Haven't we learned anything from this experience? I would rather have a husband at home than one who lands himself back in the hospital in the next few weeks because you pushed yourself too hard."

The look on Jim's face was incredulous, "I can't have you es-pecially being negative. I am tired of everyone telling me I can't or I shouldn't. I am going to do this and need for you to help me."

I took another deep breath before I answered, "Okay, you're right. We'll try it, but you have to promise me that you will listen to your body. If you need to stop, you must." Jim shook his head up and down and smiled.

Fortunately, my academic year was finishing and with no plans to teach a summer course, I had more time available to help with logistics. This helped with the transition. My time was further freed up with the help of friends and neighbors. One of my kind neighbors drove the kids to daycare, so I could drive Jim to work, wheelchair him in, and help him get settled for the day. Other neighbors and friends would occasionally bring us a dinner, walk our dog at night (so I could put the kids to bed and help Jim), play with the kids on a Saturday, so Jim and I could spend time together, or stop over to hang out with Jim in the evenings.

The help was appreciated because the act of getting Jim ready for work was laborious. In the morning, showers took a long time. Then there was a recovery rest, dressing with the help of nurses, and a time-consuming breakfast with small bites to eat slowly. It would take about two hours to get Jim ready to come down the stairs. The nurse and I often gave each other looks, and I knew she was thinking what I was: *He shouldn't be going to work. He needs more time to recover.* Some days I wondered if he would make it. He was so frail still, yet strong in a strange way. His determination and hard-headedness have always been two of his best and worst traits, and it was evident that these alone were getting Jim to work.

The first order of business was ensuring that Jim was ready to work by 9.00 a.m. sharp. Once in his building and office, I would busy myself getting Jim set there with a last-minute suction of secretions in his neck, a run to get some bottles of water, or a refilling of a humidifier. I would then quickly make my exit out the back door to not be seen.

Although we tried hard to ensure this happened every day,

there were those days that were so difficult for Jim because he had a rough night prior or because he felt ill or exhausted (or both). On these days, Jim would get to work at 9:10 or 9:20 instead of 9:00 a.m., and I could see his frustration. "I have to be here by nine a.m.! I know I'm being watched and this is going to count against me," Jim said.

"What are you talking about? Who is watching you? Everyone wants you to succeed Jim," I answered.

"That's just it, Erica. Everyone is testing me to make sure I can succeed. If I drop the ball even once, there will be a reason to get rid of me."

I was stunned. Jim worked for a company that was known for treating its employees very well. My rosy colored view of life didn't allow for the idea that people were waiting for Jim to make a mistake. My rosy view of the world focused on the good in people. "Are you sure?" I finally asked.

"Of course, Erica," Jim replied, frustrated with my naïvety.

Jim was concerned about how his colleagues and, in particular, his boss, would view him. Would they still treat him like the manager—would they respect him—how much did he have to do to prove himself all over again? It took a while for people to start coming to him again, mainly due to their sensitivity to Jim's needs as he got readjusted at work. After a few weeks, things seemed to have settled with his colleagues, and Jim decided to get reacquainted with his team, the projects, and their needs by having one-on-one meetings with each person. During one meeting with Jordan, she asked Jim, "I thought we were friends, Jim?" Jim was confused and waited for Jordan to continue. "I don't understand why you didn't tell me about your caringbridge site on the web. This really hurt my feelings."

Jim was trying to process everything. They had just moved

from talking business to personal issues, and there was no mention about Jim's health or progress or well-being. Finally able to gather something to say, Jim said, "Why, the caringbridge site is something that Erica started for our out of state family. I don't even know who is on the site."

Jordan looked irritated, "Well, I had to learn about the site from someone else who works here and she's not even in our department. Do you know how stupid I felt when she told me something about your health and I had no idea what she was talking about!"

Jim again was unable to understand why Jordan was saying these things. He replied, "Jordan, listen. Erica only told our family about the site. It was really only one of her sisters and my sister who started spreading the word. I don't know how people found out about it."

Jordan continued, "Well, again, I would have appreciated knowing about the site. I thought we were friends."

At that, Jim realized he would get nowhere with Jordan and that she probably was correct in her assessment that they were not really friends. Jim was hurt. He realized Jordan was not interested in him. Rather, she was interested in why she wasn't in the "in crowd" of people who knew information about Jim. It was Jim's first lesson upon his return to work that some people can be so disappointing.

This was just the start to the accusations and the tests that would come at Jim. About a month after he started back to work, there were questions over why Jim didn't have a report written. The report was based on information from his team, and Jim had decided to give his employees a few more weeks to finish their parts since he had been away and they voiced concern about completion. Additionally, the deadline was close to the Memorial

Day break and many people were taking vacations. Jim made the call as a manager, but his boss then told him that this was not his call to make. It would have been if Jim had been healthy.

Another time soon after his return, Jim was asked to welcome a class one day during "kick off" that occurred over a two-week training session. It was not the official welcome and it was in the middle of the week "Welcome to Wednesday. This is the agenda for the day." The kick-off was at 9:00 a.m. We worked hard to get Jim there on time, cutting it close. "Hurry, Erica," Jim said numerous times, growing more and more anxious.

"Certainly, they will give you a few minutes if you are not there, Jim. Who really starts at nine a.m. sharp?" I responded.

"As I've told you before, this is a test, Erica. I have to be there at nine to do this or it will be another strike."

I thought about this and knew this was probably true, but the co-worker, Josh, who was leading the session would certainly give Jim a few minutes if necessary. He would not start without Jim, knowing he was coming. As we were walking as quickly as possible down the hallway, we heard, "Jim Young! Is that you?" Turning around, we saw a friend that Jim hadn't seen in months. After a very quick hello and hug, we excused ourselves and turned to walk the few remaining feet and get into the meeting location. That's when we heard Josh's voice, "Welcome to Wednesday, everyone!"

Jim stopped dead in his tracks. He gave me a look to kill. His eyes pierced through me and his whole body slumped over in defeat. Then he quietly murmured, "I can't believe it. I can't believe he started without me."

I couldn't believe it, either. "Why would he do that? Why wouldn't he look into the hallway at least to see if you were on the way?"

Jim thought for a millisecond about this and stated, "You know him. He had no intention of helping me at all. He probably started the meeting at eight fifty-nine a.m., just because. I suspect that his closed door every evening translates to Josh talking to my boss about my deficiencies. This is just something else for them to talk about this evening."

I was so saddened by this lack of consideration. I added, "Well, maybe it won't be as bad as you think. I mean really it is only a welcome statement. It's not like you were giving a presentation."

Jim looked at me exhausted, "Oh, no, it's a huge deal. Just wait and see. I'll hear about it soon enough. It means I can't do my job."

I thought about this before I said, "I don't get it. If they don't think you can do your job, why don't they ask you to leave? Why not give you a severance package?"

Jim smiled weakly and said, "It may come to that, but I think everyone wants to see what I can do." I looked at my watch. It was 9:01 a.m.

About two weeks later, the boss asked Jim to present to his team. Jim's trach and his muscle weakness overall often times negatively affected his ability to project his voice the way he would like and to talk in general. He still couldn't walk much, either, but he was very competent while sitting. His mind was sharp and his skills right on. Still, asking Jim to do a presentation this early in his recovery was like asking Jim to run a marathon without any training. Jim complied—he was happy to share information with his team and thought that this was basically what the presentation was about.

The morning of his presentation, I phoned shortly after I thought he would be back in his office. "How did it go?"

I was nervous for his reply, but relieved to hear Jim say, "It actually went well. I couldn't walk of course, but the information I gave was good and helpful." Jim paused for a few seconds to regain some strength, "I don't think my boss will hold it against me that I didn't walk around or use the board much. At least I hope this is true."

I encouraged him, "Why would she? She certainly knows you can't walk well yet and that your hands are still weak. I thought you said the presentation was more about the content."

Jim replied, "Yes, that's what she told me. After the meeting, Bob told me the presentation was helpful and that I did well."

I smiled, "Oh, good. That's a great sign."

A few days after the presentation, however, a different story came to light. His boss stopped by Jim's office, "Do you have some time to talk?" Jim sensed this wasn't going to go in his direction. She sat down across from Jim and started, "Your presentation the other day was great in terms of content. You were spot on with information and actually gave your team some things they didn't know." Jim braced himself for the "but" that was to follow.

She continued, "But I had a problem with the presentation's style." Jim waited again. "For example," the boss said, "you didn't walk around the room and you didn't write on the board. It was hard to hear you at times. You need to work on your projection."

Jim tried to reply as politely as possible. "Okay, I'll work on that." He didn't know what else to say. He thought to himself, *can't you tell that I can't speak as well as normal, that I have a tube stuck in my throat that prevents me from projecting my voice? Don't you see me struggling to walk? Can't you give me some slack on that part of it?*

He continued to think about the writing aspect. He was

having a hard time holding a pen and writing, but didn't want to call attention to it. Jim was still able to type and communicate well on the computer, but his writing skills were absent with a pen. Still Jim thought to himself, *I am still able to do my job. I do need some accommodations, but I am still competent.* Then Jim reflected on the Americans with Disabilities Act that he had been told about recently. He vowed to look into the paperwork that he needed to fill out to get some protection.

In general, Jim managed well enough throughout the day as long as he was in his office. Meetings were held there and people came to him. This helped with his energy reserves. The one tricky part came if he needed to suction himself. We had the suction machine discretely tucked under his desk and a mirror handy in the drawer. Jim would have to lean down, get the suction tube, turn on the machine and then use the mirror, so he could guide his hands to the correct opening. This act, very straightforward, would take me two minutes; however, the muscle wasting in Jim's hands was much and the fine motor skill of this procedure was difficult. It could take Jim fifteen minutes to finish this task.

While Jim was at work, his physical therapy and occupational therapy sessions went to the wayside. To accomplish things at work, Jim would cancel his sessions. The balance between working and therapy was difficult. After work, he was spent. The idea of coming home to do exercises or to go to an out-patient physical therapy site was not possible. Exercising in the middle of the day was not a possibility, either, since it really did take a long time to get undressed and dressed. Eventually, several months out, Jim was able to release much of the work demands and take off work early two days a week in the late afternoon to go to physical and occupational therapy.

The shift back to an individual contributor role occurred

several weeks after Jim was back at work. It started with Jim's mid-year review, which was ironic in the first place because Jim had only been to work for a month that year. The boss treated Jim's case as if he had been working since January, and therefore comments about Jim not reaching X, Y, Z goals that had been set the past year prior to Jim's crash that landed him in the hospital, seemed very unwarranted.

These events fed into Jim's gut instinct, even when he was in the hospital, that his boss was looking to replace him. "Erica," Jim had said several weeks prior when he was in the hospital, "She already has a replacement for me."

I looked at Jim strangely, "What do you mean? You haven't even started back at work."

Jim smiled weakly, "Just mark my words. She already has Mr. Josh Colleague in mind. It is just a matter of working the system and making sure to give me the allotted pat on the back."

I replied, quite surprised, "Oh, no, that doesn't even make sense. Mr. Colleague doesn't have the experience. He wouldn't even be a logical choice."

Jim nodded and stated, "Just mark my words. I am always right about work politics."

"Yes," I replied, "you are, but in this case, you are sick and in the hospital and not thinking straight. That really makes no sense."

Reflecting on this conversation and all that had transpired since then, I frowned. Jim had been right. The gentle nudge had been in place, the tests designed to set Jim up to fail, and the unfair judgment on progress when he had just returned to work. The real blow came when we realized that another friend turned out to not be a friend. The colleague who couldn't wait those two minutes for Jim to do the "kickoff," Mr. Josh Colleague, was quick to use Jim as a mentor when he first joined the group, but was now quick to throw him under the bus in order to advance his own career.

When Jim was in the hospital, Mr. Colleague would phone almost every day. "How is Jim doing today, Erica?" he asked. It was a welcoming call to receive, thinking Jim's co-workers were concerned about him.

"Today is a good day. We found out why Jim can't breathe." And then I would explain the latest progress.

"When will Jim be back at work?" he asked.

I explained what we knew so far and what we were thinking. I thought I was talking to a friend and someone who had Jim's best interest at heart. I learned later that my rose-colored view tainted the reality. Josh wasn't calling so much to check on Jim, but to gauge how much time he had left to impress the boss. He was using my information to assess what room he had to work, what he was up against, and how to best strategize for his future.

Jim felt betrayed and exhausted. He couldn't fight the work battle, he knew his health battle was much more important. The decision had been made more or less for him and even though Jim knew he needed the release, he knew he needed the time to heal, the fact that the position was given to Mr. Colleague was a low blow. After work one evening, Jim said, "The position was listed today." I waited, trying to gauge Jim's mood. He continued, "It's the same description as it was. I was a little surprised since Mr. Colleague doesn't match some of the "must" statements in terms of experience."

I brightened a little. "Maybe this means you were wrong. Maybe your boss really is looking for the experience."

Jim didn't wait for me to finish, "No, she's not, Erica. It is Josh's job for the taking. Just wait."

The posting came down from the website after only a few days. "I told you, Erica," was Jim's comment.

"That still doesn't mean anything, Jim," I said, holding out hope.

A few more days passed. "Mr. Colleague made the cut. He has an interview scheduled," Jim told me.

"Okay, now I'm thinking maybe you are right," I replied.

"I told you in the hospital, Erica. It is a done deal."

With that I decided to focus on the positive. Trying not to be bitter or angry, I considered why this might be happening. "Okay, Jim. Let's think about this—if Josh gets the position."

Jim gave me a blank look and replied, "He will get the position, Erica."

I was annoyed, "Okay. Fine. When Mr. Colleague gets the position, it will be good because he knows what you are capable of—he knows you are a good employee. You taught him much and he will look to you for advice."

Jim still stared at me, unable to get excited. Finally, he said, "I guess you have a point. A new person might not know my strengths. Maybe Josh will cut me a bit of a break."

"I hope so," I agreed. "Maybe he will feel so guilty, he wouldn't dare do anything."

Jim stared at me again, "I guess one of the reasons I love you is that you always, and I mean always, look to the good in people. I am sure this won't turn out to be the case, but maybe Mr. Colleague will give me tasks to play to my strengths—at least for a while. I'm sure when I'm no longer useful to him, I will need to go."

I didn't even know what to say to this last comment. I couldn't believe that it would come down to that. Jim is hardworking, he's intelligent, and he had much to offer the department. Still, Josh is a mover. I wasn't quite sure what to think, but the future suddenly looked dimmer.

Other than this one conversation, Jim and I spoke of Mr. Colleague little. True to Jim's prediction, Mr. Josh Colleague was promoted the next week. Jim didn't want to talk about it. He didn't want to talk about work. He was depressed and frustrated his body wouldn't cooperate fast enough. In other ways, I knew Jim was so relieved to have the stress removed from his shoulders. He felt sorry for himself at times, and other times, he was grateful to have a job. He got angry at the sickness and angry with people he thought were friends who turned out not to be. He wanted to work and was so frustrated that it was so difficult to do so.

Still, Jim was working. He was afforded the time to do the physical therapy he needed for regaining strength. He was relieved of many obligations and the stresses that went with them. We tried to focus on the idea that this was a "blessing in disguise."

*Miracle = Strength Regained Enough to Return to Work*

✳ ✳ ✳

## CHAPTER 26

JUNE 2010

# Family

*"A group of individuals living under one roof
and usually under one head"*

ON THOSE SUMMER EVENINGS WHEN I would pick up
Jim from work, I would arrive sometimes with kids in tow
(depending on whether I was early or late for pickup at daycare)
and we would get Daddy together. The kids were thrilled to
draw on the whiteboard in Daddy's office and would charm
Jim's colleagues. The kids would ride with Daddy in his wheelchair or help him with his walker. Although Jim was sometimes
frustrated with the pleas for candy, the whining, or the fighting
that comes with a brother and sister, he was glad for family
time. If I didn't have the kids with me, Jim and I would go
together to get them. As Jim would wait in the car for us to
return, he would often see someone from work and talk for as
long as he could.

Talking could often be quite taxing on Jim physically, especially if it was at the end of the day. It was so nice seeing people
wish him well, shake his hand, give him a hug, or just say "nice
to see you, buddy." When the kids were secured in the car and
we were driving back home, it was a special time. Jim often didn't

have the energy to talk, but it was nice being a family. I would ask the kids questions, we would sing, or the kids would be arguing about something silly like who would get the last cracker.

Once we arrived home, if Jim was feeling up to it, he sat downstairs in our overstuffed olive green chair. This is the same chair where the IV antibiotics occurred—the same chair that Jim would sit in when he was so sick and tired and couldn't make it up the stairs after a day at work. It was the same chair that provided enough cushion and support for Jim, as he was withering away in 2007. But it was also the chair that he could still eat dinner in to be "near" the kitchen table where the rest of the family was eating. This chair was Jim's "home" when he was downstairs. This chair became Jim's chair.

The kids responded more positively to their daddy in a more "natural" environment. With room to play and toys scattered about, the kids could interact freely with one another, and Jim could get a better sense of who his kids were as individuals. In Jim's bedroom, there was little space to play, and lots of sounds, tubes, equipment, and medical "stuff" scattered about. The feel of Jim's room was cold. It was "Daddy's bedroom." But the feel of the downstairs was home—it was everyone's room. In particular, Annalise opened up to her daddy downstairs. Upstairs, she seemed bothered by the bedroom much more so than Braxton. Braxton treated the room more as an adventure since Jim's hospital bed has a control with it to move the head, legs, and height with the touch of a button. Often, upon entering the room, Braxton would run over and up on the bed, with a determined look on his face. "Braxton," Jim would warn, "don't throw the pillows off the bed." It was too late as the head was coming up quickly and consuming Braxton in the process. With a giggle in the background, I would call after him, "Braxton, Daddy needs his bed down and clean. Get out of there." Disappointed,

Braxton would release the bed and then start watching television with Jim. Holding Annalise in my arms, I would release her to the floor, only to have her come to me with arms extended. She wanted to be held. So I would pick her up again and bring her over to Jim. For a while, Annalise wanted only to point at Jim's trach and say "ut-oh." Many months later, she started coming into his room to drop off a treasure and at night, running in to blow kisses, hug him on the leg, or do a "flying kiss" when I zoomed her in for a landing.

Most of the time, Jim was so sad that Annalise didn't seem to want to be around him when he was in his room. I tried to place Annalise near Jim, but she would recoil, afraid of the tube in his neck and the noises coming from around his body. "Come on, Annalise," I would plead. "Daddy would love to hold you. You can sit in his lap."

Jim would look so disappointed when she refused to go to him. "Do you know how badly I want a hug from my daughter, Erica?" I would shake my head, wishing I could will Annalise to comply. "I just want one hug around my neck. She hugs you all the time. I really would like a hug from her."

"I know, sweetie," trying to be as gentle as possible. "I am so sorry. I think she is just in a mommy stage. A lot of kids go through this."

Jim gave me a doubtful look and then replied, "Really? Do you think I'm going to believe that, Erica?"

I protested, "It's true, Jim. A lot of small kids prefer their moms and then they go through a daddy phase and then they might go back to a mommy stage. It is totally normal."

"Sure," Jim said sadly, "easy for you to say. Neither of my kids have had a daddy phase."

Pained, I would try another tactic. For several months,

Annalise loved to play Dora on the computer with her daddy. When that faded, she seemed content to view photos on the computer screen. Braxton seemed more transfixed on the television and watching shows with his father. But in all cases, the interaction was always short-lived and never as engaging as Jim and I wanted. It was difficult for the kids to sit still under the best of circumstances. In this case, they were expected to be quite mature for their young, tender ages. With all the commotion of nurses coming and going, machines making all kinds of noises, and their daddy's body getting tense at times, the kids were not comfortable for long periods of time in the room.

As time has gone by, the kids have adjusted well. They seem to read their daddy well. They recognize a "good" day from a "bad" day and respond in kind. Daddy is just Daddy. Braxton has always seemed comfortable around Jim, interacting with him as these days allow. "Mom," Braxton said one memorable evening, "it's all right. Daddy is tired. I'll go play in my room. That way Daddy can still see me from his chair. He can see me play with my castle and the knights battling each other." After a slight pause and a smile from his mother, he started toward his room. "The good knight wins. He always does. He fights. Daddy can fight, too."

Outside of our home life, the kids are affected as well. Braxton told me once about a friend at school who had been absent for a while. When I asked where Bobby was, Braxton replied, "He's sick. He's really sick. He's been gone for days. I think he must have Lyme disease. That's too bad—he'll be gone a long, long, long, long time!"

The only thing I could think to say to Braxton was "Lyme disease is a horrible disease, but fortunately it is not caught like a cold. I bet Bobby is fine. I actually think he is on a vacation. I'll ask your teacher about it tomorrow."

I hate that our kids are forced to think about sickness in this way. To Braxton, it appears that you can either have a cold or you can be really sick with Lyme—there is no in-between. Even though I've tried several ways of tackling illness when we talk, Braxton still keeps this dichotomy. Considering everything, however, I do think Braxton has a good sense about health and sickness. He knows fully that mindset makes a huge difference in beating a disease. My insightful little boy has said, "You have to think about being healthy. If you don't want to be sick, try not to be sick." Braxton knows that even though things might get really bad and other people might think things will never improve, they can. Braxton knows that people help one another by praying, by walking the dog, by driving kids to daycare, and by bringing over hot meals. As Annalise grows she will realize and learn these things as well. If she doesn't, I am confident Braxton will tell her soon enough. Braxton loves being the big brother and plays the "do this" role very well. For her part, Annalise follows everything her big brother does and wants to do everything he does.

*Miracle = Love from Children to Help the Healing Process*

✳ ✳ ✳

## CHAPTER 27

JULY 2010

# Date

*"A social engagement between two persons that*
*often has a romantic character"*

ONE EVENING, OUR NURSE, AUTUMN, said, "You and Jim need to go out. I'm starting to arrange it with the help of the nurses. Figure this out with Jim and leave the rest to us."

I looked at her with gratitude and felt guilty at the same time, thinking, *how come I haven't thought about this myself? What is wrong with me?* I had been so busy, caught up in the logistics of functioning, that any "extra" fun or care had been omitted.

After a brief moment of getting my thoughts together, I headed into Jim's room and told him the story. His face turned to panic. "Erica, I don't mean to be a downer, but moving from home to work and back again is one thing, I'm not sure about deviating from that."

"I know what you mean," I replied. "It makes me a little nervous, too, but Autumn is going to have things set up for us, so that you don't have to worry. One of the other nurses volunteered to babysit, and we will have all the backup equipment ready in the event of an emergency—which, by the way, won't happen. But still, we'll have everything in order, so you feel comfortable."

Jim reflected on this and then gave a very weak smile. I knew he didn't really want to go, but he knew he should do it. "Okay, I'll try," he finally said.

"Great. How about the fancy steak restaurant? We have a gift certificate that we should really use before it expires."

"Sounds like a plan, although I don't know how much I'll be able to eat, Erica. You know how painful it is for me to eat."

"I know. Good thing for you I can eat for the two of us. You know me, I'm not shy," I smiled.

Two weeks later, we were getting ready for our date. It was a beautiful Saturday night and I was very excited for the opportunity. As I was getting dressed, I realized it had been months since I had stopped to relax and do anything "fun" for myself. How wonderful that the fun would include Jim. I hoped he was thinking these same thoughts rather than getting anxious.

Unfortunately, when I saw him, I realized instantly that he was getting very nervous. He said, "Are you sure we should be doing this, Erica?"

"Oh course, we should. Everything is set. You are nervous and anxious, which is understandable, but everything is going to be fine."

Jim stared at me too long. I was feeling strange until he finally said, "You do have Braxton's emergency inhaler in your purse, right? My backup ones are at work."

"Yes," I replied, trying to reassure him. "Please don't worry about anything, Jim. I have the inhaler downstairs on the counter actually. I had to take it out of my purse for Braxton's game, but I have it. Just remind me to get it in case I forget."

Jim did seem to be more at ease. "You're right. It's all fine. It will all work out."

"Yes, it will, Jim Young," I said very confidently. "Now, let's go."

And with that, the nurse working that evening helped get Jim downstairs and in the car. I was running from the upstairs bedroom, to the car, to the kids, then back upstairs for a last-minute retrieval of a piece of equipment, then to the car, then back to the kids to say goodbye. As the children were crying and saying, "Don't go, Mommy!," the nurse smiled kindly and said gently, "Go, Erica. Just go. They will be fine. You have reservations and you need to go. Go!"

I knew she was right, so I quickly made my exit, feeling a bit nervous about leaving the kids. I prayed they would quiet down quickly for our nurse and that the night in general would go smoothly. I didn't realize until I got into the driver's seat and pulled out of the garage that I, too, was very anxious. Even though the date was no different in many ways from going to work and helping get Jim settled into his office, this adventure felt more intimidating. It was more real in some ways and I wondered if I wasn't pushing my husband too much.

Fortunately, the restaurant is only about a ten-minute drive from the house, so I didn't have too much time for my crazy brain to start acting up. Instead, I made small talk, trying to take both my mind and Jim's mind off the details. "How great," I stated, "it's going to be a good night. We're out on the town and we have a gift certificate—can't beat that!" When we dropped off the car for valet parking, I spoke to the man about the situation and he parked the car basically next to the front door in case I needed to run out and get a piece of equipment for an emergency. All was going well.

We walked into the restaurant. Jim's gait was slow and his body slumped over slightly, but he was moving just fine. We didn't have the wheelchair and he retired the walker as well. When we got to the host stand, I said, "We have a reservation."

"Wonderful," the host said. "Shall I get the gentleman a pillow as well? Our seats are unfortunately not comfortable since they are straight-back wooden chairs."

I smiled and thanked him for his consideration. After he retrieved the pillow, he started the walk leading us to our table. He started off at a regular pace, and then upon glancing back, realized we were far behind and that Jim was walking slowly. He paused and walked back to us discretely. Then he asked, "When did your husband have back surgery? Is this his first time out since the surgery?"

I smiled and simply replied, "It is Jim's first time out for a social occasion in quite some time." I was taken back by this simple notion that what was happening to Jim was so foreign to most people. Why wouldn't the host think it was back surgery? Jim was relatively young and back surgery was a very good guess. Who would think something like Lyme disease could do such damage to a person? Then I chuckled a bit to myself, remembering that Jim had a "piece of hardware" (as Jim likes to call the trach) sticking out his neck and that obviously the host hadn't seen it.

After we were seated, I looked across the table to my husband. I felt victorious, like we had just accomplished something huge. Jim smiled back at me. He was uncomfortable in the chair, even with the pillow, and nervous to be far away from safety equipment. Still, he seemed at peace and looked like good ole Jim Young. But then I noticed it. Jim's breathing began to suffer. He was struggling to get a breath and it was likely due to anxiety. "Jim?" I asked, "Are you okay?" He was looking at me, but not really seeing me. I could see the panic on his face. Again, I asked, "Jim?" And then I added, "You are just nervous. You are fine, Jim. Really. You are breathing just fine."

Jim's eyes grew wider. He shook his head up and down as if he agreed that he was just panicking. Still, he was still struggling to breathe. Another few seconds went by and then he asked, "You have Braxton's inhaler, right? I need it."

My heart sank. My body sank. Jim saw it on my face as he said in earnest, "You left it on the counter, didn't you?"

"I think in the craziness of leaving the house, I just forgot it. It's fine though, Jim. I can drive home and get it."

If Jim had enough energy in him, he would have shot up from the table in sheer panic at the thought of being left alone in the restaurant. I, too, quickly realized this was not a good plan and said, "I can call Patty and ask her to pick it up from the house. I can also drive just down the street to the drug store—I'd be gone five minutes and I can get an over-the-counter inhaler."

Jim's eyes grew wide again. He was so mad at me for forgetting it, so frustrated that life these days was so complicated, and so worried that his body was going to fail him. I replied, "Okay, I see none of these options are good. What about asking our waitress if she or anyone in the back has an inhaler?" Jim gave me the "give me a break" look, but did not speak. So I continued. "Sometimes there are emergency inhalers at places, just like reading glasses. You never know. I'm going to ask the waitress when she comes back."

"No, no. It's all right. Let me calm down and see how I do," Jim replied.

Then we just sat in silence. I stared at Jim, looking for the subtlest sign that he was failing, so that I could spring into action. I was a nervous wreck, looking around the restaurant for exits and emergency pathways. I reached down into my purse to make sure my cell phone was there and working. I looked back at Jim, who was staring at me, trying to read my expressions.

Then he said, "Erica, don't worry about it. Just give me a little more time. It's silly for you to drive home and then turn around and come back."

I, of course, couldn't relax. I tried to make some small talk, but the entire time I was thinking, *Jim can't breathe—Jim's not comfortable—I am so sorry—what a stupid mistake* or various versions of this.

We eventually did order some food and actually ate some dinner; however, Jim struggled the whole time and barely ate anything as a result. Jim would select a small piece of food, chew it for a long time, and eventually swallow it. Then he recovered from the activity. He needed to breathe better. He waited. Noticing it seemed harder and harder for him to eat, I bypassed Jim's wishes and when our waitress returned, I blurted out, "My husband can't breathe and I forgot his inhaler! Do you happen to have an inhaler or does anyone in the kitchen have an inhaler that we could borrow?"

The waitress sensed my panic and kindly replied to Jim, "I'm so sorry you can't breathe, sir." Then she looked at me and said, "I don't have an inhaler, but let me ask in the back. It's an unusual request, but I've been shocked by some of the things we have around here. You never know."

With that, she exited, only to return several minutes later with bad news. "I'm so sorry, y'all. I asked everyone I could think of, even the front staff and no one has an inhaler." Then she waited for our response and added, "Do you want me to wrap up your food to go?"

Jim shook his head "No" and then stated, "I should be all right. I feel better already. A lot of it is nerves. It really is fine." The waitress gave a comforting smile and then waited a few more moments to be sure.

When she left, I said to Jim, "She's right, you know. We can finish up dinner at home and you'll be much more comfortable."

"Erica," Jim replied. "We decided we were going to do this and we're going to do this. Now stop."

"Okay," I replied, trying to convince myself that things were not as serious as they were. I continued, "But you know, I will be really mad if, on our first date out in over a year, you pushed yourself so hard that you found yourself back in the hospital." Jim grinned at this, and I know he worried about the same thing.

At the end of the dinner, the waitress returned. Carrying a tray with all the deserts on them, she quickly told us of the selections, "I think you would really like this pie here. It is one of our most popular deserts."

We both looked at each other, wishing we could have a slice, but knowing we couldn't. I spoke for both of us when I replied, "Thank you anyway. It does look delicious, but we really need to get going."

"Well, if you could eat here or had the desire, what would you choose?" she replied. "I could give you a piece to go." Jim said the chess pie sounded good and she said she would be back with a piece for us.

"Here's that pie for you both to enjoy when his breathing is better and under control," the waitress said.

"It's an entire pie," I said.

"I know," the waitress smiled. "And, it's on the house. I really do hope you can enjoy it soon."

*Miracle = Kindness from Strangers Making a Big Difference*

✳ ✳ ✳

*Reflection*

**W**E HAD A PERFECT STONE patio. In our backyard was a place where we could hang out with a glass of wine and watch the sunset. It was a place to invite friends and talk in the late afternoon sun. It was a patio that blended in with our suburban yard, complete with one large boulder calling attention to the inviting space. That was the plan. That was the vision. So as newlyweds, after just moving into our new home, Jim and I rushed to a local stone yard in search of the perfect stone and boulder. When Jim and I saw the boulders, we both zeroed in on one particular one. The boulder was beautiful and stood out from the rest. It was about three tons and had angles such that you could use it as a chair if you desired. Green lichens grew in strategic places and it glistened in the sun. The green complemented the silver specks of granite that were also scattered about the boulder. "You know, Jim," I said, "we have to have this particular boulder."

"I know," Jim said, heading off to speak to the owner.

"What if they can't move it to our backyard?" I asked.

"Don't worry. This boulder will be in our backyard. Somehow. I'll figure it out," he said, flashing me a great big confident smile. After speaking with the owner, Jim returned to the yard where I was still examining stones. "Good news," he said, "they have a mini-forklift and the owner told me it was no problem. This is something they do all the time for customers."

Days later, the deliverymen came with the mini-forklift, the stones, and the boulder. The stones were placed in our backyard easily enough, and then they consulted about what to do with the boulder. As Jim and one of the deliverymen were talking about the best route for the mini-forklift, the deliveryman's facial expression suddenly turned. "Oh, no," he said, "do you have an irrigation system?"

"Yes," Jim replied. "Why? Is that a problem?"

"Unfortunately, I can't drive the forklift on your grass in the event that it might damage the irrigation system."

Jim was frustrated. He thought he had talked to the owner about this and was assured it would be all right. After a moment of considering the problem, Jim asked, "How far can you get the boulder?"

"How about to the edge of your driveway?" asked the deliveryman. "That way, you only have a small incline to get the boulder down, so that it is at the edge of the patio."

After the delivery truck left, Jim assured me that he could figure out a way to move the boulder. First, we decided to borrow a dolly from work. That didn't do it. Next, we decided to get some flats on wheels and move the boulder up on it, but that didn't work, either. A few days later, we decided to hook the boulder to the car, using a strap and move it with the vehicle. Third strike; that didn't work either. At this point, I was deflated. Jim was still thinking of techniques. Day after day, the boulder stared at me when I returned home from work. "I think we bought a very expensive decoration for our driveway, Jim," I said.

"Funny," Jim said, obviously not amused. "I'll figure something out. Just give me a little more time."

The boulder sat in our driveway for weeks. Neighbors would pause on their walks, asking, "How are you guys going to move that boulder?" Others would comment "There's no way you can get that to your backyard." I was starting to believe them, but then Jim proved us all wrong.

One Saturday late morning, after breakfast, Jim jumped off the couch. "I'm going to move that boulder today. I'm sick of it." I had no idea what he had up his sleeve, but he had that resolved look that I knew well.

"Last night I was watching something on the History Channel," Jim started. "It was all about how the Egyptian pyramids were built. They moved huge stones great distances. If they can do it, so can I." And with a determined look on his face, he headed into the garage, searching for items he needed.

"Do you want my help, Jim?" I asked.

"No," he said, "it's fine. I have it all worked out in my head. It only requires one person."

Throughout the afternoon, I would visit him in the backyard. As sweat poured down his face, he would answer very optimistically, "It's going all right. This boulder will be in place soon." Another hour went by and I checked again. Same reply from Jim, "It's going fine, Erica. Don't worry. This boulder is moving. It will be in place soon." The next time I checked, I could see some progress. I could also see a look of pride on Jim's face. The boulder had moved only about ten inches, but it had moved.

And so it continued. As the day went on, the boulder inched its way down the incline and toward the patio location. By placing a part of the boulder up on a metal rod, Jim could roll it ever so slightly. Then he would remove the rod and put it elsewhere and roll the boulder another inch. At the end of that long Saturday, Jim came inside. He was exhausted, dirty, but happy. He exclaimed, "I told you I could figure it out! That boulder is finally in place."

\* \* \*

## CHAPTER 28

NOVEMBER — DECEMBER 2010

# Anniversary

*"The annual recurrence of a date marking a notable event"*

AS THE FALL SEASON BEGAN to wind down at Thanksgiving time, Jim began to crank up. Even though he was definitely better physically, his mood became more and more irritable and he seemed depressed. Physically, he was in good shape. He was interacting with the kids more often, he was able to walk up and down the stairs relatively easily, and he was driving to work and walking in himself without a walker. He was still uneasy on his feet, with his right foot sometimes not cooperating as it should, but he was successful at walking unassisted. Jim's breathing was better, but still labored at times. His overall stance was stronger than several months prior, and he was doing fine at work. We had much to be grateful for during this Thanksgiving season.

Still, the Thanksgiving break was a reminder that the holiday season was here and with it, the one-year anniversary of the major crash was upon us. My sister Monique, brother-in-law Pat, their two daughters, and my mom were headed to our house for a visit. Jim's goal was to be walking well by the time they arrived. Exhausted one evening, Jim confessed, "I'm not there yet. Erica. I thought I would be back on my feet within a year. It's been a year! I still have a hole in my neck and I'm still exhausted almost all the time. I can't believe your family is coming and I'm not in good shape."

"Stop it, Jim," I replied. "You are doing so well. Remember that the doctor in the hospital didn't even think you would live past July. Here you are months later, not only alive, but also working and recovering. You will get there. It is taking longer than either one of us expected, but you will get there. You are getting there. Now, if that isn't something to be thankful for, I don't know what is."

Jim smiled, "You're right, I know. I think the devil is just getting after me. I am just so tired of all this."

I didn't know how to respond. I couldn't imagine being in Jim's shoes. I'm not sure how well I would handle everything, and it had been so long since he had felt good. Jim interrupted my thoughts, "You know what I just realized, Erica?" He waited a moment. "I just realized that I can't remember the last time I felt good. It has been so long since I have been sick. I just want to feel all right for a change."

"I'm so sorry, Jim," I replied. "I truly wish there were something I could do. I feel so helpless. Unfortunately, the hard work is all on you. No one can do the exercises for you. No one can clear up your mind and change it to "grateful" and "positive" gear. But what I do know, and what you need to remember, is that this is temporary. You have always said that you can do anything for two years. Well, you may be over that mark in regards to how long you've had Lyme, but you have reached the one-year mark with the post-trach stage. You can do this. It's only temporary."

"Yeah," Jim said, "I have said that before. I do think you

can do anything, anything, for two years. I just don't want to in this case."

A few days later, the Dugan family arrived. It had been some time since Pat had seen Jim. They were friends and Jim was happy to see his buddy. "Do you know the last time you saw me was on that ski trip?" Jim asked Pat. "You know, the trip my college buddies planned because they all thought I was dying."

"Yeah, whatever, Jim Young," Pat joked back with Jim. "You weren't much of a skier on that trip. Get on with this already, so I can go back with you." Then the two men trailed off discussing funny incidents that occurred on the trip.

As the cousins got reacquainted with one another, Monique, my mom, and I planned Thanksgiving dinner. There was much to cook and do before Thursday arrived. As we were working out details, Monique said, "I think Jim looks good, Erica."

"Do you really? That means a lot. I think he is much better, but sometimes you can't tell when you are with someone every day."

"How is he doing at work?" my mom asked.

"All right," I replied. "I worry about him. I still wish he would take a leave of absence, so he could work on his health, but he won't. I know connecting with people and pushing himself to work helps him in some ways, but in other ways, he is taxing his body so much."

"Well," my mom responded, "remember what I always say."

Monique and I looked at one another and she rolled her eyes, "I know, I know. Miracles happen every day."

"It's true!" my mom said. "You girls stop making fun of me. Miracles happen all the time. You have to believe it."

"I do, Mom," I said smiling. "I really do."

On Thanksgiving Day, I pulled out our Thanksgiving journal.

Patty, Janet, and Patrick were guests for the feast and they protested a bit, but the deal is if you eat at our house, you are obligated to share your thoughts in the book. The burgundy journal holds statements of gratitude from Thanksgiving guests. If you can't write, you can scribble, make a drawing, or if the person is too little, I summarize what I think they would be thankful for. From the holiday of this year, these are the statements.

What we think Annalise is thankful for: "Babies, Elmo, and her cousins."

What Braxton said: "Thankful for all the wonderful things Mommy does for us. That's what I want to put in the book."

What Thea, one of the cousins, said: "Eating the chicken." (it really was turkey)

From Evie, the other cousin present: "I am thankful for my family, friends, house, and for being healthy."

From Monique and Pat: "Happy to be here this year. Excited to see how strong Jim has become. Thankful to be here, healthy, and enjoying everyday for what it brings—stress, fun, peace—all of it!"

From Wilma: "What a good and wonderful day! Jim is making great progress, kids are happy and healthy, family around me, what more could a person want? Thankful for a good year."

From me: "I am so grateful for continued support and love from family and friends—we are fortunate to have all the help. I'm also thankful for the new friends we now have at church—there are many nice people there."

When I asked Jim to write in the book, he said he couldn't and asked that I write for him, maybe the next day. He was too tired. He did come downstairs for the meal, sitting in his overstuffed olive chair at the end of the dining room table. He didn't eat much of anything in public; it was just too painfully slow to chew and swallow. Instead, he soaked up the conversation, the laughs, and seemed content.

The next day when I asked him about writing in the journal, he declined again. "Let's do it later, Erica." I could tell he needed a nap. So the rest of us decided to go shopping for a bit. As we were gathering in the car, I overheard Thea, who was the same age as Braxton, ask him, "Why does your dad not walk?"

I braced myself for his answer. He looked a little shocked at the question, but the answer was obvious to him. He shrugged his shoulders and replied, "He can walk, Thea, but he's tired a lot. He has Lyme disease and is working to get better. He has warriors and knights in him helping."

Thea shrugged her shoulders at Braxton, "Okay. Just wondering." And with that, we drove away.

After the Dugan visit, Jim seemed a little revived. He finally answered the "what are you thankful for" question with a "I am thankful for being here." He didn't elaborate and I didn't press it. I hoped this answer included happiness for his kids and for the kindness we had been shown. I, too, was much thankful that Jim was still here. Our kids needed him, and we both knew he could get healthy.

The Dugan trip served its purpose. Jim was reminded of good times and love and support. Still, with this help around, Jim's spirits started to slip further as a result of a return to the hospital for an outpatient surgery. The Ear, Nose, and Throat (ENT) doctor had noticed on Jim's last routine appointment that Jim's trach had some skin tags surrounding it. The trach would rub against these to cause irritation, and sometimes bleeding. The ENT physician commented that he could do the procedure in his office, but just for precautionary reasons, he wanted to do this in the hospital. So in early December, right after the Dugan visit, Jim and I checked into the hospital. It was a strange and eerie feeling being back there, but I tried not to focus on the feeling too much. "We'll be in and out of here in a few hours," I naively told myself. Jim was pre-registered, but there were still various paperwork items to deal with before they took Jim back to get ready for the procedure. The two of us sat in a prep room for several minutes, and then the nurses returned. One said, "Okay, Mrs. Young, I think we are ready. You can wait for your husband in the waiting room. The doctor will call you when the procedure is finished."

I looked at Jim. He looked so scared. I looked back at the nurse. I touched my bag that contained an extra trach in it, size number eight. I smiled at Jim and then looked back to the nurse, "Do you guys need Jim's trach? I brought one and it's in my bag."

The nurse quickly commented, "Oh, no. That's fine. There is a trach waiting for Jim in the operating room." Then she motioned for me to leave and showed me the door.

I paused again and thought to myself, *should I give her this trach anyway?* I kept silent and started out the door. I paused at Jim and gave him a smile and kiss. "Everything will be fine. I'll see you in a little bit." Jim gave me a nervous smile. I paused again thinking, *will the nurses be offended if I ask them about the size of the trach? Or maybe I should just tell them Jim uses a size number eight trach?* I hesitated. But then I continued out of the room. I was being too overprotective. These were professionals. She said they had the trach already. I didn't want to offend anyone. So I left and set up camp in the waiting room.

I kept busy on the computer working on items for classes. But hours later, I started to get nervous, thinking, *what are they doing back there? Did something go wrong? Why aren't they coming out to talk with me?* Fortunately, as these negative thoughts began invading my brain more quickly in succession, the ENT doctor came out to see me. "Erica," he said, as he took off his face mask, "Jim did great and is just recovering now. You should be able to see him shortly." I was thrilled. He then told me to wait for my name to be called and that someone would take me back to see my husband.

When the phone call came, it wasn't the one I had expected. "Mrs. Young," said the nurse, "there is a problem."

"How could this be?" I asked. "I just talked with the doctor who said all was fine."

"Well," the nurse continued, "it turns out that a number six trach was put in Jim's throat instead of the number eight size. We are trying to figure out what to do and waiting to hear back from the doctor. He has already left the hospital."

*Oh great!* I thought. *How on earth could this have happened?* I blamed myself for not speaking up, and then I felt sick for what this meant for Jim.

Several minutes went by and the nurse called again. "Mrs. Young, the doctor says he could come back to the hospital and we could do this again. That will be in several hours, but we could do it. The other option is that we could just leave it be and see what happens." Knowing Jim would not want to wait more hours in the hospital, I asked the nurse if she asked Jim what he wanted. "Yes, I did. He wants to leave it alone for now and think about it."

"Okay," I replied, "when can I come back and see him?"

After that, I sent an email to Dr. House, the pulmonologist. He replied to my urgent message that evening, "Well, it's unfortunate it happened this way, Erica, but we were thinking about going down a size on the trach anyway. It may be a few weeks sooner than we were going to do this, but Jim is ready. He is really in good shape."

That gave Jim and me confidence that the trach mistake was a blessing in disguise and that this was another step in the right direction. Jim was getting stronger physically, his endurance was increasing, and he desperately wanted to get the trach out of his neck. This would move us that much closer. A few days after his trach surgery, we received another set of good news from Dr. Lyme. "Looking at the latest blood results, Jim, leads me to think that your motor neuron disease is arrested." Upon hearing this, I jumped around the room, giving high-fives to Jim and the nurse. This was huge. Jim now felt like he had the Lyme on the run, and the focus was thus to build back his body.

We felt like things were starting to go our way.

## CHAPTER 29

DECEMBER 2010

# Tax

*"A charge usually of money imposed by authority on*
*persons or property for public purposes"*

I WAS WRONG. A FEW DAYS later, we received a letter from the IRS. On my way home from work, my mom, who was still in town, told me of the envelope waiting on me with the remark "It is never good when you get a letter from the IRS. I'm so sorry, Erica."

When I walked in the door, I saw the envelope on the counter. I didn't want to open it. I didn't want any bad news. I ignored the letter for several days, but eventually I knew I had to read it. Once I opened the envelope, it stated, "A problem was detected with your 2008 tax return" and we were being audited. My knees felt weak and a nauseous feeling washed over me. I was so tired of dealing with one issue after another. I was just so tired. I felt overwhelmed and didn't want to worry Jim. So I sat on the letter another few days. A few days later, I ran into a neighbor who is an accountant. "What do you think about this?" I asked.

He considered all I had told him and replied, "You were flagged because of the high medical claims. It is a given that if you claim a lot in this area, you will be audited. I can give you the name of someone who has worked for the IRS and he consults now. He's not cheap, but it may be worth a conversation."

I knew I couldn't put off telling Jim any longer. I didn't know if I should get in touch with the consultant or proceed on my own. I was running out of time regardless. The IRS gives you only thirty days after they send the letter. It was already weeks into the deadline. That evening I approached Jim and told him of the letter. I was so surprised to hear him casually say, "Ah, I figured this might happen. When you started doing our taxes this year and you asked about Dr. Lyme's bills, I realized I had mistakenly put some of the bills with last year's returns."

"What do you mean?" I asked. "I'm confused."

"I was so sick when I was doing the tax returns and didn't want to ask you to do them. I've been doing them since we have been married and didn't think it was a big deal. Plus, I thought if I did them, it would help take my mind off of being sick. But this past year, I obviously was so sick and recovering from the tracheostomy that you were forced to do them with my help. As you were asking me questions and working through TurboTax, I realized I clumped IV antibiotics all together as a treatment and I didn't pay attention to dates. That's why you had some of the previous year's medical receipts in this past year's folder."

"Okay," I replied. "I understand that part, but why aren't you more freaked out about this? I know I am. I've been sick about it for days. So worried to tell you about it because I didn't want you to worry."

"Well, Erica," Jim replied. "What are we going to do about it? It was an honest mistake. We'll just make up the difference."

Then I told Jim about my conversation with the neighbor and asked if he thought it a good idea to hire the consultant. Jim replied, "I don't think we need to do that. We just made a simple mistake. You're going to have to get lots of things in order for the IRS on your own anyway. Seems like we would be using money in the wrong place. I know we owe money, so let's just pay it."

That seemed like the obvious thing to do, although my mom kept urging me to hire the consultant. "Maybe he can help, Erica," she said. "You never know. I don't know why you want to do this all on your own. It's crazy."

"But, Mom, I have to run around gathering all the receipts and going to the bank for returned checks and getting summaries of things for doctors regardless of whether I go to the consultant. Jim knows he made the mistake and thinks they will not penalize us based on this honest mistake."

"But, Erica," my mom continued, "don't be naïve. You told me the IRS had other things listed as well, like questioning charitable contributions and travel for work. Please go see the consultant."

"Mom," I continued, "I don't even know if he has time for us and his fee is thousands of dollars. Plus, I only have another week and a half to pull this off. It's so crazy how little time the IRS gives you."

"Is there anything I can do to help?" was Mom's reply.

"You are helping. I'll run around like crazy and if you can handle the kids, that would be wonderful."

Fortunately, we have a folder with all receipts associated with deductions for the tax year. Unfortunately and understandably, the recordkeeping during Jim illness wasn't what it usually was. And I had been so busy with baby Annalise and Braxton and working full-time that I didn't pay attention. I mostly had to organize receipts, write a letter explaining our side of things, and track down proof that our insurance didn't pay for the medications and office visits—nothing difficult, but time-consuming and very frustrating.

Upon gathering receipts, I realized that our charitable contributions were actually more than what we claimed. I was pretty excited about that, naively thinking that our debt would decrease as a result. But I came to discover that the IRS doesn't work like that—they are happy to change your return if you owe then money, but they are not willing to change the return if they might owe you a little something.

The day that the return was due, I was frantically tying up all the loose ends and after realizing that our fax machine at home wasn't going to cut it, there were just too many pages for our machine to handle, I drove off to the local UPS store. I flew into the door and asked the storeowner for help. I have faxed things through them before and usually it is a five-minute process, but not that day. The document was ninety pages in length and would get fed in too many at a time. Then the line was busy. Then the machine ran out of memory (too much time had elapsed trying to contact the IRS number). It was a nightmare! I could feel my heart starting to pound stronger and stronger, with panic washing over me.

Stepping outside to get some fresh air, I re-read the letter I had in my purse. It was clearly stated in several places that, "You must have your documentation into us by the date indicated on the letter or risk further penalties." I looked at my watch. It had been over an hour since I had been at the store. I looked back at the letter and decided to call the help number. After punching a few numbers, I was placed on hold, waiting for the next agent to help me. I looked at my watch, I waited, and I paced up and down the sidewalk. I looked in at the UPS worker who shook her head "No" again. I looked at my watch. I waited some more. When a voice finally started twenty-five minutes later, I was caught off guard. "State your problem," she started.

I explained the situation and then she replied, irritated, "It's fine, ma'am."

"What do you mean?" I asked. "I don't want a penalty if I don't get it to you today."

Oh, don't worry about that," she said. "Just send it to us in the mail."

"Should I send it over-night or certified?" I asked sheepishly.

To that question, I heard a chuckle and the comment, "Really, it is no big deal. Even if you got it to us today, we won't look at it probably for another two or three weeks. You honestly can just put it in the regular mail." Still, I didn't believe this. Why was the letter in my hand worded as harshly as it was? Why such different messages? I decided to overnight it and pleaded for her to make a note of this call in our records. She told me that by calling, it was an indication that I had met the deadline. What a bomb to drop on me after such an emotionally-charged day.

I walked back into the UPS store and told my story. "Really?" she asked.

"I know," I replied, "it's bizarre. I'm so sorry. What a waste of time for us both. It has been over two hours."

"Please don't worry about that," she replied. "I was obviously doing other things, too, but I wish they would have told you sooner. For your sake."

Weeks later, we heard from the IRS with a form letter that indeed they received our documentation. Weeks later still, we received the letter, telling us what we owed. I was shocked. It was thousands of dollars more than I had expected. They also threw in several thousand dollars worth of penalties. I hid it from Jim for days, but, of course, true to form, the IRS doesn't give you much time to pay your bills—thirty days from the date they had on the letter. When I did share the news with Jim, I was equally shocked by his attitude. His reaction was "Yeah—that's about what I thought. The penalty was higher, though."

"Really, Jim? I thought you thought they would waive the penalty."

"I was hoping they would, but it doesn't surprise me. Don't worry about it, Erica. We'll figure it out. Just pay the fine and let's move on. I'm tired of thinking about this, and I'm sure you're tired of dealing with it."

With Jim's dad's help in Alabama, we secured a loan from a credit union to pay for the IRS bill. I sent our check to the IRS and two or three days later, there was another letter from the IRS. Thinking it was a confirmation of our payment, I was impressed with their speed of reply. I was quite surprised to find another letter, saying there was a problem with our taxes from 2009, the year after this audit year. *Are you kidding me?* I thought to myself. I reread the letter. This time around it wasn't an audit, but an indication that we had made a mistake with how we claimed childcare. I remember being confused when TurboTax was asking questions about daycare, so it made sense that I had made a mistake. This mistake was another $2000 out the window! There went some more of our retirement savings.

\* \* \*

## CHAPTER 30

JANUARY 2011

# The Bomb

*"Something unexpected and unpleasant"*

AFTER OUR ANNIVERSARY MARK OF one-year post tracheostomy, I began my spring semester at the college.
This semester started off well with two groups of students in
two classes that seemed eager to learn and do well. One class
contained several graduating seniors, and was a course that is
not offered often. This was a nice change of pace with the chal-
lenge of thinking about things in new ways. My teaching and
meeting schedule fell into place nicely, with my colleagues being
understanding of my desire to work from home one day a week.
This allowed me to save time on the commute drive and use
that time to run errands. I also was able to get much work done
because no one came to see me and I didn't have meetings to
attend. Because of this, I was able to get most of my work done
during the work week and during the day. I had an easier load
at night and on the weekend.

Still, it was busy, too. The kids were still so little and needed
lots of love and attention. Mornings would be a whirlwind of
trying to get them ready for daycare, helping with Jim (even
with the nurse present), and tending to my own needs. Even

though I planned for things the night before, I still forgot things and chaos ensued. Once I got the kids dropped off, the long commute was nice in a way, since I had the chance to clear my head, return phone calls, and plan out things for work and home. When I was at work, it was constant. If I wasn't in the classroom, I was in my office, helping students or preparing for class. I ate lunch at my desk, bypassing eating with colleagues, so that I could be as productive as possible. I had a drop-dead cut-off time at the end of the day to leave, in order to get the kids on time. Therefore, I found myself chatting less with my colleagues, focusing only on business, and feeling more and more isolated. But this trade-off made sense. When I did see friends at work, they would smile, ask about Jim, and fortunately understand the craziness of the situation. Still, I missed talking with them about work and their families.

About two weeks into the semester, one of my friends at work popped her head into my office, "How is your family holding up?"

"Everyone's fine, Kate," I replied. "Thanks for asking."

"So no one has the flu over there?" She asked, following it with, "I'm so glad. Seems like a lot of students around here are sick."

"You know, you're right. At Jim's work there are a lot of people absent and several kids at daycare, too, but didn't realize it was the flu. That scares me."

"Well," Kate replied, "since you know about it, you guys should be extra careful. Maybe you shouldn't let the kids around Jim for a while."

"That seems like a good idea. Thanks."

That night I told Jim about this, and he agreed it was a good idea. Then I asked, "How are you feeling?"

"I do feel a little strange and there are so many people on my hall out. I'm a little worried," Jim reflected.

A few days after this conversation, Braxton had a fever. He complained he didn't feel well. I started to panic, but then told myself to stop thinking negatively and that there was nothing I could do except help Braxton feel better. Two days after Braxton felt strange, Annalise had a fever. Both kids seemed sick for only a few days, and I wasn't even sure it was the flu. When I stopped to focus on my health, I realized that I didn't feel all that well, either. The three of us stayed as far away as we could from Jim, but he was still exposed to whatever was going around since he was still actively going to work. By the end of the week, both the kids and I were fine. It seemed to take me a little bit longer than Braxton and Annalise, but in general, I counted our blessings that we didn't seem to have the flu after all. I rationalized that it was just something minor, and that Jim had been spared as a result.

But then it happened. Jim started a fever and was having more problems breathing. When he would return from work, he would quickly get on the ventilator for some relief and help. Over the course of the next several days, his breathing became incredibly labored, complete with many secretions and mucous. He obviously could not work with this and stayed at home, trying to rest as much as possible. At night, he would beg the nurse or me to help him with the suction catheter and get further in his throat to help remove the secretions that were blocking his breathing. At one point, I said, "Jim, this is just not safe. This tube is so long, it must be punching a hole in your lungs."

Jim looked back at me in desperation, "I can't breathe, Erica. There is something deep there blocking me."

The following day, when things were still not improving, I phoned Dr. House and sent him an email, expressing my concerns.

He emailed back, saying, "Fortunately Jim is on a lot of antibiotics. The same ones I would give him if I thought he might have an infection. And, of course, if it is the flu, that is a virus, that has to run its course. But if you think it's a good idea to check him into the hospital, we could do a thorough examination and try to rule out things as well as just get a status update."

I relayed the message to Jim, who replied, "I don't want to go to the hospital. I am afraid I will get sicker in the hospital. See if Dr. House will come here."

Dr. House was kind to make the house call. When he arrived, he said, "I don't blame you, Jim. It is true that people leave the hospital sicker sometimes than when they started. But, we do need to consider it if things are not improving."

He approached Jim and did a checkup. After using his stethoscope to listen to Jim's lungs, Dr. House smiled and said, "Your lungs sound pretty good. Have things changed since we spoke via email?"

Jim shook his head, "Yes, I feel better today. I do feel like something has changed for the better. It's a small change, but I can tell."

Dr. House did some more assessments of Jim and then said, "I do think Jim just needed to rest and let the bug work its way out of his system. I feel like there is nothing I can do for you since you are already taking the antibiotics from Dr. Lyme. These would be some of the same I would prescribe for you. And, it's encouraging that Jim is starting to feel better."

Jim smiled, relieved to stay home. "Thank you, Doctor."

"No worries," said Dr. House. "But I do want to caution you. Since you are working on a lower reserve than most of us, it will take you longer to recover from this bug. I am assuming it is the flu, based on what you've told me about your symptoms.

If Erica had the flu or if I had the flu, it might knock us down for a week. In your case, I would say you would have to add several weeks on top of that." Then he paused, gave a slight smile to both Jim and me, and continued, "Please, just take it slow. Don't put too much pressure on yourself. It's all right to go on the ventilator for rest and support. You can start working back off it when you feel stronger."

Another day passed and Jim's breathing was worse. Nighttime became even more of a battle, with Jim unable to get a block of solid sleep throughout the night. He was miserable. He started losing weight and strength again . . . quickly. Dr. House phoned the following day to check up on Jim, "How is he doing, Erica?"

"Not good. I'm wondering if he just said that to you the other night because he so much does not want to go to the hospital again. I'm really scared. He can't breathe or eat and is getting weaker every day."

"Okay," Dr. House replied, "I hear you, Erica. Let's give it one or two more days at the most, and if Jim doesn't turn a corner, we really should get him in the hospital and see if something else is going on."

A few hours after this call, Jim's mom Patricia phoned, "Erica, I'm on my way. Please don't worry about it. I'm retired and have nothing else to do. And, of course, nothing else is more important. I'm leaving in the morning and should be there tomorrow night to help."

"Thanks, Patricia," I answered. I didn't want to argue. "Please drive safely." I hung up the phone, hoping her presence would help Jim. There is something about a mother that really does make all the difference in the world. When Patricia arrived the next day, she hugged the kids and ran up to see her little boy.

She gave me a look that was telling. She was just as worried about him as I was.

"Hi, Jim," she started and told him a bit about her travels. When Jim couldn't really respond due to weakness, she followed up. "Son, listen to me. You are really sick. Erica is worried about you. I'm worried about you. I think it's time you go to the hospital."

"No. Mom," Jim persisted, "I'm not going. Those places are awful, and I'm telling you I will catch something else there and I'll be worse off."

Patricia stared at him. Jim stared back. I felt uncomfortable. After a few more minutes, Patricia said, "How about if Erica calls the doctor again and we see what he has to say?"

Jim agreed and fortunately Dr. House agreed to come back out to the house. Perhaps it was the presence of his mother, or the threat of returning to the hospital, but over the course of the day, I could see Jim perk up. By the time Dr. House visited, it was late in the evening, and Jim was a transformed person. Dr. House gave me a strange look and I'm sure he was thinking "Why did Erica call me out here again? It's obvious Jim is better."

Rather than doing a thorough exam on Jim this time, we all ended up talking at length about expectations, Jim's health, his progress, and how to approach this flu. Dr. House concluded, "It seems like Jim is working through these issues. I don't hear anything negative in his lungs, and the ups and downs Jim is experiencing is not unusual. What we try to do in these situations is manage as best we can and let the patient work through things."

About two weeks from the onset of the flu, Jim started feeling more like himself. He was not well yet, but he needed to return to work or go out on short-term disability. It was too soon, and we both knew it. "Jim, you really need to stay home to recover," I pleaded.

"I don't have that luxury. If I could, I would. But if I don't go back now, it gets complicated and I can't do short-term disability again. It's too soon."

"You promised me that you would listen to your body," I protested. "If your body was saying you needed a break, you need to listen to it."

Jim looked so frustrated. "I know I promised, Erica. I do feel like I am recovering, and I have been listening to my body and stayed home."

I cut him off, "Yes, but not long enough. You need to stay home longer to fully recover."

"I can't, Erica. I can't," he sadly replied.

Jim plugged along at work, but it was getting harder and harder for him. Everyone could see the continual decline, but Jim had committed himself to some projects, and he needed to see them through.

✳ ✳ ✳

## CHAPTER 31

MARCH — APRIL 2011

# The Breaking Point

*"The point at which a person gives way under stress"*

JIM WAS STARTING TO ACT a little more like his true self about five to six weeks after the flu struck. It was mid-March. He was only given a two-week grace period, when another bug started going around work and daycare. At my workplace, students and colleagues were going down like flies. I heard it was strep throat. I heard it was some general stomach bug. I heard everyone seemed to be getting it. I knew I would not. I rarely get sick and I know I don't really have the liberty to recover from an illness, so I will myself to not get sick. Often I will say to myself, "Don't get sick, Erica. You have no time to be sick. You are healthy." This method has served me well over the years. When others around me were ill, I seemed spared.

But stress changes things. Sleep exhaustion changes things. The new bug struck me like a lightning bolt. I was teaching class one morning and my throat started feeling sore. I would clear my throat and move on—still, I could tell it was getting worse as the class period went on. Fortunately, I had a glass of water with me, and this helped keep my throat in check. The following class period, I changed things a bit, breaking the students into groups to solve problems, so that I wouldn't have to speak so much. Every time I did speak, I found my throat feeling more and more raw.

After class, I returned to my office and tried to eat the salad I brought for lunch. It was a struggle. I tried to swallow, but couldn't. I looked at the clock. It was 1:30 p.m. I had a student coming at 3:00 p.m., so I knew I had to make it to that point. I tried to eat my food again. No luck. I felt miserable. My colleague, Kate, walked past, waved, and said hello. I could hear her stop in the hallway, and then she walked back to my office. "Erica, are you all right? You look horrible," Kate said.

"Thanks a lot," I mumbled. "I do feel awful. My throat is killing me."

"You need to go home."

"I can't. A student is coming to my office at three. We've had this appointment for weeks."

Kate stared at me and finally said, "Erica, you need to go home. Go. Put a note on the door and go home. The student will understand."

"Do you really think she'll understand?" I asked. Kate shook her head. "Okay, thanks, Kate. You're right. I really need to get to bed." I could barely get these words out, my voice was so strained.

I was so weak and tired, I had to struggle to get my stuff in order. I fumbled out to my car and looked at the time. It was 2:45 p.m. Feeling a little guilty about the student, I tried to focus on the drive itself. I was nervous to make it home safely. My commute was an hour, and I was exhausted. My throat was so sore. As I drove, I stopped at McDonalds. I pulled in and ordered the largest Dr. Pepper I could. I thought this would help my throat. It didn't. The act of swallowing the liquid was painful. I only managed to drink a few sips of the drink. I phoned Patrick and asked if he could pick up the kids. When I got home, I crashed and slept for hours.

The next day, I cancelled my classes without even considering an assignment for the students to complete. This decision told me how sick I really was. Any other time in the past (including when Jim was in the hospital), I would come up with an assignment for the students to do in place of class. I felt this was important for their education and to help keep biology "fresh on their minds."

Somehow the next morning, I got the kids ready for daycare, drove them there, and then made my way to the health clinic at Jim's workplace. I didn't have an appointment and at first, the receptionist wasn't sure they could see me. Thank goodness she changed her mind and I only had to wait about ten minutes in the waiting room. When the nurse called my name, I slowly got up and considered falling back down on the ground. I felt so weak and overall miserable. The nurse and I walked back to the exam room, where she took my vitals and then said the doctor would be in shortly. Time went by so slowly. So many minutes passed that I wondered if I had been forgotten. I was struggling to keep my eyes open. While sitting, I rested my head against the table and closed my eyes. More minutes passed. I wondered if I could close my eyes on the examination table and rest a bit, so I moved up on the table and fell asleep. Eventually, the doctor came in, examined me, and gave the diagnosis of strep throat. After picking up my medication at the pharmacy, I returned home and slept all day long.

The fear was not necessarily over the kids, although certainly I didn't want them to get strep throat. The fear was Jim. I stayed away from him, but of course, I was probably infectious days prior to this point. A day or two after my illness, he felt his throat start to tickle. He started himself on antibiotics immediately. We had some extra ones from treating the Lyme disease and he didn't want to take any chances.

The next day, I could tell Jim was struggling. I was starting to feel better, but he was declining. Again. The day after that, Jim was definitely sick. He struggled through this episode, going to bed early and arriving at work late. And although he didn't get nearly as sick as I did, this second illness knocked him back even further. The flu started the downward progression and the second bug sealed the deal. Jim would struggle from this moment on.

I returned to work after the weekend rest and all seemed fine with me until about a month later. Then the sore throat started again—this time on the other side of my neck. It wasn't near as intense as before. The first time I felt like my throat was closing in on itself and that there was something physically stuck there. This time, the throat was just sore and I was beginning to have trouble swallowing. I decided to go back to the doctor's office.

A got a barrage of questions from the doctor: "Are you sneezing a lot lately?" and "Are your eyes irritated?" and "Do you notice any heartburn after you eat certain foods?"

I kept thinking, *I don't have allergies—I know what that feels like.* And, *I don't think I have acid reflux.*

Finally, the doctor said, "Well, I don't think it's very likely that you have mono. The chances of that are very rare and you really would have to be under some serious stress." She continued, "It is unlikely someone your age would have mono, but just to be sure, let's draw your blood and test for that as well as thyroid functions."

After having my blood drawn, I returned home and was telling Jim the story. About ten minutes later, my story was interrupted with a phone call from the doctor. "It's confirmed already. You do have mono."

Upon hearing this news, I jumped back from Jim. The physician continued, "You really need to rest. It's a virus, so there's really nothing we can do about it. Probably what you had a month ago was mono and this is a flare-up. That's why you need to get rest."

"I don't understand. I was tested for strep throat and treated for it."

"Actually, you were treated for it, but the test came back negative. Didn't someone call you to tell you this?"

"No," I replied. "How contagious is this? What signs do I look for with my kids?"

"Don't worry. At this point, you are not contagious. Just be mindful of your kids as you always would be. Look for a fever, sore throat, and exhaustion. If you see any of these symptoms, bring them in right away."

I hung up the phone and my next panicked thought was, *if I have mono, maybe that's what Jim had. What if he still has it? Maybe this explains why he is struggling so much to get back to where he needs to be.* Then I looked at Jim and after explaining what I just learned, I said, "Jim, you really need to go on short-term disability. You are not getting better. You are struggling. You need to pay attention to your body and stop working. Your job needs to be getting healthy."

"Erica," Jim said in an irritated tone, "I don't want to hear this again. My department is scheduled for a move, and I want to be there to get my office moved and set up the way it needs to be." He paused waiting for my response. I gave none. I was too frustrated to speak. Jim continued, "And, most importantly, I promised Mr. Josh Colleague that I would finish this project. I want to keep my word. It's my project and I need to finish it. When the project is done, I can start thinking about leave."

"Fine," I replied, "but I will bring up short-term disability to you all the time until you are so sick of hearing me say it, you will be forced to take time off." Jim smiled and nodded.

"And," I continued, "you know your body can't take much more of this. You are twenty pounds lighter as a result of the flu and this mono or whatever it is—twenty pounds you really couldn't afford to lose. If you continue on like this, you will kill yourself." I paused. "I will be so mad at you, Jim Young if you do that. Our children need a father. Work on your health. Mr. Colleague will understand."

## CHAPTER 32

MAY 2011

# Surrender

*"To give up completely or agree to forgo
especially in favor of another"*

DURING THESE HORRIBLE BREATHING DAYS, we learned
that our insurance company was ready to move on our
appeal. We had gone through all the levels internally to get
reimbursed for paying out-of-pocket for all of Jim's care associated with the IV antibiotics. Now, there was an external review
committee that would hear our case. This was our last try on
getting reimbursed thousands of dollars.

In response to the initial denial of payment, I wrote a letter
in appeal. From what we understood from the letter of denial,
our insurance company considered Jim's treatment as "investigational" and "not medically necessary." Thus, my letter was
designed to highlight that long-term IV antibiotics are standard
for fighting chronic Lyme disease and that without the treatment,
Jim would not be alive. The four-page letter included much data
from the scientific literature and supporting recent court cases.
Part of the letter follows:

We have successfully argued that our benefit booklet's

definition of medically necessary has been met. The booklet defines services or supplies that are:

*provided for the diagnosis, treatment, cure, or relief of a health condition, illness, injury, or disease; and, except for clinical trials as described under the Plan, not for experimental, investigation, or cosmetic purposes.* Jim's treatment was not experimental or investigational. Such long-term IV treatment for Lyme has been occurring for years with successful results (see references in text of letter above).

*necessary for and appropriate to the diagnosis, treatment, cure, or relief of a health condition, illness, injury, disease, or its symptoms.* As outlined above, Jim would not be alive today if he didn't have these IV treatments.

*Within generally accepted standards of medical care in the community.* The CDC states Lyme disease is a clinical diagnosis (and as in the court case above, this trumps the IDSA's guidelines which are suspect anyway due to various conflicts of interest) and there are numerous scientific publications showing that chronic Lyme disease exists and that long-term IV antibiotic treatment can be successful in treating Lyme disease.

*Not solely for the convenience of the insured, the insured's family, or the provider.* Obviously, Jim (and our family) has been hit hard by this disease and are not using such antibiotic treatment for convenience. Again, it is because of the treatments that Jim is alive today.

*[The insurance company] states that it "will provide coverage for intravenous antibiotic therapy for Lyme disease when it is determined to be medically necessary and when the medical criteria and guidelines...are met."* We know these have been accomplished. Jim received a clinical diagnosis from a leading expert in Lyme disease. [The insurance company] states that

Jim didn't have erythema migrans nor the specified serologies, but the absence of these does not mean he doesn't have Lyme disease. Any rash associated with tick bites is bad (Jim had several streaky rashes) and he was taking antibiotics at the time of testing, making the already unreliable serology tests even more unreliable. The second component of [The insurance company]'s denial about guidelines is disingenuous as well. The CDC's guidelines over-ride the IDSA's guidelines (and outline that diagnosis is based on a physician's knowledge of the disease itself and its symptoms; a clinical diagnosis is more reliable— that is from the Clinical Guidelines and Law "the legal standard of care for treating a condition is determined by the consensus of physicians who actually treat patients, not by treatment guidelines"). Additionally, the IDSA's guidelines should be viewed with suspect since various states, such as Connecticut's Attorney General, are trying to get the IDSA Board to reexamine the guidelines using all the scientific literature (not just viewing a small sub-sample).

With our letter in hand and a review of what we wanted to say during the meeting, we waited on that May afternoon for the insurance company to call us. Jim's breathing was still labored, making it difficult to speak, so the burden of arguing our case fell to me. I found myself sweating and very anxious. Precisely at the appointment time, our phone rang.

"Mr. Young and Mrs. Young, this is Sue from the insurance company. I will be representing the insurance company during our call. I also have on the phone our external reviewer, Dr. B. He is an infectious disease specialist."

"Hello," I answered. "We are both on the phone, but Jim is recovering from a bug and his voice is strained, so I'll be doing most of the talking."

"Okay, fine," Sue replied. "Let's begin. The purpose of this review is to determine if you should be reimbursed for costs associated with the care of Lyme disease. Is that correct?"

"Yes," I answered.

Sue than started reading parts of my letter. I was confused, thinking she was representing the insurance company, not summarizing my points. Sue stumbled on my points. She misread a word, corrected herself, and continued. She did this several times. Even I was confused and I penned the letter.

Then I was allowed to speak on behalf of our case. I started to speak in a cracked, nervous voice. On the one hand, I was happy it was on the phone because this reviewer, "Dr. B.," wouldn't see my nervousness. On the other hand, I thought it would be much better if we could all see each other face to face. I outlined our points as best I could, feeling so happy that we choose to write things down on paper, so I wouldn't forget to say anything. I concluded with, "So in summary, chronic Lyme disease is treated differently by different doctors based on each patient's symptoms. There is not a one-size-fits-all treatment because Lyme looks different in different people. Regardless, treating chronic Lyme with long-term antibiotics is not investigational. There are years of published results illustrating the effectiveness of long term IV use. For some patients, it might be two months, for others it may take twelve months. Again, the point is that the doctor treating the patient determines this. Using guidelines to refuse payment does not make sense. Every patient is different and therefore every treatment plan will be different."

Dr. B. responded, "I think you have made that point several times."

I continued, "Okay, well then, I would just like to say that the insurance company's other point is that the treatment was not medically necessary. It is clear from the fact that Jim is working now, rebuilding his body and not dead that the treatment was medically necessary. Jim would not be here today without the treatment. No doubt about it."

Sue then asked Jim if he wanted to say anything. Jim's voice was weak, but he wanted to speak. He cleared his throat and said, "I just want to restate that guidelines are simply that and that guidelines should not be used exclusively as the law. "

Sue replied, "Thank you, Mr. Young. And now Dr. B., do you have any questions?" My heart sank, my body tensed up, and my face went numb. There was too long a pause, so I knew there was a problem.

I briefly went over what I had said in my mind and decided we had made a tactical error when I heard Dr. B. speak, "Ah, yes. Only one question. How was Jim diagnosed with Lyme? Was the diagnosis made after the IV treatments were given because he responded well to them or was the diagnosis before? Walk me through that diagnosis."

My voice would not come. I focused our whole argument over treatment of Lyme, but Dr. B. didn't even believe Jim had Lyme! I felt nauseous, but willed myself to speak. "Well," I started, "after we got to Dr. Lyme, he asked Jim a series of many questions, taking a detailed history of symptoms. He was interested in all the symptoms Jim had and when they started. He noted that several were ALS symptoms, but that many were not. He asked Jim questions extensively for thirty or forty minutes. After this, he performed various tests in his office. He asked Jim to squeeze his fingers, looked at his gait, tested his hearing, and focused on his nervous system. We were in his office with him for about two and a half hours."

Dr. B. was impatient, "But Jim never had a blood test?"

"At the end of our office visit, Dr. Lyme asked if Jim would get the test done through a reliable lab and gave us all the necessary paperwork to make that happen. When we got home, we could go to the lab and they would draw blood and send it along. Dr. Lyme had already made the clinical diagnosis of Lyme disease with overlap ALS symptoms and we had mapped out a plan to get started with treatment right away. Dr. Lyme added that the test wasn't to verify that Jim had Lyme. He was sure he did, but because of the controversy out there on whether or not Lyme is as prevalent as it is, Dr. Lyme wanted Jim to be tested. He then told us that the testing would cost about $800 and unfortunately this was yet another thing the insurance company wouldn't cover. We decided that financially it wasn't worth it to us. If I knew then what I know now, we certainly would have done it, but we didn't. So to go back to your question, the diagnosis of Lyme was made before Jim was treated with IV antibiotics or any antibiotics for that matter. When Jim started responding nicely to them, we were reassured this was the correct diagnosis."

"I see," Dr. B. said. "So Jim never had a positive blood test."

I replied, "I just want to remind you of something you already know." I found myself gaining some confidence, and continued, "Many laboratories that test for Lyme are not reliable. Tests are not reliable. A positive test result doesn't necessarily mean you have Lyme because there are false-positives. A negative test result doesn't necessarily mean you don't have Lyme, either, because they are so unreliable. I have documented several published papers on this if you look at the letter."

"Yes," Dr. B. said, "I have that here."

"Jim has had many tick bites and many rashes associated with these tick bites.

He also had taken antibiotics for what the physicians thought might be the flu or something flu-like, and this can mask the appearance of bands on a serological test. Again, we knew all of this prior to being asked by Dr. Lyme to take the test and decided we wouldn't gain anything from it. Maybe this was a bad call, but we still contend that the test wouldn't necessarily confirm that Jim had Lyme. The best diagnosis of the disease is a clinical one made by a Lyme-literate doctor, not by a blood test."

Dr. B. really didn't have much to say or ask after that. My gut told me this was bad, but I tried to convince myself that maybe it was a good sign. Still, as the insurance company representative was trying to end the call, I decided to interrupt: "Can I say something else, please?"

"Umm, sure, please go ahead," she replied.

Trying to gain as much momentum as I could, my voice started shaking again, tears welled up in my eyes, and certainly everyone knew I was fighting back tears. "There is gray here. It isn't black and white. We know this is true from the continual back and forth over whether Lyme exists in North Carolina. Okay, now the medical community says Lyme does exist. So the fight has moved to whether or not Lyme can be chronic. Some say 'No,' but many say it can be. Obviously, there is still much to figure out—there is no black and white as the insurance company contends. There is gray." I pleaded with Dr. B. "There is enough going on with research to know that this Lyme thing is not figured out yet and new things are being discovered all the time. So having such a rigid insurance policy in place seems strange. This doesn't make sense." I paused for a moment, trying to catch my breath, trying to stop my voice from shaking. It didn't work, and I continued on for a few more moments. "I don't understand why, given this uncertainty and continual change in the field of Lyme biology, that a physician's diagnosis can be so easily discounted. This just doesn't make sense to me."

The insurance company representative, Sue, coldly responded, "Thank you, Mrs. Kosal." Dr. B. said nothing.

Then Jim and I were excused from the call and the review continued. We had been on the phone for twenty-two minutes. I am convinced Dr. B. already knew his vote for the most part from the start of the review process and nothing we could have said would have changed his mind. I am sure the outcome was determined before the phone call itself.

Verifying my gut instinct, two days after our review phone call, we received our official denial letter in the mail. It was full of legal jargon and was puzzling because it had internal review stuff in there with external review stuff. It seemed like the internal review and the external review letters were incorrectly meshed together. What was significant was the conclusion. Dr. B. summed it up, "The patient was being treated with an excessive combination of antibiotics for a disease which he is not supported to have. The medical records do not support the diagnosis of Lyme disease. Although it is said that ticks have over the years bitten him, there is no objective evidence presented to support the diagnosis of Lyme disease. There is no serological evidence presented, there is no examination of the cerebrospinal fluid to document evidence supporting central nervous system Lyme disease nor is there any abnormalities presented of his physical and neurological examination."

Wow. We were back at the beginning—they didn't even believe Jim had Lyme disease! I was so mad, disgusted, frustrated, deflated, and sad. All that effort, all that optimism, all that confidence that we could somehow "help" others was gone in an instant. We could do nothing further, short of hiring an attorney to sue the company. We knew we couldn't do this. We couldn't risk any repercussions or denials to Jim's continual care.

✳ ✳ ✳

## CHAPTER 33

MAY 2011

# The Shove

*"To push or put in a rough, careless, or hasty manner"*

ABOUT TWO WEEKS LATER, ANOTHER blow came our way. At this point, I started thinking, *how much more can we take? Where is the silver lining? Life is really so unfair.* I was at home working on my self-evaluation and assessments for our biology program as my semester had just finished. The phone rang, and it was Jim. As was usual for him during these still-struggling-to breathe days, I heard his voice only faintly, "He put me on a plan." My heart sank. Panic flooded me. I felt hot. This was what I had been afraid of—this was what Jim's closest friends were warning.

"What does that mean exactly, Jim? What is a plan?" I asked these questions, but I was really thinking, *what about the health care insurance?* The kids and I could certainly switch to my work's insurance, but with Jim's pre-existing condition, the new insurance company would certainly reject Jim. What would happen to Jim? How could we financially handle this? Why didn't Jim listen to me and take short-term disability?

My daydreaming was interrupted by Jim's response, "You remember what a corrective action plan is, Erica. It is when the company basically outlines what you need to improve and they give you a deadline to get to those improvements or they offer you the opportunity to take a severance package and leave on good terms."

My heart sank again, "So what are the improvements?"

Jim paused, trying to catch his breath and then said, "During training, I need to be able to teach a class, walking around, projecting my voice clearly, and writing on the board as well as coaching all sessions within that two week time period. All this after Josh and I concluded several weeks ago that all of my work would be done from my office."

I cut him off before he could finish, "Isn't that discrimination? Mr. Colleague knows you can't do that anytime soon, but there are lots of other productive things you can be doing to help the department. Aren't there other people at the company who are considered handicapped and have accommodations to help them with their jobs?"

Jim sighed, "Yes, but you know Josh doesn't care about that. I don't think he wants a handicapped person working for him. We both know that Mr. Colleague has wanted me gone since before I returned home from the hospital."

I was so sad and mad, trying to make sense of my emotions. "Jim, what are the other problems listed on the corrective action plan?"

I braced for the answer and Jim said, "I need to finish up the project that caused me to stay in place and not take disability leave. But the ironic thing is that Mr. Josh Colleague claims I'm not meeting the deadlines for this project, but there have never been any deadlines in place. The entire corrective action plan is full of distortions and half truths."

"Like what Jim?"

"Josh commented on the fact that there was miscommunication with a video group helping our department that was just not true. What actually happened was the group lost the original coded video. I didn't miscommunicate, they lost the video. I told him about this. He wanted me to apparently fail at something, even though he knew it wasn't my fault."

I suddenly remembered some things I had been helping Jim with on the weekends. "Wait a minute. Are some of these items related to the guy who is out on paternity leave right now?"

"Yes," Jim replied.

"And so," I continued, "you can't do your part of the project until he gets back to work and that is your fault? Didn't the baby come early?"

"Yes," Jim answered, "the baby was due a month from when the guy left for paternity leave. Obviously, everything had to be tabled until he returns."

"Did you explain this to Mr. Josh Colleague?" I asked.

"Yes, but he said that I should have planned things out better, knowing that this guy's wife was pregnant."

"Unbelievable." I said, "And the guy had his own projects he was working on, too."

"Yep," said Jim.

"So what does this mean?" I asked.

"Well, I called Human Resources before I called you and told them about my plan of taking short-term disability. Because Josh already wrote an official plan of action for me, I can take short-term disability, but when I return, the plan is in place. I have to meet the expectations at that time."

"Can Mr. Colleague take it back?" I asked. "I mean, you were planning on leaving. He knows that. Why didn't he talk to you and tell you he was going to do this unless you left. I thought he was our friend."

"Erica," Jim responded sadly, "you know that he is really not my friend. We learned that a while ago. Ironically, it turns out that HR says he can take the plan "back." He can rip it up and it goes away, but he won't do it."

"So," I asked, as I was trying to take this all in. "If you leave and get stronger and return to the department, you will still have to do these things, but the project will be completed by someone else while you are gone?"

"Exactly," he replied.

"Does that mean . . .?" I wondered.

"Yep, sure does. I can't win. I can't even look for another job within the company with this plan hanging in my folder. I have to redeem myself in the department first and then I would be eligible to look elsewhere."

"Wow," I said, "we saw this coming, but still. What does this mean? What are you thinking?"

"The good news from HR is that I can still take my leave as I was planning all along. I guess we'll just figure things out as we go."

I paused, unsure of what to say. I was crushed that Jim, after all his time working, was being "kicked to the curb" like this. I was so frustrated by Mr. Colleague's actions. He knew Jim was holding on to finish the project for him. Why didn't he talk to Jim and tell him things were not going as well as he hoped and that Jim really needed the break to work on his health? Why wouldn't he let his "friend" leave with his dignity?

I did manage to say to Jim on that phone call, "Okay, well I think it's good that you are forced to focus on your health.

You know you need to stop working and even though it is not on your terms, it is a good thing. God is helping make sure you stop working and that you don't have the stress involved with trying to finish up this project and that there will be no doubt in your mind that you need to be off of work. That part of the decision is taken off the table, and that is not a bad thing."

There was silence on the other end of the phone. I could hear Jim struggling to talk and could hear the labored breathing. I added, "It's all right, Jim. I'm so sorry, but it's okay. Do you want me to come get you?"

Jim responded, "I made an appointment with HR tomorrow to talk about things and need for you to come to that meeting with me. I'm fine now. I'll be coming home soon."

When Jim got home, I gave him the biggest hug I could, but the correct words didn't come. We were both silent and then sat on the couch. Jim finally said, "The ironic thing is that I could work on much of this project at home. That way I could get on the vent if I needed to for a break and still work on the computer. I wouldn't have to spend all my energy getting dressed and getting to work."

I responded, "I know you talked to Josh about that. Considering how many other employees work from home on occasion, I still don't understand why he was so against it."

Jim smiled, "I think he needed to prove to the rest of the department that I wasn't being treated differently. You are supposed to put in a twenty-four-hour request to work from home and then be approved."

"So why can't you just ask for a Monday and Wednesday standard every week and work from home?"

"Because the times are supposed to be occasional, not routine.

Mr. Colleague said he didn't want the group thinking I was getting special treatment."

"You know," I responded, "your team would totally support you working at home routinely as you got stronger. That is a bunch of crock. Really. He just didn't even want to ask them."

"I know, Erica. But I can't talk about this right now. I don't want to think about it anymore today."

"Okay," I said, smiling, "but just one more thing. I need you to do me a favor. When you meet with Mr. Josh Colleague tomorrow, before we go to HR, I want you to say something like, "I need to be associated with this company. I have two small children who depend on me and if you terminate me, you will literally be putting a nail in my coffin. I can't get on Erica's insurance policy because of pre-existing conditions."

Jim stared at me. I waited for him to say something, but he didn't. I repeated again, "Seriously, Jim, I need you to say that. I wonder if Mr. Colleague has thought about it that way. I'm sure he didn't. Obviously. I just can't believe that a person could act so coldly to another given the present circumstances. And, considering you two are friends."

Jim responded dryly, "Supposedly friends."

When they met the next morning, Jim honored my request and tried to emphasize his need to be associated with the company. Josh gave Jim a long stare in response. He was irritated, but finally stumbled around and said, "Well, short-term disability will give you that. You are still associated with the company if you are on disability." He paused, gauging Jim's response. It was obvious to Jim that Mr. Colleague did not consider the totality of his actions and what "the plan" meant to Jim's future and to the future of our family. Indeed, it became clear that Josh cared only about his own future.

When Jim said nothing, Mr. Colleague continued, "Jim, don't come back until you are 100 percent healthy." Jim remained silent, stunned at the condescending tone he was hearing.

That afternoon, I picked up Jim at his office and we went to HR together. A plan for how to proceed was carved out, and we all knew that Jim needed to leave as soon as possible. When Jim met with Mr. Colleague again, he told him that he would be gone in a few days. Josh was surprised, "I didn't think you were going to leave that quickly. I was hoping you would finish up some loose ends on the project."

"That is why I am staying a few days," Jim said. "If you had asked me about the project before you went to HR and worked on my plan, you would have realized how close I was to finishing. Even though that guy has been gone on paternity leave, I figured out another way around things, and he was kind enough to do some things for me while he was out. All you had to do was ask. Just talk to me."

✳ ✳ ✳

## CHAPTER 34

OCTOBER 2011 — JANUARY 2012

# Perspective

*"The interrelation in which a subject or its
parts are mentally viewed"*

W E EMBRACED JIM'S NEW FREEDOM with optimism. He
was afforded the time to heal, to be relieved of stress,
and to focus on the important things in life. Jim and I were
trying to make sense of things and trying to stay positive. We
decided to try to stick to a schedule, where exercise was built in
and therefore done more often throughout the day. This proved
to be more difficult than imaginable. Jim was exhausted again
much of the time and struggling more and more to breathe.

The breathing problems led to more time on the ventilator
and a new wave of fear rushed over both Jim and me. Things
were not moving in the right direction. I called Dr. House, the
pulmonologist, and told him of the problem. "Well, Erica," Dr.
House replied, "it probably wouldn't be a bad idea to have Jim
stay at the hospital for a few days, so we can thoroughly check
things out. We talked about manipulating the ventilator settings
and seeing how Jim responded. The hospital is the best place
for that."

I told Jim of Dr. House's suggestion, and although he was not happy to return to the hospital, he couldn't deny his breathing problems. "I guess that would be a good idea," Jim struggled to say one time he was off the ventilator, "I can't believe how much time I am spending on the ventilator. I don't get what is happening to my body, but I feel like I can't breathe well. Any time—even when I'm on the ventilator."

The reason Jim was struggling became clear when we arrived at the hospital. The first thing performed on Jim was a chest x-ray that revealed a hole in his lung. His lung was punctured, deflated, and not working at all.

"How long has Jim been functioning like this?" I asked Dr. House.

"It's hard to know," he replied. "I must say I was shocked to see the x-ray. Usually when people have punctured lungs, they can't function at all and are at the emergency room quickly. This is another testament to how strong your husband is."

"How did he get the hole?" I asked.

"Well, it's not uncommon for long-term ventilator patients to get one," Dr. House commented. "The ventilator can push hard at times to get oxygen into the lungs, depending on what the patient is doing himself, so the ventilator itself can cause the problem."

"Does this mean that he is now more susceptible to get another puncture in his lung?"

"Unfortunately, yes," Dr. House said, "but at least you will now know what to look for and it's on your radar."

Within a few days, the fluid had been drained from Jim's lungs and the hole was self-healing, so that his lung reinflated. Jim was discharged and once home, we both knew it was time to reconsider our strategy.

"Okay," I said, "let's figure this out already. We can't actively visit with Dr. Lyme. He's too far away and it's too difficult to travel. Why don't we try the local Lyme-literate doctor? You need to see someone who can physically touch you and physically see you."

"I know what you mean," Jim replied. "I didn't see the need to visit someone local because I was already seeing one of the best Lyme-literate physicians in the world. I was worried they would have me down different paths and that things would get complicated."

"Do you still feel that way?"

"I'm not sure, but it's worth a visit."

I was so happy to hear this. For months, friends and family suggested this, hoping that a physician who could examine Jim more closely might be able to offer some insights. I had bothered Jim, too, but the task of visiting a new physician was too daunting for him. Jim didn't want to retell the story again, didn't want a new regime to follow that might interfere with Dr. Lyme's protocols, and was scared to find out any new, bad news. The punctured lung was God's way of saying, "Wake up, Jim! Get some help locally."

So when Jim made the comment, I moved as quickly as I could. After setting up the appointment and filling out all the paperwork, we arrived at Dr. Holistic's office. His approach is to concentrate at the cellular level, treating stress, toxins, and nutritional gaps. Initially, Jim was given a Meridian Stress Assessment test (MSA). A technician used a probe to see how much energy was going in and out of the body at specific points that are related to a frequency keyed into the instrument. Based on Eastern medicine in a large part, the idea is that a balance of energy should be seen. If there is an imbalance, it is telling of a potential problem.

As a result of this test, we learned Jim was full of fungi (among other things) and allergic to eggs and cheese.

Next, we answered many questions from a nurse as she filled in gaps to Jim's medical history. Finally, we were shown to Dr. Holistic's office. He welcomed us with a bright smile. A slender balding man full of energy, he explained his philosophies and shared insight on what he was learning as he collaborated with other Lyme-literate physicians around the country. We appreciated his directness, his thoroughness, and his obvious constant interest in learning more from the literature and his peers.

"What I would like to concentrate on now is cleaning up the battlefield." Dr. Holistic explained. "You've had a major fight going on internally and Dr. Lyme has hit the bacteria hard. Now we have a lot of debris in there that may be causing your problems. I've seen this often with my other patients. They are doing well fighting off the Lyme bacteria and then they reach a plateau and can't quite get well. What I have found is that if we clean up your system—get rid of toxins, give your cells what they need to function well with, your body can start to heal."

Jim and I smiled. We liked what we heard and thought everything Dr. Holistic was saying made a lot of sense.

"So the plan at this point," he continued, "is to get rid of that fungus we found and tackle the toxicity and nutritional issues. I want to run a bunch of tests to see what's going on with that endocrine system of yours. I also want you to have a newer test called My Lyme Immune ID test. We in the Lyme world are really excited about this test because it looks at various factors in the body, not just antibodies, that are indicative of Lyme. There is an immune tolerance test and a Lyme stimulated cytokines test. The Lyme Immune Tolerance Test measures the body's cell mediated immune response to the bacteria's antigens. I don't expect this will help me understand much due to the high levels of cortisol you are taking. This will interfere with the test and not give reliable results. The part of the test though that should help with your case is the Cytokines Test, which measures the inflammatory processes within the body. The cytokines, or chemical messengers of the immune system, will be released if there is a parasite infection. Once we have these results and you've been on the new protocol for a few weeks, we'll get back together and see where to go from there."

We left his office hours later, feeling a renewed sense of hope and possibility.

At the next visit, we learned that Jim's results from the Cytokines Test were off the charts. In many of the categories' tests, he showed highly elevated results, indicative of probable Lyme. For example, one category had a normal range of 1,9664 to 33,631 pg/mL of cytokines. In Jim's case, his value was 59,695 pg/mL. We finally got our "positive blood test" that all the conventional doctors wanted. Based on Jim's results, Dr. Holistic decided that the intravenous antibiotics worked well in the past and that he wanted to return to them after several weeks of "prepping" Jim's system with good nutrition and flushing the body of toxins..Additionally, from the medical history that his nurse acquired, Dr. Holistic learned that there were some antibiotics that are commonly used to treat Lyme that Jim was never given. At the time when we first saw Dr. Lyme, Jim was so far advanced with his neurological symptoms that Dr. Lyme wanted to use certain antibiotics over others. Dr. Holistic wanted to include these antibiotics into the protocol, acknowledging that some new insights had been reached with how to treat Lyme since Jim had his initial IV antibiotic therapy years prior.

But then, true to form—one step forward and two steps back—Jim struggled again. He was struggling to walk and seemed to be getting weaker again. He wasn't moving much or doing exercises, and this was the rationale we envisioned for his troubles. Then one afternoon, he moved one way in his chair, and his blood pressure shot up. Fortunately, the nurse acted quickly and after a rush to the hospital, we learned he had a blood clot in his leg that, after being dislodged, resulted in several pulmonary embolisms.

The assault never seems to end. Seeing the images of Jim's lungs on the computer screen with the physician pointing out the embolisms was alarming. I didn't think about multiple ones, but there they were. I didn't think about large ones, but there they were, too. Poor Jim. He was so depressed as a result of these setbacks. And to add insult to injury, while in the hospital recovering, Jim could never get off the ventilator (they are worried about infections), and he couldn't eat with the tube feedings the way we had been doing at home (grinding up regular food and injecting it directly into his stomach). Instead, he was fed constantly with a liquid diet, which not only had less calories, but also messed up his digestive tract. Jim returned from the hospital exhausted, more vent-dependent, and skinnier than before.

Still, the "nine-lives" of my cat husband does make me think there is a reason for Jim surviving all this horribleness. His uncle wrote a note to us that could always make us chuckle, but I must say, it also was very insightful. He wrote "Jim, if God wanted you dead, you would be dead already."

*Miracles = Surviving a Collapsed Lung and*
*Pulmonary Embolisms*

✳ ✳ ✳

## CHAPTER 35

FEBRUARY 2012

# Deliverance

*"The state of being delivered; especially...rescued"*

ALTHOUGH HE WASN'T DEAD, JIM was still so weak, couldn't breathe on his own for any extended period of time, and was struggling to walk and move efficiently. Then another assault came. The day after Jim switched officially to long-term disability, I received a phone call from the Human Resources department at Jim's work. "I have to go over a few things with you, Erica," began the call. Mr. HR went through a checklist of what was to be expected now that this switch occurred. "Don't worry," he continued, "I know this is a lot to take in right now, but I'm outlining all of this in a letter and will mail it out tomorrow."

"Okay," I replied, "that would be helpful."

"Sure. No problem. Do you have any questions right now?"

"Yes," I said, "how will daycare work for my daughter with this switch?" I was excited for Annalise to start pre-school at Jim's workplace. I had just visited the new building where she would transition to, had a tour, talked with the teachers, and they were preparing for her arrival.

"Oh, yeah," Mr. HR casually said, "I knew there was one more thing we needed to cover." He paused, cleared his throat, and asked, "Do you have other arrangements for Annalise?"

"What do you mean?" I questioned.

"Well," Mr. HR coldly said, "there is no longer a spot for Annalise at daycare. She can't go to daycare anymore."

This was my worst nightmare. This was the one thing that Jim was terrified of happening. I couldn't believe such an insult was happening to my sweet just-turned three-year-old daughter. I was so confused. "I don't understand," I started. "I just had a tour of the new building where she is moving to and there is a spot for her."

"Well . . . since Jim is on long-term now, this is no longer a benefit." Again, there was such coldness in his voice.

I protested, "But Jim is still considered a full-time employee. We asked several months ago what would happen when Jim switched to long-term disability and someone else in HR assured us that Annalise would be fine."

"That person gave you incorrect information. I know Jim is technically still a full-time employee, but because he is not actively working, there is no spot for your daughter."

"But I am working full-time obviously or our daughter wouldn't be in daycare. And, since Jim is on long-term disability, he obviously can't take care of our daughter while I work."

There was a long pause. I could feel my heart racing. Then Mr. HR said, "The problem is that this is the policy, Erica. If we make an exception for your husband, we would have to make an exception for everyone in this situation."

I was outraged, "And how many people are really in this situation? I can't imagine you have that many people who are on long-term disability and who also have a child in daycare at the same time."

"Exactly," said Mr. HR, "usually people on long-term disability are much older and they don't need the daycare."

"Exactly," I replied. "So it makes sense to make an exception."

"I'm afraid I can't do that, Erica."

"Well, then who can? There must be someone I can talk with and argue our case. We're not asking for free daycare. Of course, we would pay for it as we are right now, but I just want my daughter to stay there, where she is loved, taken good care of, and has stability."

"Well," Mr. HR said, "I could talk to the woman who runs pre-school on your behalf. I'm not sure she'll be able to help, though. I don't want you to get your hopes up too much."

I pleaded with him to have some leeway on a child. "Well, I guess she can continue going to daycare for the next week until you make arrangements otherwise" was his response.

After we hung up the phone, I sat motionless and stunned. Did this really happen? After a short cry, I pulled myself together and thought, *there is no way this company would do this.* I knew Jim would know whom I could call or perhaps Jim could call in a favor. Hating to have to tell Jim this news, I did so, hoping for that valuable information. Jim was as stunned as I was.

The next morning, without any information from Jim, I called Annalise's current teachers and told them the story. The lead teacher jumped into action. "Honey," she reassured me, "we're going to the top. You don't have any time to waste. Time in this case is of the essence. I am going to tell you exactly what to do. Mrs. Kind Soul, as you know, is a wonderful person, and has a place in her heart for children and education. She will help you, I am confident. But she's very busy, so what you'll need to do is call her assistant. Email her as well. You want to make sure you make contact as quickly as possible before anything is done with our sweet Annalise." The teacher then followed this with the email address, the phone number, and some tips and encouragement.

I knew the teacher was correct. There was a golden heart out there who would see that this was just not right. I compiled an email and sent it off. I remember looking at my watch and thinking to myself, *oh, no, I'm late for my meeting.* It was a Friday afternoon. I didn't even know if the assistant would get my email before the weekend was upon us all. But I couldn't do anything more with this 3:00 p.m. meeting out there. The meeting proved to be a good distraction, but when I returned to my office at 5:00 p.m., I was eager to check my email inbox. There was a flashing light on my phone as well, indicating that there was a voicemail waiting for me. In both cases, it was the assistant to Mrs. Kind Soul.

The email message read, "Erica, thank you for your note. First, let me say that Mrs. Kind Soul is so sorry that this happened to you. She was very sad to hear about this and wants you to know that there is a spot for Annalise for however long you need it. This is such a small thing we can do for your family, but we are happy to help. I hope your husband is able to recover now that he is at home. Best to you and your whole family."

I ran out of my office, screaming with joy. When my colleague and friend popped out of her office to figure out what was happening, I rush over to her and gave her a huge hug. Another angel rescued us. I was so grateful. I was so happy. "Thank you, God!" I sang out.

I told my friend what happened and then she asked, "Do you know Mrs. Kind Soul?"

"No," I answered. "I've never met her, but I know about her. She's very active with the company and does a ton of good things for the community. I really owe this woman so much. I wonder if she knows she has just saved my family."

My friend smiled, "I bet she has some idea."

"I hope so. How amazing to be able to help people like that. I really know there are good people in the world. We've been so lucky in so many ways, but it doesn't seem like we have much going for us these days. This has given me new hope. I feel like my faith has been restored."

My friend smiled and gave me another hug. "Have a good weekend, Erica."

"Absolutely! You, too!"

I learned on Monday that after receiving calls from Mrs. Kind Soul, things were shaken up at the company. The teacher was called in an effort to learn more details. The director of the pre-school was contacted as well as Mrs. Kind Soul wanted to know who gave me that information. After sorting through things, it was decided that the policy needed to be changed. Upon learning this news, Jim began to cry. We were, not only so happy and very much appreciative that Mrs. Kind Soul came to our rescue, but we were also relieved to know this would never happen to another family.

*Miracle = Another Angel Helping Us*

✳ ✳ ✳

## CHAPTER 36

MARCH 2012

# Paradox

*"A statement that is seemingly contradictory or opposed to
common sense and yet is perhaps true"*

"ERICA, THIS IS THE CASE manager at the nursing company.
How are you today?"

I was a bit confused by the call. It seemed random and out of
the blue. "I'm all right, Sue," I replied. "How are you today?"

"I'm fine. Sorry to have to tell you this, though. I know you
guys have a lot on your plate right now, but I'm very concerned
about Jim's eligibility to stay with our nursing company. Every
three months, the overseeing physician, a general practitioner,
has to sign off on various forms to continue nursing care. Your
GP doesn't feel comfortable anymore because he hasn't seen Jim
in so long."

"Okay, I never knew that," I replied. "Why can't the physician that Jim sees the most, right now his pulmonologist, Dr.
House, do that? "

"It's the way the insurance company works. We asked Dr.
House to do it last time and he did as a one-time deal, but the
GP really needs to be overseeing your case. I've actually spoken

with Dr. GP at length about this, and he says he won't sign off until you visit him again."

"That's fine, now that I understand this. I just didn't know and obviously Jim didn't understand this, either. It is amazing to me how much people assume you know about how the health-care industry works. I think people who are in that field forget what it would be like if you weren't in that field."

Sue chuckled nervously. "I'm afraid we are partially to blame on that. I thought someone would have explained that to you."

"That's part of the problem with the nursing company—whomever I speak with assumes that someone else who has spoken to me must have told me about whatever it is that we are talking about. Very frustrating. But anyway, I'll call and make an appointment with Dr. GP."

I could feel the hesitation with Sue because she didn't say anything immediately. So I asked, "What is the problem now?"

"Well," Sue said, "Dr. GP wants to see Jim by the end of the week."

"Did you explain to him what a difficult time Jim is having at the moment and that he has just seen several doctors?"

"I did, but he was most insistent. If you don't somehow get Jim there this week, I am really worried about what that will mean for his care."

I took a deep breath, "Fine, I'll figure it out. Jim is not going to be happy, but he'll understand the urgency, too."

"Thanks, Erica, I really do appreciate it," Sue said as she hung up the phone.

A few days later, the nurse, Jim, and I were at the GP's office. Getting Jim to the physician's office in his current weak state was quite tricky. Many lifts and wheelchairs and maneuvering ventilators from place to car, and then back to the wheelchair, was interesting.

The visit itself was routine enough. Dr. GP came into the examination room with hand extended, "Jim, it is good to see you. Tell me how you have been over the past several months."

The nurse and I took him off the ventilator, but Jim was struggling to breathe and talk. Still, he did his best to convey all the crazy things that had happened over the past many weeks. As I saw him really struggling to speak, I filled in the gaps.

Dr. GP then checked on Jim's lungs and heart, and asked him to do some simple tasks, like squeezing his hands to assess Jim's strength. When he was finished, he looked at Jim directly in the eyes and said, "Jim, we've known each other a long time. I feel we have a connection since we are both older fathers." Dr. GP laughed and Jim smiled. I remembered that Jim and his physician had both become fathers later in life and that Dr. GP's children were about the same age as ours. "Here's the thing, Jim. I'm glad you are doing better. Obviously right now you are having a bad spell, and I need to see you more often. I want you to continue getting better, but I want to see you regularly, so I feel comfortable signing these forms."

Jim shook his head and I explained that we just learned how it important it was to see a GP, but up until earlier this week, we thought that if Jim was seeing any doctor, that was fine.

"I understand," said Dr. GP. "How about you come back in three months and we keep to that schedule? Also, what time of the day works best for you? I think you mentioned mornings are not good. If this is the case, I can put a note in your file to give you preference. From my point of view, I'd like you to come just after lunch. That way I won't be delayed and you won't have to wait. In general, it is a slower time, too, so you can avoid all the potential germs that might be floating around the office."

Jim and I both smiled, thanked Dr. GP, and left feeling pretty good about the appointment.

The next day, the phone rang and it was Sue. She started with, "I have bad news for you."

I was confused, trying to figure out what we needed to do now. "I don't understand Sue. We left Dr. GP's office yesterday with a three-month follow-up scheduled and all was well."

"I thought so, too," Sue explained. "And then Dr. GP phoned. He apparently didn't understand how ill Jim was until he saw him and now he doesn't feel comfortable being the overseeing physician."

I could feel my face get hot as anger started to boil up inside me, "What do you mean? Dr. GP doesn't want to take care of Jim? Why did he shake our hands and tell us to come back? Why didn't he have the guts to tell us this directly?"

"He says Jim's case is very complicated."

"And what, he can't or really, he chooses not to help Jim? Isn't that unethical? Don't physicians all take an oath to help their patients?"

"Erica, I understand your anger," Sue said, trying to calm me, "I talked with him for quite some time about it, explaining that you see so many specialists who are taking care of the complicated parts of your case. He still felt uncomfortable and frankly, you don't want a physician who isn't comfortable."

"Do you know Jim has been seeing Dr. GP for over twenty years?" I paused and continued, "I just can't believe this is how a physician would treat a man he has seen for twenty years. I am floored."

There was a nervous giggle on the other end of the phone. Sue said, "Well, the good news is that given this, Dr. House has agreed again to sign the paperwork. But in three more months, you guys will need to find a new physician. Do you remember that service we spoke about weeks ago—the one that sends doctors directly to your house?"

"Yes," I replied, "I'll give them a call. It would make it a lot easier on Jim to not have to leave the house at this point."

"Maybe this really will be a better solution, Erica," Sue sounded genuine. "What are the doctors saying about Jim's prognosis?"

"Ah," I said, "that is the question. No one really knows. No one has ever really known. Jim doesn't fit any criteria nicely. There are so many considerations and most of the time, it seems a guessing game. I just can't believe that in a relatively short amount of time Jim has started to struggle so much. We went from the flu to this bug to taking time off of work to now really having trouble walking and staying off the ventilator for any period of time."

"I'm so sorry, Erica," Sue responded. "But Jim showed amazing recovery the first time. Let's hope he can do it again. What's going on with the new physician?"

"Dr. Holistic is great. He has some new ideas from all his collaboration with other Lyme-literate doctors across the States. Now that he has definite confirmation that Jim has Lyme, he is going to aggressively treat the Lyme symptoms again with the IV antibiotics. There's one other fantastic bit of news, too."

"What?" asked Sue. "I don't have any new documentation on Jim's charts."

"We just learned about this," I explained. "Jim and I have been trying to get human growth hormone for years. It is incredibly difficult to get and the test that you have to go through can be very stressful on your body. And there must be a reason to have the test conducted in the first place, so it throws in another complication."

"So did Dr. Holistic help with this?" Sue asked.

"Yes, as things started to become more clear with the Lyme test results, blood work, and other contributing factors, Dr. Holistic thought it would be fine to test Jim. And, for the first time, we are so excited that Jim failed this test that stressed his body to see how much human growth hormone the body was releasing."

"And obviously," Sue continued, "Jim is not making any or very little which can justify the injections of human growth hormone."

"Exactly," I confirmed. "The goal is to stimulate Jim's body into making muscle."

"Oh, yeah," Sue said. "The reason human growth hormone is so highly regulated and controlled is because of all the athletic scandals."

"Yep," I said, "those baseball players really changed the playing field on this one."

"Wow, Erica," Sue said, "that really is great news."

"I know," I said. "I keep thinking all of this is going to come together and Jim's body can take over to heal itself. I really think the body is capable of some amazing things if the field is set up fairly."

"Here's hoping you guys can get that fair shake."

"Thanks, Sue," I said as we hung up the phone.

I paused before going to tell Jim the news of Dr. GP and the "drop." It seems I live in a world of dichotomies. I am grateful for the health care system, but the health care system has major problems. I am in awe of a few doctors (and owe them so much!), but most physicians do not impress me as they should. I have seen the best of people, but I have also seen such ugliness in people. I own a house, but have no place of my own in it. I am married, but also a single mother. I have a solid marriage, but my husband and I do not sleep in the same bed, go out as a couple, or engage in conversations, as you would expect. I am very grateful for many things, yet I remain confused as to why this is all happening. I have faith and knowledge that Jim will be all right, but the pace of his recovery is so stressful at times. I believe, but I have doubts as well.

Whenever the stress comes at us, something tends to happen to remind me that it will be all right. For example, both Jim and I had "signs" come our way at the same particularly stressful time during a period when Jim's body wasn't cooperating and his mental state was low. One evening, Jim cried out to God, "Please give me a sign—something so that I know all will be well." That night, he had a vivid dream. He was on the beach and he started walking slowly along the water's edge. Then Jim increased his pace and started "power walking." After another few seconds, Jim broke out in a jog. The thought of Jim moving so easily and so freely brought tears to my eyes. He, too, felt such an impact from this dream.

On my end, during this same time period, I was driving to work one morning and contemplating things. This was a regular occurrence for me, and I often found myself talking and praying out loud. As I rounded the corner on the highway, much fog impaired my vision. It was difficult to see clearly, so I slowed my speed. Then suddenly, there was a clearing on the side of the road where there was a very tiny farm. I saw a donkey, just strolling along alone and with purpose. On previous commutes,

I would catch a glimpse of a donkey among the cows every once in a while. On this particular morning, I saw only the donkey—no cows.

Donkeys have a significant meaning for me. When I was younger, my mom and my oldest sister Lisa both had horses. We would often go to the boarding stables and take care of the horses and, of course, my mom and sister would ride their horses. There was a donkey there that caught my attention. For some reason, I was attracted to its quietness, its smartness, and its overall sweet nature. Eventually, the owners of the stable let me ride the donkey. I was thrilled—riding the donkey was so much better than riding a horse. The donkey was very gentle and seemed to know what to do before I knew what was happening.

Many years later, when I was in graduate school, completely out of the blue, I took out a piece of paper and wrote a poem. It was the only poem I have ever written in my adult life and it focused on a burro. A few years after this, I decided to get a tattoo. I chose a donkey. The donkey is the Native American totem for "seeking knowledge," something that I strive for on a daily basis. The donkey symbolizes strength, intelligence, dedication, and determination. Since I consider these all to be highly desirable traits, I thought the donkey tattoo was ideal. If you search the Internet for donkey totems, you will find that the, "Donkey can teach much about patience and humility. [It] has wisdom and teaches when to use it with timing. [It] aids in realizing outer recognition of inner potentials and the strength that comes from internal fortitude. He can aid in showing one how to move with the flow and allow Spirit to work and/or trusting your strengths . . . [He] will teach you how to listen to your head and heart."[1] When a donkey "shows up as a totem, you have a trusty companion to help lift your burdened spirit. Donkey reminds us that we do not have to shoulder our responsibilities alone. Help is available."[2]

I knew years prior that there was a "reason" that I was drawn to donkeys. I never could truly explain it, but just like choosing the name Annalise for our daughter and later learning it means "Gift from God." Now that I know more about the donkey, it is reassuring to claim it as my own.

The clearing in the road during my commute to work that morning of despair was no coincidence. The donkey that came out of that fog reminded me that things were going to be okay. We still had a long road ahead of us. We knew the road was as you would expect any road to be—turning around blind corners at times, hills that slow you down, times of fast movement and times of slow movement, and the unexpected bump or obstacle in the road that seems to have come from nowhere.

1.   from http://www.starstuffs.com/animal_totems/dictionary_of_animals.html

2.   from http://healing.about.com/od/animaltotems/ig/Animal-Totems-Photo-Gallery/Donkey.htm

## CHAPTER 37

SEPTEMBER — DECEMBER 2012

# Future

*"An expectation of advancement or progressive development"*

PEOPLE ARE PLACED IN YOUR life often times for a specific reason. Things sometimes happen at the time they happen to help you along your path in some way. Sometimes these ways are not understandable, and other times, things seem so clear.

One afternoon, I signed up for a computer deal that landed me in a hypnosis therapist's office. "What can I help you with today, Erica?" the kind therapist asked.

"I'm not sure," I responded sincerely.

She looked at me strangely. Her eyes narrowed a bit and then she said, "There must be a reason you signed up for this deal. What are you hoping to get out of the sessions?"

I smiled and responded as honestly as I could, "I don't know. I have always been intrigued with hypnosis. I saw the deal and thought 'why not'?"

"Okay," the therapist replied, "let's try this a different way. Tell me a little bit about your life."

Well, the floodgate was opened and I rattled off my elevator speech about Jim, my kids, my job, and the craziness of it all. The longer I spoke, the wider her eyes grew. When I finally paused for a breath, the therapist gently touched my knee and said, "Well, I'm thinking managing stress would be a good thing for you. How about we start there?"

"Yes," I said, "that seems reasonable." I paused, reflecting on what I had heard about hypnosis and helping with addictions. "And, how about you throw in a little bit about me avoiding chocolate?"

The therapist smiled and waited for me to clarify. I continued, "I do seem to eat more chocolate than I should. I think it is the stress. I never really understood the whole 'eating for comfort' thing I have heard about for years. But now I get it."

"Okay, no problem," the therapist replied. We went into another room, a small room with white walls, a large black leather Lazy-Boy chair, and a strobe dance light sitting on a table. She asked me to lay back and watch the neon colors swirl around and around as I listened to her speak about relaxing. As she promised, I heard everything, remembered everything, and was in complete control. I tried to resist closing my eyes or drifting off, so I could stay focused. Finally, the therapist said, "Erica, when I say your eyes are getting heavy, I do want you to close them. Close your eyes. It's all right."

So I did and found myself liking this form of therapy. I only had to talk about ten minutes on the front end of it and then I relaxed. And I was surprisingly very relaxed, indeed. The idea is that in this state, something scientists are still trying to understand, your subconscious is more open to the messages it hears and upon "waking up," your conscious brain is more likely to act on them.

Weeks later, I still wasn't craving chocolate and I was excited about this technique in general. Just as I was considering this,

I received an email (from a non-related source) with a link to an interview with a man who also does hypnosis therapy. In the interview, he spoke about using hypnosis to help a client regrow muscles, when he was not able to see results from any of the conventional Western medicine techniques. I was stunned at this message and the commonality to Jim.

I phoned the therapist and asked her about this interview I saw. "Oh yes, Erica. There is a lot of anecdotal evidence that hypnosis can work with medical problems."

"Would you be willing to come to our house to do hypnosis on Jim here?"

Without any hesitation, she replied, "Of course. That's not a problem at all. But I need for you to understand, there are no guarantees with Jim."

"Oh, of course," I replied, "but I am excited for this possibility. And, if nothing else, from my own experience, hypnosis is like a meditation session and that cannot do anything but help Jim."

Weeks after the sessions started with Jim, the therapist asked him what he thought of the sessions. Jim smiled and spelled out "legs stronger." I ran over to the therapist and gave her a high-five. I was thrilled and a little surprised that I didn't know this. It was not something Jim and I had talked about since the sessions started.

Another series of incidents occurred all around the same time that pointed Jim and me in one direction. After doing a radio blog interview, the interviewer asked if I had ever considered allergies for Jim. I explained that he was allergic to eggs, milk, and dairy. "No," she continued, "I mean severe allergies. There are known cases of people with Lyme who actually have allergies. Once the allergy is fixed, the Lyme goes away."

I considered this, "You mean, the allergy is controlled and the body can take over and fight the Lyme effectively in its absence?"

"Exactly, Erica," she continued. "I really think you and Jim need to check on this much more than you have."

Another two weeks passed, and I was still working on this allergy idea when I found myself eating lunch at a large round table with strangers at a conference for work. When first sitting down, I chose an empty seat next to a plate. Someone had obviously saved a seat, but I didn't know who. I simply chose the seat and didn't think much about it. Several minutes later, an attractive blonde woman in her fifties came to the table, "Is this my food?" she asked.

"I'm not sure," I replied.

"I guess it must be," she said and took the seat. We then started talking business and exchanged pleasantries. "Now, tell me again," she said, "what do you speak on—I think I missed that."

"I speak to audiences about resilience. The need to steer things in the direction of your own choosing, even when adversity strikes you hard."

"This focuses primarily around your husband?" she asked. "Tell me about him."

So I did, trying to summarize in a few minutes all the craziness that had transpired over the past years.

When I was finished, she looked up at the ceiling. She looked around her to see if anyone else was listening to our conversation. Then she looked up again. Finally, she stared directly in my eyes and asked, "Are you a religious person?"

"Yes."

"Okay. So I just need to tell you something." She paused and then continued, staring directly in the eyes, to the point that I was slightly uncomfortable. "It is all about allergies with your husband."

"What did you just say?" I could feel my eyes starting to water.

"I'm not sure if you have even considered allergies, but I'm just telling you, it is all about allergies for your husband. Fix the allergies, everything else will come into equilibrium."

"You don't understand how weird it is that you are telling me this . . ." I was cut off by her reply.

"It doesn't matter. What I'm telling you is it is allergies. You and your husband have been seeing some good physicians, but you are not targeting the real problem. You are seeing experts, but the wrong experts."

I sat staring at this woman, shocked at what was coming out of her mouth. She then looked up at the ceiling again and back to me and then the ceiling once more. "Okay, I told her already. Will you leave me alone now?" she said.

Then she looked at me again and smiled. I smiled back, trying to process all that was being said. "Are you going to be around for the afternoon sessions?" she asked.

I nodded "Yes."

"Okay, I'm going to write down some physicians' names that you need to look up. If you can get Jim to see them, do it. But if traveling is too difficult, consider what they have to say." She smiled at me gently and then continued, "One more thing. I feel like you and Jim have been talking to the zoologists when you should have been talking to Dr. Jane Goodall."

Because I looked very confused by her statement, the woman continued, "Let me explain. If you want to know something about chimpanzees, you could go to the zoo and talk with the zookeepers there and they would give you some great information. But if you really want to understand chimpanzees, you need to go to the expert of chimpanzees. You and your husband have been talking to zookeepers when you need to be talking to Jane Goodall."

"I see," I replied with a smile, wondering if this woman somehow picked up on my biology roots.

"Good. Now act on it already," and with that, she stood up and excused herself to the restroom.

I left my work conference feeling uplifted, as if a message from God had been given to me through this woman. Several weeks after this incident, when Jim and I returned to Dr. Holistic, I asked about testing Jim for more allergies.

"Strange that you should bring this up right now, Erica," he said. "I was just at a Lyme conference last weekend where there was some really interesting research on mold. There is a lot of talk in the Lyme world about allergies to mold. If you can clear this up, in many cases, you really give the body a fighting chance."

The timing of these events all together was not a coincidence. I was getting excited, thinking about how things, finally, might be coming together. I panicked thinking we were too late. "So are you thinking, Dr. Holistic," I asked, "if Jim is allergic to mold, and we take care of that, the walking and breathing will come back?"

I braced myself for his answer. It was the first time I asked Dr. Holistic this direct question and I wasn't sure what would come out of his mouth. Because Jim had been struggling so much, saying the IV antibiotics were killing him, and talking about dying again, it was risky asking this sensitive question. "Well," Dr. Holistic said, "I am very optimistic about the latest routine of IV antibiotics Jim has had over the past two months. You say his cramps are gone again and the fasiculations are very minimized. This is real progress." He smiled wide and I clapped, realizing we hadn't celebrated this positive milestone. Instead, we had been focusing on the negatives. I was happy for the reminder to focus on the good.

"What is still not clear at this point," Dr. Holistic continued, "is how all the changes we are making are interacting with one another. We changed three things—the IV antibiotics, the testosterone pellet injection, and the human growth hormone. I feel good that the human growth hormone will be able to help."

He paused, looked at Jim and me and then back at his assistant and the computer screen. Dr. Holistic is always running from room to room, helping his patients and you can tell he is constantly in thought mode. After a slight pause to catch his bearings, Dr. Holistic continued, "The thing about late-stage chronic Lyme is that the treatment is long and the progress is slow. If there was a way I could take shortcuts and help people get well sooner, I would do it." He chuckled a bit and said, "Actually, I have tried that because I want people to get well as soon as they can. But I have learned that this doesn't work. You have to move slowly because the progress is slow. When I was studying with Dr. Lyme a few months back, he explained his protocols to me and his logic about treating Lyme. I'll share with you his analogy because I think it's really good. What's going on in Jim's body is a pendulum and it is swinging like crazy. The bacteria are pulling it in one direction and Jim's immune system—that is the oversensitivity to that Lyme bacteria—is pulling it back in the other direction. What we need to do is control the pendulum swing and get it moving so slowly that Jim's body can work as it should. So if you get the pendulum to stop swinging so widely, you can start fighting effectively and rebuilding efficiently."

He paused for another moment and readjusted himself in the chair. He smiled again, giving me the opportunity to ask a clarifying question. "So if the pendulum is in control, you think Jim's body can be rebuilt?"

"I think the human growth hormone is going to make a difference here. I'm very optimistic about it. Did I tell you about Dr. New York Lyme and sending some neurological patients to India for stem-cell transplant treatment?"

We shook our heads "Yes," as I remembered this conversation months back and my asking when Jim could go for the treatment.

"So," Dr. Holistic said, "that's what we need to work toward. Let's first think about mold. Have your house tested and we'll test Jim here. We'll then look at metals in the body and if Jim has them, we'll work to remove those as well. Then we'll see what happens and take it from there. Again, the progress will be slow."

After wrapping up the conversation, we moved to another room where a technician tested Jim for allergies. He did have mold in him and sensitivities to mold, so Dr. Holistic prescribed medications to help with these. As the technician was working on Jim, I asked her, "Can you think of any strange allergies that Jim might have?"

"Dr. Holistic has asked me to look for mold. That stuff will kill you if you have it in your system unchecked."

"I know that you're checking on that, but I feel like we need to be thinking about strange allergies, something we've missed that no one would think to check out."

She paused and continued working on Jim. After a couple of minutes, she said, "You know what? I was just in Canada studying with a physician and he was telling me about one of his patients who was paralyzed by some allergen that was found on the grains he was harvesting."

I jumped out of my chair, so excited and screamed, "That's

what I'm talking about. I could hug you!" I glanced at Jim who was fighting back a tear.

"Don't get too excited about that," she replied. "We don't know if Jim has that and I can't remember exactly what the story was. You know what I'll do? I'll get in touch with the physician and find out what that allergen was. In the meantime, I wouldn't give Jim any wheat, just to be safe."

Although we are trying to uncover this potential puzzle piece that once found may hold a major key in Jim's recovery process, we do see glimmers of hope and have the faith that things can turn around for him and for our family. As another Christmas season is upon us, my renewed hope is that this is the time, this is the year for total healing. Jesus was sent to provide hope to all people. He was a living reminder of God's love and taught that impossible things are possible with God's help.

Although my husband is on the ventilator most of the day, cannot walk or stand on his own, and communicates by spelling out words on his hands, our faith tells us that too many signs, help, people, and love have come our way, indicating that although none of this makes sense, Jim can get well.

There are glimmers here and there, reminding Jim to keep fighting and believing. During this hopeful and joyful season, a physical therapist commented, "Wow, Jim. I must say you surprise me. I wouldn't have thought you could do this much exercise given your muscle wasting. You are strong."

Indeed my husband is strong. My kids are strong. They are tough and full of optimism for the future. I am resilient and grateful for all we have. In particular, I have come to realize that many miracles have occurred in our lives—many miracles for which we are indebted.

Some of these miracles were very overt and others subtle. But none of these miracles is less than that. Truly amazing things have happened at just the right time, and many provided just the right insight into what was needed. Prior to this experience in my life, I would have said a miracle was something truly impressive and powerful in the sense that the improbable happens instantly—a "walking on water" type of incident. I have since learned to appreciate that miracles come in all shapes and sizes and that many occur all the time if you just pay attention. Miracles are those things that propel us forward when we doubt or don't think something is possible. Miracles are those things that keep us motivated and remind us that there is good in the world and kindness in all places. Miracles are those advances in technology that allow for life.

Yes, miracles are powerful and they do allow things to happen that you thought improbable. But miracles are made when the belief in them are there. Miracles are made when we ask and expect them.

There is a framed sign in the kids' bathroom, a quote from Teddy Roosevelt that says:

"Believe you can and you're half way there." I read it to the kids on occasion and then tell them the other half is that they have to work hard to get there fully. This is definitely the case with Jim. We believe and know he will be well—he is halfway there. The hard work that is still in progress is the rebuilding of his body.

So for this next Christmas season—celebrating the birth of Jesus, a miracle and an event that changed everything—I am reminded that amazing things are possible. When I consider the season of light, the promise, and the possibility, I know that amazing things have happened, do still happen today, and that with faith, anything is possible. God has gifted me with resiliency and has given my family many gifts of kindness. Jesus, who has taught us resilience by example, compassion, and belief in both the seeing and unseeing world, was the greatest gift to the world.

As the holiday season is here again, it is not a reminder that another year has gone by without Jim being healed. Instead, it is a reminder that gifts come in a variety of packages, and that blessings are to be counted. During this Christmas season, we will celebrate the birth of Jesus, but also the other gifts God has given us all. Remember that one of the most precious gifts He gave was the ability to make things happen with belief that rocks you to the core. Amazing things are possible. Amazing things—miracles—happen if you believe.

*Miracle = "If you have faith as small as a mustard seed, you can say to this mountain, 'Move from here to there,' and it will move. Nothing will be impossible for you."*

*(Matthew 17:20)*

✳ ✳ ✳

# Appendix

W HAT FOLLOWS IS NOT MEANT to be an absolute guide to Lyme testing, but rather an indication of what many have gone through, including our family, on their way down a troubling path full of uncertainty.

When we go to the doctor with an ache, a pain, or an illness, we go with an expectation that the tending physician will be able to perform a careful and thorough diagnosis of the difficulty or issue. We expect that the resulting diagnosis will lead to a solution to the problem and will ultimately lead us down a path to wellness. Perhaps the diagnosis will involve various testing—reliable, trustworthy, and dependable testing—and the doctor will use that information to propose a treatment or a procedure. It doesn't work that way in the Lyme world. There are **no** reliable tests. This makes for a big problem as it relates to our healthcare community. Still, most people want a test and most physicians seem to want a test to "confirm" Lyme.

There are a number of laboratory tests for Lyme and a host of other means to determine if a person is infected with the Lyme bacteria (*Borrelia burgdorferi* ). The accuracy of any of these tests may be determined by a number of items including: when

the testing took place, what type of test is used, what lab performed the test, the interpretation by the laboratory or physician,
and what a person had done prior to the testing. Even the day
of the week could affect testing outcomes. Tests run early in the
week tend to be more accurate. Tests that look for antibodies in
the blood (our immune system's reaction to an infection) may be
affected by any one of the following conditions:

The test may have been performed before the body has had
a chance to make antibodies. (The generally accepted "ideal"
time for an antibody test is six weeks after a tick bite.)

Antibiotics taken in the early stage of the disease may prevent a person from ever making antibodies.

If the test is taken after a course of antibiotics, there may be
a decrease in the level of antibodies present.

In addition, all Lyme testing may be called into question,
depending on the laboratory performing the tests. Many labs,
especially the ones that are non-tick-borne illness familiar, have
quite a reputation for getting Lyme testing wrong. A number of
studies have been performed using the blood of confirmed positive patients with dismal results.

Further, depending on the type of test, the results may be
affected by the interpretation of the lab or by the physician, especially doctors who are not familiar with tick-borne illness. Jim
likes to say, "You can roll all of the Lyme testing together, throw
it out to the general medical community, and you might get a 50
percent accurate result."

There are four commonly accepted (although not necessarily
reliable) tests for Lyme. There are, of course, many other tests
and procedures to determine if a person has Lyme, but the four
indicated below are widely used and recognized by physicians
and the medical community:

**Lyme Titer**—This is a test that looks for Lyme antibodies in the blood. Antibodies are the proteins that our body, the immune system, makes in response to an infection—in this case, an infection of *Borrelia burgdorferi*. A titer is a measure of how much the sample can be diluted before the antibodies to the Lyme disease bacteria can no longer be detected. A titer of one to eight means that antibodies can be detected when one part of the blood sample is diluted by up to eight parts of saline. A larger second number means there are more antibodies in the blood. A Lyme titer also might indicate a past or a current infection, given that once Lyme antibodies are in your system, they never clear. The Lyme titer appears to be the "standard" of the non-Lyme literate doctor community. If a physician suspects Lyme, he will frequently order a Lyme titer—simple to run, but can produce quite unreliable results. This test is well known for giving "false negatives." Several other Lyme disease tests (ELISA, IFA, and Western Blot) may also be reported in titers.

**PCR**—(Polymerase Chain Reaction)—This test identifies DNA found in Lyme bacteria. Some believe that the PCR test is the best; however, most PCR tests are performed by laboratories that appear to have difficulty identifying it in positive people. A PCR might show that Lyme DNA is contained in the sample, but may not be an indicator of an active infection. You can appreciate the difficulty associated with that result. In addition, there are countless reasons Lyme DNA might not show up in the blood or other fluid samples (blood serum, whole blood, and urine) and if the test is not performed by a specialty lab (IGeneX or Medical Diagnostic Labs), the tests are fairly useless. It is a reported and medically known fact that PCR testing can potentially produce a false negative of 30 percent in those positive with the Lyme bacteria.

**ELISA**—(Enzyme-Linked Immunosorbant Serum Assay)
— This is another test that identifies Lyme antibodies that our
bodies make in response to being exposed to *Borrelia bugdorferi*.
It is one of the simplest, least expensive, and easiest to perform,
and one of the more common Lyme test ordered. It is a test preferred by many laboratories, not due to the accuracy, but because
it is automated. Laboratories, health departments, and clinics
indicate that the Lyme ELISA tests are good and useful. But in
two blinded studies that tested the laboratories for accuracy, the
labs failed miserably. In the first study, [1] the tested laboratories
produced correct results 55 percent of the time. In the second
study, the laboratories in question could only show a correct
result 45 percent of the time. There were almost as many false
positives as false negatives. Even identical samples sent to the
same lab often resulted in different outcomes. The International
Lyme and Associated Diseases Society (ILDAS) indicates that
"the ELISA screening test is unreliable. The test **misses 35 percent**
of culture proven Lyme disease (only 65 percent sensitivity) and
is unacceptable as the first step of a two-step screening protocol.
By definition, a screening test should have at least 95 percent sensitivity." One last negative for the ELISA test is that it can only
detect free antibodies, not any antibody that has bonded with an
antigen, something that Lyme antibodies are known to do.

**Western Blot**—This is another antibody test that looks at the
specific parts of the Lyme bacteria to which antibodies attach.
The test is generally not run unless a Lyme titer or ELISA test
is positive—to ensure against a false positive. It is most often
used as a "confirmatory" test, after a Lyme titer or an ELISA
indicates positive. It's unfortunate that this test is used mainly
to confirm, given that it is possibly the most accurate of the four
tests listed here, if executed in the correct way, and performed by
a lab that specializes in Lyme testing. Many believe the Western

Blot to be among the most reliable of all Lyme testing, although it does have its issues as well. Once again, any test that looks for antibodies in the system is subject to the three conditions stated at the beginning of this section on the specific tests. The ILADS (2011) states: "Of patients with acute culture-proven Lyme disease, **20 to 30 percent remain seronegative** on serial Western Blot sampling. Antibody titers also appear to decline over time; thus, while the Western Blot may remain positive for months, it may not always be sensitive enough to detect chronic infection with the Lyme spirochete. For "epidemiological purposes," the CDC eliminated from the Western Blot analysis the reading of bands thirty-one and thirty-four. These bands are so specific to *Borrelia burgdorferi* that they were chosen for vaccine development. Since a vaccine for Lyme disease is currently unavailable, however, a positive thirty-one or thirty-four band is highly indicative of *Borrelia burgdorferi* exposure. Yet these bands are not reported in commercial Lyme tests."

The four tests indicated above may appear simple and straightforward, but each one has major flaws that can produce poor results. To begin with, the Lyme bacteria are one of the most polymorphic bacteria known to exist. It has the ability to change its surface proteins during cell division enough to elude the immune system, and may differ from the laboratory stains of the disease enough to result in negative tests—even though antibodies may be present in the blood. Again, if the Lyme is well hidden in your body and your immune system is in good condition, any one of these tests might come up negative.

A few words about ticks and the problematic co-infection issue. Most people believe that the only insects that carry Lyme disease are deer ticks. But from recent studies and a practical point of view, that seems unlikely. All ticks that attach themselves to mammals for the purpose of extracting blood have the potential to carry a series of infectious agents, including the Lyme bacteria. However, one study[2] does indicate that the lone star tick (*Amblyomma americanum*) may be immune to *Borrelia burgdorferi*, but carries another spirochete (*Borrelia lonestari*) that causes Lyme-like symptoms and a Lyme-like illness. So the argument that we have no deer and thus no deer ticks and thus no Lyme is faulty reasoning at best. No community is immune. Furthermore, ticks not only carry Lyme, but have also become a cesspool of other pathogens that can make you equally as sick. *Babesiosis* and *Erlichiosis*, both parasitic infections, and Bartonellosis, an infection caused from the bacteria *Bartonella*, are perhaps the most common. These co-infections must be independently diagnosed and separately treated with entirely different medications and different protocols than the primary Lyme. When one or more of these co-infections are combined with Lyme, the results can be devastating on the body and in-crease the complexity of treatment. Jim had at least one other infection (*Babesiosis*), in conjunction with the Lyme bacteria that took several treatment cycles to clear. The medication, typically used to treat malaria, was to be taken with a "fatty food"—peanut butter was Jim's choice. To this day, Jim does not want anything to do with food that remotely smells or taste of peanut butter.

During the "Lyme years," our family has learned a lot about what is and isn't true regarding Lyme disease. There are widespread misperceptions about the diagnosing and testing, the manner in which the disease shows itself on and in the body, the various treatment protocols (what works and what doesn't), and the overall attitude of physicians and the medical community. As a result, we decided to include the "Top five myths regarding Lyme disease" to foster a better understanding and perhaps steer people down a decidedly different path than we initially took.

## Top five myths regarding Lyme disease:

**Lyme is easy to diagnose and easy to cure**—Not true. This is factual only if your body reacts with a bulls-eye rash and you seek immediate medical treatment. Your doctor will likely be convinced that you have been potentially infected with Lyme and prescribe the standard two weeks of antibiotics. Most Lyme disease-literate physicians, and a hosts of Lyme groups and associations, will recommend four weeks of antibiotics—if you can convince your doctor to prescribe them. Remember, Lyme tests are not reliable and many with chronic Lyme are never really cured, just treated with heavy-duty antibiotics, or some other manner of treatment, until the Lyme is in remission.

**A bulls-eye rash is required to indicate Lyme**—Not true. If your body reacts with a bulls-eye rash, it is a good indicator that you've been infected, but this is reported to happen less than 50 percent of the time. Jim and I both believed this to be true at one time, and as a result, have paid a very significant price.

**If there is no rash, then there is no Lyme**—Not true. A lot of people with late stage Lyme, close to 60 percent, never had a rash at all. Further, many of those with Lyme, close to 30 percent, don't remember ever being bitten at all. Any tick bite should be taken seriously and whether there is a rash or not, seek treatment.

**How the tick is removed can prevent Lyme**—Not true. Many have heard, or perhaps experienced in their life, the "hot match" approach to tick removal. Strike a match, blow it out, and touch it to the tick. The tick retracts and falls off. Even if this method is successful, it makes no difference to the transfer of Lyme bacteria. Once the tick has latched onto your skin—the potential transfer of Lyme is taking place. However, proper removal of the tick is important. It should be gripped, preferably with a pair of needle-nose tweezers, at the point of contact with the skin and pulled out, ensuring that all mouth parts are removed. Embedded mouth parts can contain the Lyme bacteria and continue to leach or infect if left behind. The area should then be soaked with antiseptic to kill any pathogens on the skin. In addition, care should be taken not to grip the tick's body when removing, as this could potentially squeeze the bacteria into your system. But again, don't be mistaken that how the tick is removed will prevent Lyme infection.

**Chronic or late stage Lyme doesn't exist**—Not true. Perhaps one argument to counter this statement is the thousands of Lyme groups and associations worldwide that have thousands of members all with chronic Lyme. Some physicians, including some at the US based board of the Infectious Disease Society of America (IDSA), will tell you that any symptoms or illness beyond the initial infection is something other than Lyme. All Lyme-literate doctors will tell you this is absolutely not true. But maybe the best argument to contradict this alleged statement would be a quick discussion with my husband. He'll tell you very quickly that his symptoms began approximately four to six months after his tick bites (the two that produced a serious rash) and that his condition was absolutely associated with the Lyme infection—and he suffered three plus years of hell, with ongoing issues, to prove it.

✳ ✳ ✳

1. Grier, T. 2012. Laboratory Tests. Canadian Lyme Disease Foundation. Available at http://www.canlyme.com/labtests.html

2. Stromdal, EY., Williamson, PC., Kollars Jr, TM., Evans, SR., Barry, RK., Vince, MA., and NA . 2003. Evidence of Borrelia lonestari DNA in Amblyomma americanum (Acari: Ixodidae) Removed from Humans. Journal of Clinical Microbiology 41(12): 5557-5562.

## For Additional Information on Lyme disease, please consult any of the following excellent references:

Jemsek, J. 2010. Overview of Lyme disease found at http://www.jemsekspecialty.com/lyme_detail.php (with many references cited for further consideration and other valuable links).

International Lyme and Associated Diseases Society (ILADS) main website (contains lots of information and video clips from the DVD Under Our Skin referenced below) found at http://www.ilads.org/lyme_disease/about_lyme.html

North Carolina Lyme Disease Foundation found at http://www.nclyme.org/ (they have other links on the site as well).

Treatment Guidelines from International Lyme and Associated Diseases Society (ILADS) found at http://www.lymediseaseassociation.org/index.php?option=com_content&view=article&id=89&Itemid=564

Open Eye Pictures. Under Our Skin DVD.

Weintraub, P. 2008. Cure Unknown: Inside the Lyme Epidemic. St. Martins Press.

# Acknowledgments

AFTER READING MITCH ALBOM'S BOOK, *Have a Little Faith,* an idea came to me. Motivated by the last sentence of the book, "I am in love with hope," a fire in me screamed: Get Jim's story out there. Then, with the encouragement of friends, my writing journey began. Specifically, if it weren't for two wonderful people, Bart and Glenna, I would never have thought to write this book in the first place. They gave me the push I needed to start writing. Whenever I would get a bit down, I would remind myself of what Bart said: You know the story better than anyone else. Teresa was also a wonderful promoter and friend, believing in me when I didn't and helping me stay focused and on task.

My family (my sisters Monique and Lisa, my brothers-in-law Patrick and Brian, and my mother Wilma) provided the first comments on helping to make the book a more readable story.

My friends in town were always encouraging, asking about the book, and helping with the children so I could work on the manuscript. Thank you to Patty, Patrick, Janet, and Melanie.

I am also grateful to the people who I met along the way that provided good advice, leads, ideas, and technical support. My editor Gail Kearns and book designer Peri Poloni-Gabriel were most helpful and made the book so much better than it was when they first received it from me.

Much gratitude is extended to the wonderful nurses who have helped Jim and my family over the past several years. Their competent care of Jim put my mind at ease and allowed me to take the time to write.

I also want to thank the incredibly kind neighbors, family members, and friends who have helped us along the way. Prayers, meals, dog walks, babysitting, encouraging notes, and other random acts of kindness gave me hope and reminded me to stay positive, that the world is overall a good place, and to get Jim's story out there. It is also true that without this support I would never have had the time to write this book. I received their gifts of time that allowed me to write for short periods.

# About the Author

D R. ERICA KOSAL IS A WIFE, mother, biology professor, author, speaker, and hidden strength champion. She blogs *Traveling Troubled Times*, found at http://ericakosal. wordpress.com/, where she writes about her experiences with raising two children, caring for her ill husband, and juggling a full-time career. She and her husband, Jim, also maintain a website, *Bounce to Resilience*, which can be found at http:// www.bouncetoresilience.com and is designed to provide help to people experiencing extreme stress and adversity. Please visit both sites and sign up for the newsletter, where you can continue to gain insight from Erica and keep up with Jim's progress, as well as learn about her new forthcoming book.

Erica and her family live in Raleigh, North Carolina, where she continues to advocate for her family with an unending optimism and ability to take the ugly and make it positive.

✳ ✳ ✳

CPSIA information can be obtained at www.ICGtesting.com
Printed in the USA
BVOW010440181212

308403BV00005B/8/P